CONTENTS

FOREWORD by James Callaghan
PREFACE   1
1   Early Imprisonment   3
2   London Prisons in the Middle Ages   13
3   The Rituals of Punishment   26
4   The Hidden Years   39
5   The Castle of Misery   47
6   Newgate Revealed   59
7   More Revelations   70
8   Prisoners for Debt   81
9   Eighteenth Century Lassitude   92
10   John Howard's Pilgrimage   102
11   The Mystique of Newgate   113
12   The Utilitarians   125
13   Newgate Restored   136
14   Elizabeth Fry   148
15   The Movement Towards Reform   161
16   New Conceptions   175
17   The Silent and Separate Systems   190
18   London Prisons in the Mid-Nineteenth Century   205
19   A Policy of Deterrence   219
20   The Demolition of Newgate   233
ACKNOWLEDGEMENTS   238
BIBLIOGRAPHY   239
INDEX   245

LIST OF ILLUSTRATIONS
between pages 116 and 117

The re-built and enlarged Newgate Gaol completed in 1780

A prisoners' yard inside Newgate

A view of Newgate Gaol at the corner of Newgate Street and the Old Bailey in about 1800

A service for the condemned in the Chapel of Newgate Gaol, 1808

Portable gallows outside the debtors' entrance to Newgate

Elizabeth Fry reading to prisoners in the women's section

A condemned cell at Newgate in 1873

The tread-wheel and exercise yards at Coldbath Fields in about 1870

A prisoner picking oakum in his cell at Newgate

A school-class in the Chapel of the Surrey House of Correction at Wandsworth

Prisoners at exercise at Pentonville

Prisoners at exercise at Newgate

A view of Newgate from the corner of Newgate Street and the Old Bailey shortly before its demolition

The pictures are by courtesy of the Radio Times Hulton Picture Library.

Whoever knows London knows Newgate
HEPWORTH DIXON, 1850

FOREWORD

I am very pleased to have been asked to write a foreword to this most interesting book. In the course of telling in detail the history of Newgate Gaol, Mr Anthony Babington, a Metropolitan Stipendiary Magistrate, also opens up the much wider story of our attitude to crime and punishment through the ages. It is hardly one to be proud of for he summarizes in a telling phrase the history of prison conditions as 'a chronicle of brutality, corruption, thoughtlessness and neglect'. This book certainly proves his point. We tend to forget that public opinion acquiesced in the public flogging of women even in the early nineteenth century and that public hangings did not cease until 1868.

Mr Babington's book throws a great deal of light on society's thinking about crime and punishment – or perhaps it would be more accurate to describe it as the absence of thought about such matters. Public opinion was fickle and forgetful. Prisons would be completely neglected for years while abuses grew rampant. Suddenly a reformer would momentarily awaken a flickering public conscience; and the accounts of the abuses and arbitrary treatment would shock official opinion and shame the public into calling for some reforms. Then such periods would be followed by further decades of neglect.

We can take some limited comfort from the fact that no writer today could describe our prisons in the same terms that Mr Babington uses about Newgate Gaol over the years. But we cannot be complacent by any means. At the margins there are some abuses of authority but, on the whole, discipline is exact and not arbitrary, and at the back of the Prison Service stands a Home Office staff with a sense of dedication and care about prison institutions. Prison officers themselves have a growing sense of responsibility and insight into the problems of dealing with prisoners and the means of treatment.

One obvious lesson that we must draw from Mr Babington's book is the need for a constant openness in the administration of the prison system and public vigilance by M.P.s, visiting magistrates, prison visitors and so on.

To further this end, whilst I was Home Secretary in 1969 I published a White Paper called *People in Prison* (Command 4214) which contained a hundred pages of description of the prison system, its strategy and its tasks. It is, to my mind, the most accurate account that exists and although written with an official bias, it nevertheless does not hide all the warts. I was greatly disappointed when it was greeted by the press and public with a massive yawn [but now I have read this book, I understand why]. Most people are not interested in prisons except when there is a scandal: they prefer to lock up their prisoners and then forget them.

I hope it will not be thought frivolous if I suggest that prisons should have 'Open Days' when members of the public could be invited to visit prisons and see and learn for themselves what is going on inside our gaols today.

In his concluding paragraphs Mr Babington raises a number of questions although, unfortunately, as a serving magistrate, he is not free to comment publicly on the questions he asks. I hope that some day he will do so. The questions that any reader will also ask are: what are the purposes of imprisonment as a policy? Is there an alternative? What are the causes of criminality? We have no satisfactory answers to these questions. We do know that the prison system and regime are not adequate for their defined tasks, either in resources or manpower. We have to face the fact that of men who serve sentences longer than eighteen months, more than 50% are reconvicted within two years of their release. Even worse, 80–85% of young men released from Borstal with previous experience in juvenile institutions are reconvicted within three years. Whatever else it may be, prison is not a deterrent for this type of person.

So a number of proposals have been put forward to find out whether there are more successful alternatives, and a tentative start has been made in the Home Office and in the proposals made by the Younger Committee on Penal Reform. There are proposals for semi-custody, in which a man is based in prison but goes out to work all week; or week-end semi-custody in which he is allowed out all week but has to return at the week-end; hostels for the large number of prisoners who are not criminals in the normal sense of the term but are basically inadequate persons: and, most imaginative of all, the possibility of making some recompense to society by service to the community. Such projects can include the reclaiming of canals, clearing country paths, helping in hospital kitchens, keeping up the Meals on Wheels Service for old people at week ends when usually this is stopped. Some of these proposals would need legislation and also a great deal of assistance from trade unions and voluntary bodies, and I firmly believe that such help would be forthcoming. It will need a strong lead from the Home Secretary backed by his colleagues if we are to make a start.

We also need much more research into the causes of criminality, of which we know next to nothing. But we know where to make a start because there is an identikit picture of the delinquent who commits a serious crime. He is male, he is young, he has been in trouble since he was a child, he lives in a large city, he has had an inadequate education, and he comes from a broken home. At least half of our crimes are committed by young men under the age of twenty, and we know already that a man's past criminal history is more closely related to his future criminal behaviour than either the sentence of the court or what happens to him in prison. Some research goes on but much more needs to be done if we are to avoid these irrational pendulum swings between the aims of permissiveness at one extreme and harsh punishment at the other. How should we combine the various purposes of imprisonment such as retribution, deterrence, reform and restitution? Despite the lack of sustained public interest in the subject, anyone reading this book must feel that it is time that we made a fresh attack on such problems.

And finally, if we listen carefully enough, the criminal in each generation tells us something about the nature of our society as well as our own moral standards. There is no blanket remedy to the problem of crime for there is no one disease. If that is understood at the beginning, then perhaps some of the work that needs to be done may be successful.

Meanwhile, we owe a debt of gratitude to Mr Babington for reminding us of the evils that arise when society condemns men and women and then pushes them out of its sight to forget and neglect them.

JAMES CALLAGHAN

PREFACE

IN this book I have endeavoured to trace the history of conditions in Newgate Gaol against a background of the treatment of prisoners and the theories of imprisonment in Britain as a whole.

I chose Newgate for this purpose for several reasons. First, due to its incredible longevity – it was used from around 1188 until as recently as 1902 – it spanned a greater period of time than any other of the large, general prisons. Secondly, a series of personal accounts, public reports and official records down the years have made it possible to form a fairly accurate impression of the day-to-day existence of the men and women imprisoned at the gaol.

In addition, the image of Newgate has always been enveloped with an atmosphere of morbid fascination. Its grey, massive walls exerted a sinister domination – physical, mental and emotional – over the lives of successive generations of Londoners. This was partly due to the close connection of the gaol with the gallows at Tyburn and with the entire macabre ritual of public execution; partly, to the fact that Newgate was viewed with particular horror as a prison, and its wards and dungeons were associated in the public mind with cruelty, disease, despair and death. It is remarkable how often in ancient documents mention of the goal is prefixed by such epithets as 'infamous', 'miserable', or 'loathsome'. In later years Newgate was known as 'the English Bastille', an indication of the persistence of its hateful reputation.

Any history of prison conditions is of necessity an abject chronicle of brutality, corruption, thoughtlessness and neglect. Yet it is a subject which we cannot regard with a sense of entire detachment, for the prison system of today was directly developed from the prison system of the past, and almost the whole of our present conception of the nature and purposes of imprisonment is evolved from the muddled notions, the forlorn aspirations and the total nihilism which prevailed in

1

former ages. Newgate Goal was finally demolished more than half a century ago, but its shadow still lingers, and probably it will continue to linger for many years to come.

CHAPTER ONE

EARLY IMPRISONMENT

THE concept of imprisonment did not arise in any particular country or at any particular time. Indeed, the primitive inclination amongst the rulers and the powerful to seize their enemies and to thrust them into captivity seems to have been both basic and universal.

The first prisons in Britain consisted, for the most part, of the dungeons and strongrooms in castles, manors and gate-houses – which were equally available for the confinement of lawbreakers or for the victims of personal vengeance. After the invasion of 1066 the Norman barons and the local auto-crats continued, and even extended the practice of private detention. In the same era the official prison system also began to take shape, originating from an eleventh century require-ment that the sheriffs, who were the king's officers in the counties, should become responsible for the safe custody until trial of all those suspected of committing crimes within their localities.

Faced with this onerous, new duty the sheriffs either had to make their own arrangements for finding secure accommod-ation for their prisoners, or to persuade their various counties to provide them with special gaols for the purpose. Initially no obligation was placed on the county authorities to supply their own gaols, nor even to maintain them where they had done so, although it is recorded that the sheriffs of the City of London and Middlesex made a successful application to the city treasury in 1155 for an allowance to cover repairs at the Fleet in which, at the time, they were holding all their pre-trial prisoners. However, it was decreed by the Assizes of Clarendon in 1166 that all those counties which had not already provided their sheriffs with gaols should do so without delay, and that the cost of building and maintaining them in a good state of repair would be borne by the Crown. Thence-

3

forth the County Gaol became a regular feature of the British penal structure.

In theory, all the prisons in the country belonged to the king, whether they were actually controlled by the sheriffs or by private individuals, but no grants were made from the national exchequer towards their running expenses, nor even towards the maintenance of the prisoners in them. Based as they were upon this hopelessly uneconomic foundation, the British gaols developed a multitude of abuses which were to bedevil them for many generations to come.

Probably a large number of counties complied with the Assizes of Clarendon not by erecting new gaols, but by arranging for their sheriffs to make use of existing prison accommodation in the neighbourhood, for instance the dungeons in the castle of the county town. It was the duty of the sheriffs to make all the necessary administrative arrangements, including the appointment of a gaoler. Usually they played very little part in the actual day-to-day control of the County Gaol, but they remained accountable for its proper management. Considering the financial liabilities entailed in the possession of a prison it is surprising that so many private owners were willing to undertake the responsibility. In fact, it was considered a mark of power – even an honour – and during the fourteenth century it became a custom for the king to bestow charters upon named individuals, or upon the inhabitants of certain localities, expressly authorizing the recipients to keep their own gaols.

Two other early types of gaol which should be mentioned at this stage were Bishops' Prisons and Tuns. A clerk in Holy Orders could not be imprisoned in an ordinary gaol, so archbishops, bishops and other prelates with an episcopal jurisdiction kept their own prisons in which they could detain servants of the Church, as well as other persons suspected of committing ecclesiastical offences. Tuns were temporary lockups for minor wrongdoers and were found in most large towns.

The principal official in every prison was the gaoler or keeper, who might have purchased his appointment or might have received it as a gift of patronage. Normally a gaoler was unpaid or else he received a very small and inadequate salary, and he was obliged to make his living in the best manner he could devise. Nevertheless, a gaolership usually afforded the holder an adequate livelihood; indeed, in some of the larger prisons his income could be lucrative, and sheriffs experienced little trouble in the disposal of these appointments. Gaolers, said Blackstone, writing some years later, were 'frequently a merciless race of men, and by being conversant with scenes of misery steeled against any tender sensation'.

The gaolers' main sources of remuneration were the fees which they exacted from their prisoners. The fee system was universal throughout the country, only the actual amounts varying from prison to prison. On entering a gaol the prisoner was expected to pay an admission fee, and if his sojourn there was ended by pardon or acquittal, he was supposed to pay a release fee before he could obtain his discharge. These fees were officially recognized as being the prisoners' contribution towards the running costs of the gaol. In addition, most prisons had special apartments which the gaoler could let out to selected, wealthier prisoners, often at exorbitant rents. It became customary for a gaol to be divided into what was known as the 'common side', where the penniless prisoners eked out their days in circumstances of extreme squalor and privation, and the 'master's side', where prisoners might obtain a graduated scale of comfort and service according to the amount of the rents they were paying.

As the gaoler had to employ, and pay, his own turnkeys, the majority of prisons were grossly under-staffed, and security was achieved by loading the prisoners with irons. A wide variety of contraptions was used, including manacles for the wrists, fetters and shackles for the ankles, and iron collars for the neck – any of these could, if necessary, be chained to a ring in the floor or to a staple in the wall. Irons provided the gaolers with another form of income for it became the practice that a prisoner might gain exemption from ironing on the payment of a special fee. The size of the exemption charge depended on the avariciousness of the gaoler and also on the amount which he thought his victim could afford. Although the custom of wholesale ironing was forbidden by law it was permitted to continue for many centuries; as late as 1776 William Smith protested that, 'if [prisoners] have the money to pay, their irons are knocked off, for fettering is a trade by which some gaolers derive considerable emolument.'

The gaoler ran his prison as a commercial enterprise. There were no beds, blankets, sheets or mattresses except those which he hired out. It was he who acted as retailer for all the food, firewood, coals and candles which were sold in the gaol. He also kept his own tap for the prisoners, at which they could buy ales and spirits at any prices he saw fit to charge. In fact, his prison was a small, closed community in which his word and his will were paramount. Although the prisoners had a nominal, common law protection against acts of 'hard usage', they were habitually ill-treated by gaolers and turn-keys alike, and sometimes the most terrible atrocities were perpetrated upon them. The savage whipping of prisoners of both sexes was commonplace, and deliberate starvation and torture was not infrequent. It should be added that certain of the relevant authorities, particularly the Court of Alder-men which was responsible for the prisons in the City of London, endeavoured repeatedly to control the excesses of the gaolers, both in their general conduct and in the manner of their administration. Sometimes stern measures were taken; for instance, the records show that in 1290 a gaoler of New-gate who had murdered one of his prisoners was convicted and hanged for his offence.

The lives of the gaolers and the turnkeys were never free from danger as the prisoners, especially those in the criminal wards, had so little to lose through insubordination that they constantly indulged in violence and rioting. A turnkey at Newgate was killed in 1325; so were the keepers of the Cam-bridge gaol in 1346 and 1349; and the warden of the Marshal-sea prison suffered mortal injuries in 1381. Furthermore, it was a gaoler's essential duty to hold his prisoners in safe cus-tody, and if any person escaped from his charge he was likely to suffer dismissal, or an even more severe punishment. Where an escape was attributable to the gaoler's own negligence it was by no means unusual for him to be placed in irons and incarcerated in some neighbouring prison.

Inside a gaol the debtor and criminal prisoners were nor-mally kept apart, but there was no additional segregation according to age, record or type of offence. Most prisons allowed their male and female inmates to mingle indiscriminately and this, coupled with the availability of unlimited supplies of alcohol, resulted in an orgy of sexual promiscuity. The prisoners had no work to do and nothing to occupy their minds except their day-to-day existence. On the common side the gaols were bare and cold and few had an adequate supply of fresh water.

If a prisoner could not afford to buy his food and the other necessities of life from the gaoler it was expected that he would be supplied with them by his relatives and friends. In consequence, many destitute prisoners died of starvation. However, to alleviate the harshness of the system prisoners were habitually permitted to beg from the sides of their gaols, and also to send out parties in the charge of turnkeys to make collections from passers-by in the streets. In addition, charitable donations of food and money were frequently made to prisons by the guilds and by other societies and institutions, and certainly from the fourteenth century onwards philanthropically-minded individuals were accustomed to make specific bequests in their wills for the alleviation of distress amongst poor prisoners in the gaols.

One of the most dreaded afflictions in the prisons was an outbreak of the illness known as 'gaol fever'. It was believed that this deadly infection was both natural and endemic to the lives of prisoners and since the causes remained uninvestigated and unknown no protective measures were taken against the disease. Gaol fever was rampant from the earliest times until the end of the eighteenth century. Stow mentions an epidemic in the London prisons in 1414 which killed off sixty-four prisoners. It is recorded that a bad outbreak occurred at Cambridge Assizes in 1521, spreading from the gaols to the courts and infecting judges, jurors, lawyers and witnesses; a similar pattern of events took place at the Oxford Assizes in 1577 when about three hundred people died, including the Lord Chief Baron. It is scarcely credible that these constant occurrences were accepted and were allowed to continue unchecked for so long. One reads of a 'contagious disease' marked by fever, purple spots, twitching and delirium which swept through the court at the Somerset Assizes as late as 1730, causing the deaths of some hundreds of people including the presiding judge and the sheriffs. The notorious Black Assizes at the Old Bailey in 1750 will be mentioned later.

Gaol fever is now believed to have been a form of typhus, resulting from poverty, overcrowding, dirt and lack of sanitation. It was first identified by Dr John Hunter in 1779 as being a similar infection to the perennial outbreaks in London and other large cities, and also in closed institutions like workhouses and hospitals.

The jurist Bracton, writing around the year 1250, stated that prisons were for confinement and not for punishment. It has already been observed that the Assizes of Clarendon in 1166 imposed on all sheriffs the duty of detaining suspect lawbreakers until they could be brought to trial; but at that time a set term of imprisonment was never contemplated as being, in itself, a recognized sentence of a court of justice. However, Professor Ralph B. Pugh has pointed out in his recent and valuable study of medieval imprisonment that during the period 1272–1421 a number of statutes authorized specific prison sentences, some of definite length and others indefinite, for a wide variety of offences. For example, in 1285 it was decreed that a lawyer who deceived the court should be sent to prison for one year, and that kidnappers could suffer perpetual imprisonment; in 1361 the sentence for stealing hawks was fixed at two years, and an indefinite sentence was empowered for a juror who accepted a bribe. Some idea of the incongruous sense of values existing in that era can be gleaned from the fact that in 1406 indefinite imprisonment was prescribed as the penalty for an offender who made arrows with unsuitable points. On the whole, the commonest fixed sentences laid down in these statutes seem to have been either a year or a year and a day.

In spite of these statutory terms of imprisonment for certain specified offences the British gaols, for the most part, were used for purposes other than punishment. Prisoners who had been convicted in the courts were returned to their gaols to await the carrying out of their sentences – which usually consisted of branding, whipping, pillorying or execution. In those days, long before there was any procedure of appeal, the punishment was inflicted with the minimum of delay. Other prisoners were detained in the gaols on a coercive basis until they paid fines or were able to find sureties for their good behaviour in the future.

A large proportion of the prison population were debtors. Imprisonment for debt developed in time into one of the strangest and the most illogical features of the British penal system. It originated as a strategem employed by the Crown as a means of compelling the payment of outstanding debts to the Exchequer; it is likely that it was used principally where the victim had the means but lacked the inclination to discharge his liabilities. A statute in 1352 placed private creditors in a similar position to the Crown by granting them the power to imprison their debtors pending the full settlement of an outstanding liability. The creditor was not responsible for the maintenance of the debtor whom he sent to gaol unless the latter was completely destitute, in which case the creditor was supposed to keep him supplied with sufficient bread and water to sustain life. It was not until 1759 that this obligation was enlarged and it was enacted that every debtor in gaol should be allowed the sum of four pence a day towards his subsistence by the creditor who had imposed his confinement on him.

A debtor was not discharged from prison until his creditor relented or the debt had been discharged in full. As he was unable to earn a livelihood himself it usually meant that he would have to rely on the assistance of his family, his friends or some charitable donor. Doctor Johnson, with his usual perspicuity, summed up the position: 'The confinement, therefore, of any man in the sloth and darkness of a prison, is a loss to the nation and no gain to the creditor. For of the multitudes who are pining in those cells of misery, a small part is suspected of any fraudulent act by which they retain what belongs to others. The rest are imprisoned by the wantonness of pride, the malignity of revenge, or the acrimony of disappointed expectations.'

In company with the criminal prisoners those detained for debt were obliged to pay entrance and discharge fees to their gaolers. Prisoners of every description were also subjected, when they were first admitted to the common side of a gaol, to make a peculiar form of payment which bore the name of 'garnish'. Unlike the other financial exactions in the prisons, garnish was arranged and collected by the prisoners themselves. It is possible that the custom began as a legitimate contribution by a newcomer towards the cost of cleaning materials, coals and candles for the wards; indeed, a proportion of the garnish-money continued to be expended on such items in some of the prisons. But garnish soon degenerated into a cruel and squalid toll extorted from the newcomer, to be used in providing an evening of drunken debauchery for his fellows. If the entrant could not pay he was liable to have his clothes stripped off him and confiscated; further, he might have to undergo a long period of ostracism, bullying and intimidation against which he had no redress, for the authorities and the prison officials granted their tacit consent to all the most repulsive features of the garnish system.

An untried prisoner remained in confinement until his gaol was next delivered. The process of 'gaol delivery' was merely the clearing of the prison by bringing to trial all the inmates who were being detained on suspicion of having committed criminal offences. In very early times the gaols were delivered spasmodically by the sheriffs and the local justices on their own initiative, but later the whole procedure was placed on a more formal basis when the Crown began to issue specific commissions of Gaol Delivery to certain officials to clear a named prison. It was during the reign of Henry II (1154–89) that the king's judges started to tour the country delivering the gaols in all the localities through which they passed; but commissions continued to be granted to the local justices, as visits from the king's judges were few and far between. Even then the unfortunate prisoners might have to spend a period of months, perhaps years, in prison before they were brought to trial.

When an itinerant judge was carrying out a commission of gaol delivery in a county he usually sat at a specially constituted assize court in the county town. In time, assize circuits were governed by statute and an effort was made to ensure that every county should hold their assizes at regular intervals; however, the difficulties of travel and communication made this aspiration very difficult to fulfil. The justices often held their gaol deliveries inside a prison and the full procedure of a criminal trial would then be enacted in a ward or a large room set aside for the purpose.

Another type of prison, which started as a completely separate institution from the gaols for criminals and debtors, was the House of Correction. Even since 1383 idlers and vagabonds had been the objects of a series of periodical statutes which prescribed the various punishments to which they should be sentenced by the justices of the peace. From time to time it was ordered that they should be gaoled, whipped, branded or placed in the stocks. During the sixteenth century the problem of vagrants and beggars became far more acute owing to the gradual disruption of the feudal system, with the consequence that so many unemployed serfs either took to the roads or set out for the nearest neighbouring town. The situation was considerably worsened by the dissolution of the monasteries in which a number of the destitute and the homeless would have found temporary shelter. Henry VIII's solution to the problem was the simple one of attempting to terrorize the 'sturdy beggars' by the imposition of ferocious penalties, but punishment alone proved to be an ineffectual antidote for a situation which resulted almost wholly from the prevalent economic conditions.

A more realistic appraisal of the position was made during the reign of Elizabeth I, and in 1576 the justices in every county were directed to set up establishments to be known as 'Houses of Correction' for the detention of 'rogues, vagabonds, and sturdy beggars'. These places, says Blackstone, 'were originally designed for the penal confinement, after conviction, of paupers refusing to work, and other persons falling under the legal description of vagrant'; their inmates were supposed to undergo a period of compulsory, forced labour in order to instil them with a desire for hard and honest toil. However, Houses of Corrections, or 'Bridewells' as they were sometimes called, were embodied into the Poor Law system at its foundation in 1597, and from then on they were utilized by the justices both for their intended purpose and for the disposal of the aged and the infirm, classified under this new scheme as 'the deserving poor'.

It will be noticed that Houses of Correction differed from County Gaols inasmuch as they were controlled by the justices of the peace rather than by the sheriffs. As will be seen later, the distinctions between the two types of institution gradually vanished and by the eighteenth century the justices were allowed to commit a large number of offenders to a House of Correction or to a County Gaol as they thought fit. Moreover, Houses of Correction soon became affected by most of the defects and depravities of the ordinary gaols, until, in general, there was little or nothing to choose between the administration of either.

CHAPTER TWO

LONDON PRISONS IN THE MIDDLE AGES

IT is generally believed that the Tower was the earliest building in the City of London to be used as a prison. According to tradition the Tower began its long and turbulent history during the Roman occupation of Britain; it was considerably enlarged and strengthened by William the Conqueror who transformed it into a fortified royal residence, standing partly inside and partly outside the city walls, and dominating the whole of the capital with its imposing stature.

Although the Tower was not designed primarily for the purpose of imprisonment, like any other fortress-castle of the period it would have been amply provided with all the facilities for holding captives in close confinement, and King William and his immediate successors started to use it as a repository for their personal prisoners. At one time in the thirteenth century a number of ordinary felons from the City were committed there too, but it was never seriously intended to turn the Tower into a general, criminal gaol.

The accommodation and treatment in the Tower varied enormously in accordance with the importance of the prisoner. Persons of note – and it must be remembered that Richard II, Henry VI, and Edward V were all confined there at various times – might be lodged in suites of rooms and allowed to live in comparative comfort, whereas those of a meaner status would probably be consigned to some putrid dungeon. Very little is known about the less favourable conditions, but it may be assumed that they were as terrible as those which were found in the other early gaols. There are the customary records of escapes, attempted escapes, epidemics, and wholesale deaths, and in 1295 the pool which supplied the inmates with their drinking water was graphically described as a place 'where rats drown themselves'. Although the Tower continued as the prison for State and political prisoners for a great many years, it seems to have been used very rarely for this purpose after the beginning of the eighteenth century.

The first building in London to be erected specifically as a prison was the Fleet, which stood on the east side of the present Farringdon Street, just to the north of Ludgate Hill. Its exact date of origin is unknown, but there are grounds for believing that it was already in existence in 1130, and it was certainly being repaired in 1155. The Fleet was called 'the Gaol of London' until shortly after the opening of Newgate, when it began to be known by its more familiar name, owing to its position on the banks of the Fleet Stream.

The Fleet was built of stone, and its site was probably chosen deliberately on account of the availability of an adequate supply of water, an asset lacking in many of the gaols established at a later date. Initially it was surrounded by a moat, which provided a high degree of security; however, this was subsequently permitted to dry up, perhaps at a time when all the worst types of criminal were being committed to Newgate. The Fleet then became the special gaol for the Common Pleas and Exchequer courts at Westminster, and in the fourteenth century it was also used by the Privy Council and the Court of Chancery. Its inmates invariably included a high proportion of debtors.

The same family provided the warders of the Fleet on an hereditary basis from its inception until about 1550. The living conditions in the prison were better than those in the average gaol, especially after it was rebuilt around the year 1335; discipline, too, was less harsh and the prisoners, particularly those confined for debt, were free on occasion to leave the prison for limited periods. In its later history the Fleet became the gaol of the Star Chamber, and on the abolition of that detested court in 1640 it was turned into a general prison for debtors and bankrupts. The Fleet was burnt down during the Great Fire of 1666, and again in the Gordon Riots of 1780. It was finally demolished in 1845.

The Pipe Rolls record that in 1188 Henry II ordered that a piece of land adjoining Newgate should be bought and a prison should be erected on it. The site of this original gaol cost a mere three pounds, six shillings and eight pence and the building work was carried out by two carpenters and a smith. According to Stow there were at that time seven double gates in the ancient walls which encircled the City of London, and of these he decribes Newgate as being the fifth principal gate. It is not clear whether the 1188 gaol was entirely separate from the gatehouse or was attached to it. In the years which followed a number of grants were made by the Crown for the mending of the prison, but the burden of maintenance fell partly upon the City authorities, and in 1218, says Stow, 'the king writeth unto the sheriffs of London commanding them to repair the gaol of Newgate for the safekeeping of his prisoners, promising that the charges laid out should be allowed unto them upon their account in the Exchequer.'

The gaol was either enlarged or reconstructed in 1236 when Henry III directed the sheriffs to convert one of the turrets on the actual gate into a part of the prison. The King contributed towards the cost, which came to about one hundred pounds, and ordered that the citizens of London should provide the residue, 'to the protection and improvement of the City'. Certainly from this point forward the gaol of Newgate comprised a section of the gatehouse including the dungeons underneath, and it did not undergo any substantial alterations for close on two centuries. In 1399 Henry IV granted the custody of the seven gates in the walls to the citizens of London which meant, in effect, that they became responsible for the execution of all the repairs which were necessary at the prison, a responsibility which they, in their turn, passed on to the gaolers who, no doubt, recouped themselves as best they could at the expense of the unfortunate prisoners.

From its inception Newgate became a prison for the very worst types of criminal in the City of London and the county of Middlesex, both before and immediately after their trials; it was also used for the confinement of a number of rebels, traitors, heretics, spies and debtors. All through the ages a considerable proportion of the prisoners in the gaol were under sentence of death. Owing to the fact that Newgate was regarded as being more secure than a great many of the outlying prisons, instructions were often issued to the sheriffs of counties all over England and Wales to convey certain of their most dangerous or most difficult prisoners to Newgate, and to hand them over to the keeper there for custody and trial in

London. The whole gaol was placed at the disposal of the sheriffs of Essex in 1259 until their county had constructed a prison of its own.

During the thirteenth and fourteenth centuries prisoners were committed to Newgate Gaol for a wide variety of offences, some endemic to city life, such as murder, assault, burglary and theft, and some less usual or less serious. In 1241 a group of Jews were detained in the prison on a charge of circumcising a Christian child; in 1320, some men charged with carrying arms in the streets at night; in 1327, ten male and female bakers, alleged to have swindled their customers. By a proclamation in 1329 Edward III ordained that certain disturbances of the peace in the City would be punishable by imprisonment in Newgate for a year and a day. In 1380 two men were brought before the mayor, aldermen and sheriffs and it was alleged that 'whereas they were stout enough to work for their food and raiment, and had tongues to talk with, they did pretend they were mutes and had been deprived of their tongues.' These imposters were sentenced to be detained in Newgate for an indefinite time.

The sort of prisoner to be found in Newgate was altered considerably in 1378 by the opening of Ludgate Gaol, which was intended for the confinement of freemen and women from the City. The Court of Aldermen ordered in 1382 that thenceforth 'all freemen of this city should for debt, trespasses, accounts and contempts, be imprisoned in Ludgate, and for treasons, felonies, and other criminal offences be committed to Newgate.' In other words, some effort was to be made to divide the more privileged citizens who were detained for debt or for some minor offence from the ordinary debtors and the overt criminals. The new prison was another gatehouse gaol, situated at the Lud gates in the city walls, south of Newgate and just to the west of the present-day position of St Paul's Cathedral. The accommodation in Ludgate seems to have been quite comfortable by contemporary prison standards; so much so that in 1419 it was closed down and the prisoners were transferred to Newgate, because it was said that the debtors in Ludgate were 'more willing to keep abode there than to pay their debts', and that the other inmates were turning the gaol into a hotbed of subversion. The transfer was only temporary, however, as Newgate was already over-crowded, and a few months later the prisoners were returned to Ludgate. Shortly afterwards, to ease the congestion at Newgate, it was decided that Ludgate should become a prison for all minor offenders; it continued as such twenty-four years until 1463 when it reverted to its original function of being the gaol for freemen of the City imprisoned for debt or for less heinous offences.

From medieval times the City of London was governed by its own council, whose powers were derived under various successive royal charters. The Court of Aldermen comprised a part of this ruling authority, and the Lord Mayor and the twenty-five aldermen were also ex officio members of the Court of Common Council, the legislative body of the City. The responsibility for the administration of the City prisons rested primarily upon the sheriffs; the sheriffs were answerable to the Court of Aldermen who, in their turn, were accountable to the Common Council and the Crown. In 1258 Henry III, angered at the escape of a prisoner from Newgate, summoned the Mayor and sheriffs to appear before him. As a result of their explanations the mayor was permitted to return to his duties, but the sheriffs were committed to the Tower until a few months later when the king's displeasure had abated.

The Court of Aldermen seem to have been well aware of the principal defects in the gaols and from time to time they endeavoured to eradicate, or at least to control them, although their edicts were seldom sufficiently enforced. In 1356 they drew up a complete code of regulations for the good management of Newgate, which forbade, amongst other customs, the exaction of fees for the removal of irons; this was retracted in 1393 when a maximum fee of £5 was officially authorized. About the same time the gaoler of Newgate, called the keeper, was forbidden to charge his prisoners for beds or candles and the fee which was payable on their discharge was limited to four pence except in cases of treason or felony. In 1431, after the security of Newgate had been further strengthened, the ironing of freemen prisoners, except those detained for serious offences, was expressly prohibited. Perhaps the most constructive step to ensure the proper administration of the gaols was taken in 1463 when it was decided by the aldermen that from then on four visitors would be appointed annually to carry out regular inspections at Newgate and Ludgate, primarily to see that their ordinances were being obeyed.

At a very early stage the Court of Aldermen realized that the standard of administration of the City prisons would depend very largely upon the quality of the gaolers. In 1356 it was decreed that the keepership of Newgate was not to be farmed out by the sheriffs, and that they were only to bestow the appointment on men of good character; for his part, a new keeper was to swear an oath that he would not extort money from his prisoners. A few years later the sheriffs were obliged to enter an undertaking that the keepership of Newgate would never be sold, and in 1421 the same provision was extended to the gaolerships of the other prisons in the City. In order to increase their control, the aldermen directed in 1431 that the keeper of Newgate should be nominated annually, though there is little doubt that the last incumbent might be re-appointed if suitable; this regulation also became applicable to the other City prisons during the following years. The keeper of Newgate had to give security to the sheriffs in the form of a bond against any of his prisoners being permitted to escape. Any grossly improper conduct or dereliction of duty by the keeper which came to the notice of the aldermen was dealt with very severely; in 1449 a keeper was removed and imprisoned for raping a female prisoner, and in 1450 his successor was dismissed for an unspecified act of negligence.

The keeper of Newgate used to take up his appointment at the same time as the two new sheriffs; and his installation was governed by a series of prescribed formalities. First of all he had to take an oath of office before the Lord Mayor and the aldermen; then, accompanied by his clerk he would attend at the gaol whilst the incoming sheriffs took over the prisoners from their predecessors by legal indenture. Having discharged their responsibilities, the outgoing sheriffs would surrender the keys and the seal of Newgate to the Mayor. Although the keeper was actually chosen by the sheriffs he was nominally selected by the Court of Aldermen who sometimes received specific requests to appoint a royal nominee. On one occasion during the sixteenth century when they had refused to comply with such a demand they were forced to do so by the Privy Council.

Originally the sheriffs of the City of London and Middlesex used their own houses for holding their personal courts and for confining their prisoners. As they grew busier they began to sit at the Guildhall for the exercise of their judicial duties, and they each took over a separate building known as a compter or counter, which combined the functions of an office and a prison. The first two compters were established in Bread Street and in the Poultry; the former of these was moved to Wood Street in 1555. The size and security of the compters may be judged by the fact that in 1425 they were used for the temporary accommodation of the entire population of Newgate Gaol, and for a short time in 1431 all the prisoners from Ludgate were transferred to them in addition to their own inmates. The primary purpose of the compters was the detention of newly-arrested offenders until they could be removed to Newgate or Ludgate. However, owing to the congestion at the major city prisons, it was decreed in 1393 that any prisoners other than those charged with treason or felony could remain at the compters for much longer periods. An ordinance in 1431 provided that penniless prisoners of every sort must be transferred from the compters to Newgate as rapidly as possible.

It has been suggested that living conditions at the compters were generally superior to those at Newgate or Ludgate, especially for the prisoners who were able to pay for better treatment. Even then the inmates were very much at the mercy of the gaolers. Stow has recorded that in 1550 the gaoler of Bread Street Compter, Richard Husband, was 'a wilful and headstrong man who dealt hard with the prisoners for his own advantage.' His excesses were such that the mayor and aldermen displaced him and committed him to Newgate where 'it was commanded to the keeper to set those irons on his legs which are called widows' alms.' Later on, Husband was released on the payment of a fine, and restored to the gaolership of Bread Street. Apparently he soon reverted to his former behaviour because in 1552 he was tried again and it was proved, not only that he had maltreated the prisoners in his compter, but that 'thieves and strumpets were lodged there for four pence a night, where they might be safe from searches that were made abroad.' Stow does not give any details of Husband's second sentence or of what became of him thereafter.

Another City prison was the Tun in Cornhill, built by the Mayor in 1283 as an overnight lock-up for prowlers, vagabonds and other suspicious persons who had been arrested during the hours of darkness. It was given that name because it was shaped like a tun, one of the large casks used for storing wines and spirits, standing on one end. Almost three hundred years after the establishment of the Cornhill Tun, the City obtained a second gaol for less serious offenders when in 1552 King Edward VI presented the Mayor and aldermen with the Palace of Bridewell to be used for the confinement of vagrants and beggars. This formed the model upon which the Houses of Correction were based and, indeed, it was to become in due course the House of Correction for the City of London.

The independent Borough of Southwark, which stood on the south bank of the River Thames, was placed under the jurisdiction of the City of London in 1327. It continued to retain many of the privileges of autonomy until 1550 when it became an ordinary Ward of the City. Southwark possessed its own compter and it also contained two other well known prisons, the Marshalsea and the King's Bench. The Marshals of England had the traditional right of holding in custody all prisoners who were awaiting trial at, or had been sentenced by, the king's central courts. The prison of the Marshals, called the Marshalsea, was built at Southwark in 1373; for some time it seems to have been used as a common gaol, but eventually it became notorious as a prison for debtors. The King's Bench prison, as its name implies, belonged to the Court of King's Bench; it was probably established in Southwark a short while after the building there of the Marshalsea, and at a later stage it was also used mainly for the imprisonment of debtors. Stow speaks of another early prison in Southwark called 'The Clinke' which, he says, was kept for such persons 'as should brabble, frey, or break the peace'; in other words, it was a lock-up for minor offenders.

It is difficult to formulate an exact account of the conditions

under which the prisoners existed in Newgate, or indeed in
any of the other prisons in Britain, in the Middle Ages as the
documentary material is so sparse; but it is just possible to
obtain a fleeting glimpse of the lives of the inmates, and the
ordeals and privations which they had to endure. Very soon
after it had been opened Newgate Gaol had acquired an
especially terrible reputation for its unwholesome environ-
ment, the distresses of its prisoners and the cruelties of its
staff. In the original building there seems to have been very
little segregation of any sort except that the lower dungeons,
most of which were fitted with stocks, were used principally
for the serious offenders. In 1314 a prisoner complained that
he had been detained in the depths of the gaol with the
felons, and loaded with irons until he had paid a large sum
of money to the keeper. The separation of the women from
the men was only partial, as in 1404 the sheriffs and the
Common Serjeant* disclosed to the mayor and alderman that
the women were cramped in a small, unhealthy room and that
in order to reach the nearest privy they had to walk through a
part of the gaol where male prisoners were confined, 'to their
great shame and hurt'. In consequence, a stone tower was
built exclusively for women prisoners. The smells of Newgate
were renowned and for centuries they polluted the
whole of the surrounding locality. Lack of hygiene and faulty
sanitation caused frequent outbreaks of fever and the annual
death-rate was extremely high; it is recorded that in 1419
alone the keeper and sixty-four of his prisoners died in a particularly virulent epidemic.

The better-off prisoners in Newgate, as in other gaols,
either had their food and clothing sent in from outside or
bought them from the keeper; the poorer had to rely on
charity and on the occasional free issues by the City authorities. There were no regular prison rations but it was customary when food was confiscated, for instance where it had
been offered for sale underweight or had contravened the
stringent requirements of the City guilds, to have it
distributed to the needy prisoners in the gaols. Also

---

* The Common Serjeant is one of the judicial officers of the City of
London.

some manufacturers, tradesmen and societies made voluntary donations of food from time to time as in
1303 when a private association in the City resolved
that in future the remains of all its feasts should be
dispensed among the poor prisoners in Newgate, the sick in
the hospitals, and others in want. A number of donations and
bequests were made by public-spirited individuals to the
various city prisons from the thirteenth century onwards. In
1237 Sir John Poultney, a draper who had been Mayor of
London four times, gave a small annuity for the use of poor
prisoners in Newgate and the Fleet; and in 1385 the serving
Mayor presented an annuity for relief of the distress of the
prisoners in Newgate. Ludgate, the Marshalsea and the compters came in for their share of charitable offerings as well. The
money received was not only spent on food and clothing but
on such other necessities as candles, coal, blankets and bedding. The City prisons also provided for the maintenance of
their poor prisoners by allowing them to collect alms in the
streets. In 1431 this system was regulated for Newgate Gaol
by the Court of Aldermen, who stipulated that future collections were to be made by two pairs of prisoners, one begging
by the riverside and the other in the interior of the City, each
carrying a sealed box and saucer clearly marked with the
name of the gaol; the boxes were to be opened every month
under the supervision of the sheriffs or the City Chamberlain.

All through the Middle Ages the London prisons were the
scenes of constant escapes, rescues and riots. During the
twelfth and thirteenth centuries to escape from gaol was a
capital offence, which rendered the prisoner liable to instant
beheading if he was recaptured. After 1295, however, this
penalty was ameliorated and escaping prisoners were generally treated with less severity. As has been noticed the gaoler
was usually held responsible when an escape had occurred and
could be punished with a fine, dismissal or imprisonment. In
1254 Henry III ordered the citizens of London to account for
an escape from Newgate; the citizens replied that their responsibility lay in the selection, rather than in the conduct of
their sheriffs, and the king appears to have accepted this con-
tention. Since Newgate accommodated so many desperate
criminals, and so many who were destined for eventual execu-

tion, the escape-rate was comparatively high. The methods of getting out of the gaol varied; sometimes it was via the roof, sometimes by rushing the gates, and sometimes by cutting a hole in the walls. In 1456 a crowd of prisoners climbed on to the leads and held the sheriffs and prison officials at bay until they were encircled and forced to capitulate by a specially-recruited force of citizens. The Statute of Escapes in 1504 introduced a scale of fines to be imposed on gaolers, the amount depending on the seriousness of the charge against the prisoner who had absconded.

Despite the efforts of the Court of Aldermen the cruelties and corruptions in Newgate continued without abatement. Ironing was wholesale among the criminal prisoners, except for those who were able to afford the exemption fee; in 1290 a man was fettered so tightly around the neck that his spine was broken. An additional cause of concern was that the gaol was falling into a condition of chronic disrepair. In 1313 the king directed the City to carry out immediate renovations; his order was ignored, and in 1329 it was reported that the walls of Newgate had become 'so weak and threatened with ruin' that they no longer afforded any real security. Thereafter the sheriffs were instructed repeatedly to execute repairs but they invariably declined to do so. About this time the keeper, Edmund le Lorimer, was committed to the Fleet for torturing and blackmailing his prisoners, loading them unmercifully with irons and subjecting them to excessive fees. A few years later one of his successors was dismissed for confining minor offenders in the dungeons of the gaol and torturing them until they had given him large sums of money. The aldermen were becoming so alarmed about the state of their prisons that in 1356 they issued an ordinance that there should be quarterly proclamations in the City inviting those who had grievances against the sheriffs or keepers to lay them before the civic authorities. In 1370 a further ordinance forbade the brewing of beer, the baking of bread or the retailing of victuals within the precincts of Newgate Gaol, but in 1393 this regulation was amended so as to permit the prison officials to resume the sale of food to the inmates provided they did not charge exorbitant prices for it. It is noticeable that around this period the aldermen were so aware of the appalling conditions in Newgate that they took steps to ensure that as many of the freemen as possible would be committed to Ludgate.

When the Court of Aldermen decided to re-open Ludgate after its brief closure between 1419 and 1420 they issued an ordinance declaring that 'by reason of the foetid and corrupt atmosphere that is in the hateful gaol of Newgate' many freemen who had been transferred there were dead, 'who might have been living, it is said, if they had remained in Ludgate abiding in peace'. Richard Whittington, Lord Mayor of London at the time, and his aldermen decided that thenceforth Ludgate should be maintained as a prison for 'all citizens and other reputable persons'. Whittington, who has been immortalized in folklore and pantomime, was a mercer who served as Lord Mayor three times; he was also a philanthropist and when he died in 1423 he bequeathed a sum of money sufficient for the complete rebuilding of Newgate Gaol. The reconstruction started almost immediately and the new prison, which was completed within a few years, stretched up from the Old Bailey in a northerly direction forming an arch over Newgate Street. It was a much larger building than its predecessor, with a central hall, a chapel, day and night wards, and separate compartments for women; in addition, there were the inevitable dungeons, and superior rooms for those prisoners who were able to pay for them. Some effort was now made to house the debtors and the minor offenders apart from the more serious criminals. Despite the manifold improvements, however, the chronicler Raphael Holinshed writing in the following century was constrained to describe Newgate as 'a most ugly and loathsome prison'.

The rebuilt Newgate drew its water supply from a fountain on the north side of the gaol, but this was scarcely suitable for drinking and caused a great deal of illness. About 1435 the Priory and the Hospital of St Bartholomew offered to make their surplus water available for the prisoners both at Newgate and at Ludgate. Thomas Knolles, a grocer who had been Lord Mayor of London in 1400, undertook to pay for the installation and upkeep of the necessary leaden pipes and, as Stow says, 'he caused sweet water to be conveyed to the gates of Newgate and Ludgate for the relief of the prisoners there.'

For the most part, the time spent by a prisoner awaiting trial in London was not so protracted as it might be in other parts of the country, both because of the more regular sittings of the City courts and the more frequent Commissions of Gaol Delivery in the City prisons. A statute in 1328 provided that Newgate was to be delivered at least three times a year; even this, apparently, was sometimes inadequate for in 1341 Edward III complained to the Mayor that the gaol was 'so full of prisoners that they are continually dying of hunger and oppression'; on the other hand the same monarch became resentful if Newgate was delivered without his specific commission, and he rebuked the Mayor and the Recorder* in 1375, saying he had been informed 'that they have many times held such sessions in the absense of his justices appointed for the delivery thereof'. It was decided in 1475 that Newgate should be delivered at least five times a year, four times by the sheriffs and once – twice if necessary – by the Mayor.

The number of commissioners appointed for each session of gaol delivery at Newgate usually varied between two and twelve, but exceptionally there might be as many as eighteen; they always included a number of professional judges, and from 1327 the serving mayor became an ex officio member of every commission. It was customary to hold the Newgate sessions in a room at the gaol, though the justices disliked entering prisons because of the dirt, the stench and the risk of infection. In 1334 Newgate was provided with a special sessions house, when a building consisting of 'a hall and three fit chambers' was erected on a vacant plot to the north of the gaol; for some reason this fell into disuse soon afterwards, and in 1365 the Newgate gaol deliveries were being held at the Guildhall. It was not until 1539 that another sessions house for Newgate Gaol was built in the Old Bailey; more will be said about this – the original Old Bailey courthouse – in a later chapter.

* The senior judicial officer of the City of London.

CHAPTER THREE

THE RITUALS OF PUNISHMENT

IT is scarcely surprising that the word 'penology' did not originate until well into the nineteenth century, since the theory and principles of punishment were as basic as they were crude until the advent of the moral philosophers of the utilitarian school. Although Britain was nominally a Christian country the treatment of criminals was governed, not by the compassionate doctrines of the New Testament but by the implacable concepts of the Old; amongst the harsher precepts which Christianity had inherited from Hebraism was the axiom that the righteous should rejoice at the sufferings of the sinner. In consequence the State endeavoured to punish law-breakers in such a manner that their afflictions would be witnessed by as many people as possible both for the retributive satisfaction and the deterrent effect.

During the reign of William the Conqueror the death penalty for more serious offences was almost entirely superseded by the sentence of mutilation; it might be bodily mutilation, such as the removal of the hands or the feet, and it might be facial, like the severance of the nose or ears, or the excision of the eyes. The sentence was usually carried out in public and might well be followed by a period of imprisonment. During the thirteenth century execution was reestablished as the common punishment for all felonies except the very minor; mutilation was still continued, but it was rarely applied in its more severe forms, and in later years it largely survived in the branding of convicted criminals.

Another form of punishment which always aroused a great deal of interest was a public flogging. This was either inflicted at a fixed whipping post, or else the victim's hands were tied to the tail of a cart, which was drawn slowly through the crowds whilst the chastisement was in progress. Prisoners of

26

any age and of either sex were liable to be flogged, the ordinary procedure being to strip them to the waist and to administer the lashes across the bare back and shoulders. Whipping was, in fact, considered to be a fairly moderate penalty and especially appropriate to beggars, vagrants and vagabonds; it was also the normal punishment for common law misdemeanours, and even for statutory misdemeanours when no other penalty was specifically authorised. Women and girls were still flogged in public until 1817, and in private until 1820.

The pillory was used in Britain from the Anglo-Saxon era. It was intended to expose the victim to indignity and ridicule rather than to physical pain, and it became a regular punishment for cheats, brawlers, nagging females and prostitutes. When a prisoner was ordered to stand in the pillory the court laid down the places and the duration, and any other embellishments which they thought fit to impose; the sentence was often accompanied by a period of imprisonment. For example, in 1364 a certain John de Hakford was convicted of perjury and sentenced to imprisonment in Newgate for a year and a day and 'within that year to be pilloried four times, once in every quarter of the City'. The court specified that on each of the four occasions he should emerge from Newgate 'without hood or girdle, barefoot and unshod, with a whetstone hung by a chain from his neck and lying on his breast, it being marked with the words "a false liar", and there shall be a pair of trumpets trumpeting before him on his way to the pillory.' De Hakford was to remain locked in the pillory for three hours each time and then be taken back to Newgate. In the seventeenth and eighteenth centuries the pillory became the centre of demonstrations by hostile crowds and a number of prisoners were severely injured or even killed as they stood imprisoned and powerless before the fury of the mob. The pillory was abolished as a punishment in Britain in 1837.

The development of capital punishment in Britain is closely interwoven with the growth of the strange and illogical doctrine known as 'Benefit of Clergy'; this, as Sir James Stephen commented in his authoritative study of criminal legal history, for a great length of time 'reduced the administration of justice to a sort of farce'. The underlying principle of Benefit was that clerks in holy orders were exempted from the jurisdiction of the ordinary criminal courts and were subject only to ecclesiastical authority. The scope of the immunity was enlarged in 1350 when it was granted by statute to the holders of a number of subsidiary clerical appointments including sub-deacons, exorcists and ecclesiastical doorkeepers; by a sweeping extension soon afterwards it was made to embrace all those male defendants who were able to read, whether they had any connections with the clergy or not. Since women could not be ordained they were considered to be ineligible for Benefit unless, up to the time of the Reformation, they happened to be members of one of the recognized orders of nunnery. In 1622, when it had become clearly established that this privilege had little or no connection with clerical office, female defendants were permitted to claim Benefit for certain minor felonies; in 1692 the remaining distinctions were removed and they were placed on exactly the same footing as men.

There can be no doubt that Benefit of Clergy was deliberately expanded by the judiciary in order to ameliorate the harshness of a criminal code, which prescribed the death penalty as a mandatory sentence upon every person convicted of felony. If a prisoner was successful in claiming Benefit, theoretically he would be handed over to the ecclesiastical courts for trial and punishment, but in practice the worst that that was likely to befall him was that he might be made to perform some penance or to undergo demotion in his clerical status. This created a ludicrous situation in which a man might commit one crime after another and still be immune from punishment. The position was modified by statute in 1487 when it was provided that a defendant who had been granted Benefit for the first time should be branded in the thumb, and that thereafter he might never claim the privilege again unless he was genuinely in holy orders. A further encroachment into the lavish application of the doctrine was brought about by the gradual division of felonies in two categories, clergyable and non-clergyable, in the latter of which an application for Benefit could never be made.

A prisoner who wished to claim Benefit of Clergy fell on his knees in the dock and then, with an open prayer-book in his hand, he had to read the first verse of the 51st Psalm, commencing with the words: 'Have mercy upon me, Oh God, according to thy loving kindness.' Many completely illiterate prisoners were astute enough to evade a death sentence by memorizing the vital lines; the judges turned a blind eye to this practice and eventually, at the beginning of the eighteenth century, it was officially recognized as a permissible alternative to the actual reading of the verse. Before its abolition in 1827 Benefit had become a means of escaping the gallows rather than a total exemption from punishment; a person convicted of a clergyable offence who had succeeded in his claim could still be imprisoned for one year or transported for seven; and up to 1779 he might also have been branded or whipped.

One of the most barbarous incidents of a British criminal trial was the procedure known as 'peine forte et dure' – the strong and the hard pain. In addition to any other penalty a court might impose, a conviction for felony resulted in the automatic forfeiture to the Crown of the defendant's entire property and possessions. By a strange anomaly a prisoner could not be convicted of a charge unless he had previously pleaded to the indictment; accordingly, if he was sufficiently determined to retain his estate for his next-of-kin he might refuse to reply when asked to say whether he was 'guilty' or 'not guilty'. From very early times a defendant charged with a felony who refused to plead was ordered by the judge to be taken back to prison and there, in the words of the sentence:

that you be laid out on your back on a bare floor with a cloth round your loins but elsewhere naked; there shall be set upon your body a weight of iron or stone as great as you can bear – and greater; that you have no sustenance, save the first day three morsels of the coarsest bread, on the second day three draughts of stagnant water from the pool nearest to the prison door, on the third day again three morsels of bread as before, and such bread and such water alternately from day to day till you die.

In fact there were very few prisoners who did not submit after a short while, as increasing weights were heaped upon their bodies in this dreaded torture known succinctly as 'the press'. When they yielded and begged to be taken back to the court a message would be passed to the judge who had an unfettered discretion whether he would allow them to return or would leave them to be pressed to death. Sometimes a defendant of exceptional resolution would maintain his defiance to the end for the sake of his wife or family; the ancient volumes of the State Trials contain several such examples. Another method of inducing recalcitrant prisoners to plead to an indictment was to tie their thumbs tightly with whipcord. This was used particularly on women, whose refusal to plead was often motivated by nothing more than sheer obstinacy. Again, a prisoner usually gave way, but sometimes it was only after a protracted spell of resistance; in 1721 a girl called Mary Andrews held out until three successive cords had been wound so tightly around her thumbs that they had snapped with the strain. Newgate Gaol had a special press room set aside for the infliction of peine forte et dure and all prisoners were brought there who had refused to plead at the Sessions House until the abolition of this particular form of torture in the reign of George III.

For many centuries – indeed for almost the whole of its long history – Newgate was very closely associated with the morbid ritual of public execution. A hanging was supposed to be a horrifying, solemn and salutary occasion, but in fact it achieved none of the desired effects. Execution days were eagerly awaited and were treated by the masses as a form of sadistic pageant; a widely-recognized jargon developed: the condemned prisoner became the 'malefactor', his last journey was called 'condemned procession', the gallows was known as 'the fatal tree' and standing beneath it in his last moments the prisoner would be excepted to make his 'death speech'. Eventually, at the climax of the drama, he would be 'turned off' and the fascinated crowds would watch his gradual strangulation until the moment of 'cutting down' by the executioner, which marked the finish of the proceedings.

Death by hanging was by no means instantaneous. There were cases where a reprieve was notified some minutes after the prisoner had been suspended and he still could be brought down and revived; on other more rare occasions the 'corpse' had been taken away by friends and relations and successfully resuscitated. In the Newgate Calendar there is an account of his sensations on the gallows by a man who was cut down while he still lived and was later restored to normal health. John Smith (afterwards known as 'Half-hanged Smith') was convicted of robbery in December 1705. His execution was ordered for Christmas Eve of that year, 'in consequence of which', says the report, 'he was carried to Tyburn, where he performed his devotions, and was turned off in the usual manner; but when he had hung for near fifteen minutes, the people present cried out, "A reprieve". Hereupon the malefactor was cut down, and being conveyed to a house in the neighbourhood he soon recovered, in consequence of bleeding and other applications.' Afterwards he was asked to recount his feelings at the scaffold to which he replied:

That when he was turned off he for some time was sensible of very great pain, occasioned by the weight of his body, and felt his spirits in a strange commotion, violently pressing upwards; that having forced their way to his head he, as it were, saw a great blaze, or glaring light, which seemed to go out at his eyes with a flash, and then he lost all sense of pain. That after he was cut down and began to come to himself, the blood and spirits, forcing themselves into their former channels put him, by a sort of pricking or shooting to such intolerable pain, that he could have wished those hanged who had cut him down.

John Smith was granted a complete pardon two months later, but he soon reverted to his former life of crime. He was incredibly fortunate as he was tried twice more on capital charges and acquitted on both occasions, once on a point of law, and once because the prosecutor died the day before he was due to give his evidence. After Smith's second acquittal he was never heard of again.

The theoretical purpose of public execution was based on two blatant psychological misconceptions, one with regard to the attitude of the condemned prisoners, and the other concerning the reactions of the onlookers. In fact very few prisoners experienced any feelings of ignominy on their last day, nor were they impressed by the solemnity of the occasion; the vast majority were only conscious that this was their brief hour of glory during which they would be the central figures and the focal point of all attention. Nathaniel Hawes, a high-wayman, refused to plead at his trial because his best clothes had been taken away from him when he was apprehended. He maintained that he had always lived like a gentleman and would like to die like one; 'I will not plead,' he is reputed to have said, 'for none shall say that I was hanged in a dirty shirt and a ragged coat.' Dick Turpin bought himself a new suit and a new pair of shoes to wear on the gallows, and he hired five men to follow the condemned cart from Newgate to Tyburn, all dressed in mourning habit. Another highway-man, Jack Rann, known as 'Sixteen String Jack', gave a fare-well dinner party at Newgate on the eve of his execution and according to one report the mixed gathering 'were all re-markably cheerful, nor was Rann less joyous than his com-panions'. Kingsmill, writing about public hanging at a much later period, tells of the demeanour of a murderer after being sentenced to death. He liked to talk about the crowded court-room at his trial and his counsel's address, said Kingsmill:

All were elements that seemed to have greatly gratified his vanity, and to have drugged him into a forgetfulness of the bitterness of his doom. He then dwelt on the speech he would make from the scaffold; [he] was sure there would be an immense concourse of people at his execution as it was a holiday week; and from these, and numerous other considerations, he drew nourishment to that vanity and that love of distinction which had, in no small degree, determined, perhaps, the commission of his crime.

The condemned procession used to set out from Newgate Gaol in the early hours of the morning and to travel slowly past St Sepulchre's Church, along Snow Hill and Holborn Hill into Holborn. From there it went down Oxford Street to the Tyburn Road. Poor prisoners were carried in the con-demned cart, sometimes seated on their own coffins; the wealthier were allowed to use their own coaches with a hearse following behind it.

The low scum of the citizens, in those days [wrote Mayhew and Binny] were regaled by those gloomy exhibitions; and at the peal of the bell of St Sepulchre's Church, assembled around Newgate, from the slums and the disreputable localities in the City, and accompanied the cart conveying the criminals to Tyburn on its dismal procession . . . On certain occasions when a noted highwayman, or burglar, or other criminal, was to be executed, crowds of most respectable citizens might be seen wending their way from all parts of the City towards the fatal tree.

The largest throngs of all assembled round the gallows at Tyburn, but at times the route from Newgate was so congested that the procession had great difficulty in getting through; a condemned man once told the sheriffs on his arrival at Tyburn, that passing through such multitudes was worse than death itself.

For the public an execution was simply an enthralling spectacle. At a time when recognized holidays were few and far between there was a growing acceptance of the fact that absenteeism amongst the working-class in London would be excessive on hanging-days at Tyburn.

It was common through the whole metropolis [said Angelo, writing about conditions in the early eighteenth century] for master-coach-makers, frame-makers, tailors, shoe-makers, and others who had engaged to complete orders within a given time, to bear in mind to observe to their customers 'that will be a hanging-day and my men will not be at work.'

The way in which the mob behaved at the scaffold was described by John Laurence:

Frightful scenes were witnessed at executions, the crowd standing awestruck as it watched the convulsions of the strangling culprit. Every contortion of the limbs was hailed with a cheer or a groan according to whether the sufferer was popular or not; appalling curses and execrations occasionally rent the air and rendered the last moments of the unfortunate criminal more odious; hawkers boldly sang the praises of their wares while a fellow-creature was being done to death. Rich and poor, thief and lord, gentle and simple attended 'the hanging' and cracked jokes at the sufferer's expense.

Although Tyburn became recognized as the regular place for executions in London, these were sometimes performed in the locality where the crime had been committed as late as the eighteenth century; for example, the notorious Sarah Malcolm was hanged in Fleet Street in 1733 for a triple murder committed in the Temple. Also, pirates and sea-robbers

by tradition were hanged at Execution Dock, and most be-
headings took place on Tower Hill. The usual hanging-day
was a Monday and the previous day a special funeral service
was held in the chapel at Newgate Gaol, with the condemned
prisoners seated around a symbolic coffin whilst the Chaplain
harangued them for their wickedness. The condemned pew
was in a most conspicuous position at the centre of the chapel
just below the pulpit, and the seats at a funeral service were
always in great demand by men and women – especially
amongst the well-to-do – who wished to gratify a morbid
curiosity by gazing for an hour or two on the wretches who
were so soon to die. A similar macabre desire led to countless
persons bribing the turnkeys at Newgate to allow them the
opportunity of peering into the condemned hold just prior to
an execution; it is said that over two hundred pounds was
paid for the privilege of seeing Jack Sheppard during the last
few days before his death.

The Church of St Sepulchre, dating from the twelfth century, stood on the north side of Newgate Street in close
proximity to the gaol. In 1605 a wealthy merchant-tailor
named Robert Dow established a charity fund of twenty-six
shillings and eightpence a year in perpetuity to associate St
Sepulchre's with the religious preparation of condemned
prisoners at Newgate. The money was paid to the clerk of the
church who visited the condemned hold at the gaol on the
night before executions and, whilst ringing his handbell, he
had to repeat a chant which began:

> All you that in the condemned hold do lie,
> Prepare you, for tomorrow you shall die;
> Watch all, and pray, the hour is drawing near
> That you before the Almighty must appear;
> Examine well yourselves, in time repent,
> That you may not to eternal flames be sent.
> And when St Sepulchre's bell tomorrow tolls
> The Lord above have mercy on your souls.

The following morning as the condemned procession was
passing St Sepulchre's the principal bell of the church pealed
a funeral knell, and the clerk intoned another canticle to the
prisoners commencing, 'You that are condemned to die, re-
pent with lamentable tears; ask mercy of the Lord for the

salvation of your souls . . .' When the procession had passed, the clerk had to perform his final duty which was to exhort the bystanders with the words, 'All good people, pray heartily unto God for these poor sinners who are now going to their death, for whom the great bell tolls.' Another ceremony which took place when the cortege was wending its way past St Sepulchre's was the presentation of brightly coloured nosegays to the malefactors; it is said that the last recipient of this particular favour was Jack Rann in 1774, and the jaunty highwayman travelled to Tyburn with a massive bouquet adorning the buttonhole of the pea-green coat which he had put on especially for the occasion.

The rites attendant upon a public execution were at the same time bestial, pious and bacchanalian. Many of the prisoners were either wholly or partially intoxicated at the time they set out for Tyburn. It is reported that in 1729, during his last hour at Newgate on the morning fixed for his execution, Major Oneby called for a beaker of brandy and composed his will; indeed such an occurrence was not at all unusual. On a busy hanging-day there might be several condemned carts with as many as five or six prisoners in each. Highwaymen had the ancient privilege of heading the procession of malefactors and if there was a well-known and popular figure amongst them he would probably be mobbed by the throngs lining the route, who strove to obtain from him, said Kingsmill, 'some slight memorial – such as a lock of his hair, or some small part of his dress, which they would cherish with a sentiment for which veneration is the only appropriate term'. Sometimes the procession would pause for refreshment outside a tavern on the road to Tyburn; the Half-Way House in Holborn was a favourite place for the hangman and his victims to join together for a farewell drink.

For a noteworthy malefactor the crowd surrounding the gallows at Tyburn might number as many as 30,000 people. A foreign visitor who watched the execution of a group of men there in 1725 has described the scene:

When all the prisoners arrive at their destination they are made to mount on a very wide cart made expressly for the purpose, and a cord is passed round their necks and the end fastened to a gibbet, which is not very high. The Chaplain who accompanied the condemned men is also in the cart; he makes them pray and sing a few verses of Psalms. The relatives are permitted to mount the cart and take farewell. When the time is up – about a quarter of an hour – the Chaplain and the relatives get off the cart, the executioner covers the eyes and faces of the prisoners with caps, lashes the horses that draw the cart, which slips from under the condemned men's feet, and in this way they remain hanging together.

The public executioner, who presided at Tyburn, was formally appointed to his gruesome office. He was often a reprieved felon and he was paid on a per capita basis for each hanging or flogging he carried out. Every 'Jack Ketch' – after the seventeenth century all public executioners were called by the name of the well-known hangman who died in 1686 – was allowed almost limitless discretion as to how the actual hanging was to be performed. He chose the length of rope, the position of the knot and the duration of the suspension. Also, he decided whether or not death should be accelerated; some hangmen swung on the legs of the strangling prisoners; others sat across their shoulders; and most allowed the victims' friends and relatives to tug at their bodies and to beat them around the region of the heart with lumps of wood or stone. When the rope broke before process of strangulation was complete the hanging started afresh; this happened to Captain Kidd, the pirate, at Execution Dock in 1701. Like all the other officials connected with the penal system the public executioners made a substantial income out of forced gifts and bribes. In a tract on Newgate, published in 1696, the author remarked that the hangman expected payment from his victim, 'demanding his fees and higgling too, as nicely with him as if he was going to do him a mighty favour'; and one of the regicides complained that while he was awaiting execution in 1661 the executioner visited him and demanded money 'that he might be favourable to him at his death', asking first for twenty pounds, then ten, and finally threatening that if he did not receive five pounds 'he would torture him exceedingly'.

The inadvisability, though not perhaps the barbarity, of this execution procedure was stressed by Henry Fielding in 1751 when he wrote:

The Day appointed by Law for the Thief's Shame is a Day of
Glory in his own Opinion. His procession to Tyburn, and his last
Moments there, are all triumphant; attended with the compassion
of the meek and tender-hearted, and with the Applause, Admir-
ation, and Envy of all the bold and hardened. His Behaviour in
his present Condition, not the Crimes, however atrocious, which
have brought him to it, are the Subject of Contemplation. And if
he hath sense enough to temper his Boldness with any Degree of
Decency, his Death is spoke of by many with Honour, by most
with Pity, and by all with Approbation.

Mere hanging was considered too easy a death for those
convicted of treason. The sentence known as 'hanging, drawing and quartering' when applied in its full rigour, is almost
too ghastly to visualize; however, many hangmen deliberately
omitted some of the incidents, or at any rate allowed the
prisoners to die before they were carried out. The full punishment consisted of the condemned man being dragged to the
scaffold, hanged, cut down while he was still alive, castrated
and disembowelled, having his entrails burnt before his eyes,
and finally being chopped into quarters. It has been suggested
by some writers that each of these phases may have had a
symbolic significance, but it seems equally likely that they
were devised in their totality as a particularly unpleasant
method of killing.

A different form of execution was used for women who had
been convicted of high and petty treason – a term which included the murder of a husband by his wife or of an employer
by his servant. The reason for this variation was explained by
Blackstone: 'as the decency due to their sex,' he said 'forbids
the exposing and publicly mangling of their bodies, the sentence is to be drawn to the gallows, and there to be burnt
alive.' In practice the hangman usually strangled the condemned woman before she was actually set alight, but sometimes he did not perform even this small mercy. Catherine
Hayes was sentenced to death in 1726 for killing her husband.
The Newgate Calendar describes her execution. At Tyburn
she 'spent some time in devotion', and then she was fastened
to the stake by an iron chain which encircled her body. The
account goes on, 'A rope was drawn round her neck by the
executioner, to strangle her, which he pulled as tight as he

could; but the flames beginning to reach his hands, he was obliged to let go, and she was seen, in the middle of the fire, pushing the faggots from her, and crying out in such a terrible manner, that those who were present remembered the expressions made use of by her many years afterwards.' Although the hangman and his assistants had heaped fuel on to the fire, 'yet it was a considerable time before she was dead, and three hours before she was reduced to ashes.'

The prisoners in Newgate Gaol lived from day to day under the shadow of punishments such as these.

CHAPTER FOUR

THE HIDDEN YEARS

To the average, thoughtful person in sixteenth century Britain prisons must have seemed as inevitable a component of civilized existence as crime, famine and the plague. Before the awakening of a national, social conscience poverty, disease, hunger and privation were accepted in an attitude of selfish fatalism, and even those of a more humane disposition would have considered it extremely illogical if the living conditions in the common sides of the gaols had been made in any way superior to the meanest standards of the poor. True, there should be enough food to prevent starvation; discipline should stop short of sheer brutality; and the basic needs of the prisoners should be met on a scale just sufficient for the maintenance of sanity and health. Such a viewpoint was exemplified in the approach of the Court of Aldermen to the management of the prisons in the City of London.

There is a dearth of reliable information about the internal conditions of the British gaols in the sixteenth century. A useful supplement to the other available material is provided by the repertories of the Court of Aldermen, in which are recorded all their deliberations and decisions from the year 1495; these show that the City authorities were remarkably well informed about the defects and oppressions of contemporary prison life. Indeed, the pages of the repertories disclose a constant preoccupation with the excesses and the disobedience of the gaolers; this is apparent even in the initial volumes covering the period between 1495 and 1560. It is revealed, for example, that in 1508 the keeper of Ludgate was dismissed for misconduct, and that a few years later complaints were received from the prisoners of the same gaol, first against the behaviour of the keeper, and secondly on account of the 'exactions and oblations of a visiting clergyman'. About the same time the keeper of Marshalsea was ordered

39

to be set in the stocks 'for falsehood in taking fees from prisoners'; and the keeper of the Poultry compter was admonished 'for receiving money from a prisoner for not wearing irons'. In 1550 the keepers of all City gaols were 'commanded to order their prisoners according to the laws and not suffering them to have such liberty as they now have'. In these early volumes there are regular mentions of visitors being appointed to the various prisons, either to carry out a general inspection or to report on some specific matter, as for instance in 1500 when seven persons were nominated 'to visit Newgate and to report on the general decay of the prison'.

The repertories set out the appointment of every Commission of Gaol Delivery at Newgate, at times adding some informal detail, such as in 1535 when it was noted: 'The sessions to be kept at Newgate as accustomed, and the justices to dine with the sheriffs at their own homes.' Four years later, in 1539, a decision was recorded to erect a new house 'for keeping the Gaol Delivery of Newgate, on the void ground against the Fleet Lane in the Old Bailey'. The Sessions House, with its central chamber called the Justice Hall, was duly erected; under its colloquial name of 'The Old Bailey' it was to become the most famous criminal court in the world. Soon after the new building was completed the repertories refer to the inspection of 'the void ground adjoining the Justice Hall', with a view to assigning a portion of land 'for the recreation of the Lord Mayor and other justices'. One can imagine the commissioners of Gaol Delivery strolling in this secluded enclosure in moments of relaxation between their cases. There is no reliable contemporary description of the original Old Bailey. During the succeeding years it was altered and enlarged, and in 1720 it was, according to John Strype, 'a fair and stately building, very commodious, and with large galleries on both sides for spectators'. The courtroom, he says, 'being advanced by stone steps from the ground, with rails and banisters, is enclosed from the yard before it, and the bail-dock where the prisoners are kept until brought to their trials is also enclosed'. Certainly in Strype's day it was unnecessary for the justices to be entertained by the sheriffs at their own homes for he says that over the court was 'a stately dining-room, sustained by ten stone pillars'. It seems probable that the original Sessions House was comparatively simple and unadorned. There is an entry in the repertories for 1550, 'The Chamberlain to make a hovel at the Justice Hall to keep the prisoners dry at the time of their arraignment,' and another, twelve years later, 'A shed to be made at the Justice Hall for the jury to stand dry at the time of the sessions when it shall snow or rain.'

For the rest, the repertories covering the first half of the sixteenth century show that the Court of Aldermen, in their management of the City gaols, concerned themselves with re-pairs, escapes and the administration of prison charity. There are sporadic allusions to the subject of fees; in one instance the keepers of the compters are directed to account for all the money they take from their prisoners, and in another, they are ordered to exhibit tables of fees in places where the prisoners can see them. From the intermittent records of committals to Newgate it is apparent that the aldermen regarded the gaol as being suitable for purely civic offenders as well as for crimi-nals; in 1510 Thomas Yong was sent there 'for his contempt against the liberties of this city', and William Clark, 'for his disobedience and using himself contrary to the ancient laws of the City'.

The information in regard to Newgate during the period, apart from that contained in the repertories, is very sparse; however, it is sufficient to show that in spite of the apparently diligent supervision of the Court of Aldermen the gaol was mismanaged and overcrowded, and the prisoners were sub-jected to continual extortion and cruelty. During the reign of Henry VIII Newgate was first used for the victims of religious persecution, at the instigation in particular of the uncom-promising Edmund Bonner who became Bishop of London in 1539. On one occasion a preacher named John Porter dis-pleased Bishop Bonner who had him seized and imprisoned in Newgate, 'where he was miserably fettered in irons,' says John Foxe, 'both arms and legs, with a collar of iron about his neck, fastened to the wall in the dungeon.' Eventually the keeper was bribed by one of Porter's relations to remove his fetters and to transfer him to a felon's ward. On his arrival there Porter began to propagate his religious views amongst his fellow prisoners, and in consequence he was 'carried down and laid in the lower dungeon of all, oppressed with bolts and irons, where, within six or eight days he was found dead'.

The first keeper of Newgate to become notorious was Andrew Alexander. His brutality has been described by Foxe who wrote, 'Of gaolers, Alexander, keeper of Newgate, exceeded all others – a cruel enemy of those that lay for religion. The cruel wretch, to hasten poor lambs to the slaughter would go to Bonner, Story, Chomley, and others crying "Rid my prison! Rid my prison! I am too old to be pestered by these heretics." ' Although Andrew Alexander is principally remembered for his savage persecution of his protestant prisoners in the reign of Queen Mary, the repertories show that he was appointed keeper of Newgate during the reign of Henry VIII. Like so many merciless men he had a strange, enigmatic side to his character which was revealed in a letter from Edward Underhill, a prisoner at Newgate in 1553. According to Underhill, Alexander and his wife used to take supper with the prisoners, presumably on the master's side, every evening. Underhill was an accomplished musician and on his first evening in the gaol another prisoner said to him, 'I will show you the nature and manner of them [the Alexanders]. They do both love music very well; wherefore, you with your lute, and I with you on my rebeck, will please them greatly. He loveth to be merry and drink wine, and she also. If you will bestow upon them, every dinner and supper, a quart of wine and some music, you shall be their white son, and have any favour they can show you.'

In 1554 John Rogers, the Vicar of St Sepulchre's, was imprisoned in Newgate as a heretic. He was kept on the master's side but during his year at the gaol, says Foxe, he devoted himself to the service of the ordinary prisoners. At one time he proposed 'that he and his fellows should have but one meal a day, they paying, notwithstanding, the charges of the whole; the other meals should be given to them that lacked on the other (or common) side of the prison. But Alexander, their keeper . . . would in no case suffer that.' Finally, Mrs Alexander came to Rogers and told him to prepare himself for the fire. He was taken to Smithfield by the sheriffs and burnt on the scaffold.

Alexander's methods were well illustrated by the treatment

of John Philpot, the Archdeacon of Winchester. Directly Philpot arrived at Newgate Alexander said to him, 'If you will recant I will show you any pleasure I can;' to which his new prisoner replied, 'I will never recant whilst I have my life.' Alexander then 'commanded him to be set upon the block with as many irons upon his legs as he could bear'. When Philpot pleaded for mercy, Alexander said, 'Give me my fees and I will take them off; if not, thou shalt wear them still.' Philpot offered him a pound which was all the money he had available. Alexander scornfully rejected this sum commenting, 'What use is that to me?' and ordered Philpot to be removed to a dungeon. Foxe adds a postscript on the death of Andrew Alexander; 'he died very miserably', he says, 'being so swollen that he was more like a monster than a man.'

During the forty-five year reign of Elizabeth I Newgate was used increasingly as a State prison. Felons and debtors were still sent there, but they shared the gaol with those imprisoned for their religious or political beliefs, or for their alleged treasonable activities. 'All this time within Newgate,' wrote the first historian of the prison, 'there was turbulence, rioting and disorders, accompanied by seemingly constant oppression.' A careful study of the repertories for the period confirms the view that the prisoners in the gaol, and indeed in all the City prisons, were subjected to an unscrupulous tyranny, especially at the hands of the keepers.

During the first years of Elizabeth's reign the Court of Aldermen set up one committee, 'to survey and consider the price of meat, drink etc., mentioned in the two tables of Ludgate and Newgate', and another 'to peruse the ordinances touching Ludgate and Newgate'; they also discussed the 'reformation of abuses by the keeper of Newgate against the poor prisoners' in his gaol, and investigated the 'abuses of the City prisons' generally. In 1574 the keeper of Newgate was fined for persistent disobedience of orders, and in 1580 the repertories record the decision of the aldermen to consider the request of the prisoners of Newgate 're. the hard dealing of the officers there'. Shortly afterwards a committee was nominated to examine complaints against William Crowder, the recently appointed Newgate keeper. Crowder was, in fact, another of the long line of ill-famed keepers of the gaol; he was alleged to have habitually exacted bribes from his prisoners and to have levied inordinate fines upon them. In addition, according to the State Papers, 'Crowder and his wife were the most horrible blasphemers and swearers.' As a result of the aldermanic enquiry Crowder was dismissed from his position, but the Lord Chancellor, Sir Thomas Bromley, took up the matter and informed the Lord Mayor that the late keeper had been harshly treated. In the outcome Crowder was granted an annuity for life. During the years which followed the Court of Aldermen were hearing a succession of complaints by the prisoners of Newgate, Ludgate and the compters; on one occasion they determined to draft an answer to the accusation that the keeperships of their prisons were being 'reserved for decayed citizens'.

The precise and impersonal records in the repertories for the Elizabethan era do not provide any significant revelations concerning the daily lives of prisoners in the City gaols. It is clear that those detained on the common sides continued to be largely dependent on charity for their subsistence. There are references to collections in St Paul's for the poor prisoners in Newgate; and in 1558 the aldermen made an order 'staying prisoners from going abroad to beg their fees', but this practice was not ended, for in 1570 a resolution was passed that the sheriffs should retain the keys of the new boxes used for collecting alms by the poor prisoners in the compters. Security in Newgate seems to have improved as there are few mentions of escapes; however, on two occasions it is stated that prisoners had been awarded punishments for possessing in the gaol iron files 'for striking off bolts'. One method of obtaining release from prison which was prevalent at that time was by volunteering for service in the army or the navy; the primitive horrors of foreign campaigns or of life at sea seemed to many prisoners to be infinitely preferable to the endless uncertainties of existence in the gaols. In 1559 there is an entry in the repertories to the effect that certain prisoners were to remain in Newgate until they were sent for by the Lord High Admiral.

The repertories reflect the concern of the aldermen that the City prisons should be maintained in a relatively sound and adequate condition. About 1554 there was a fire in Newgate which necessitated fairly extensive renovations; a few months afterwards the keeper was summoned to attend before the Court of Aldermen 'for an order touching the repair of Newgate and re-edifying the part lately burnt', and the City Chamberlain was instructed to repair the kitchens which had also been damaged. In 1568 it was decided that the Justice Hall should be enlarged; in 1584 that the privies of Ludgate were to be cleansed; in 1593 that the 'decay of Newgate was to be viewed and repaired', and in 1598 that the bail-dock at the Sessions House was to be enlarged 'and convenient forms to be provided for the juries to sit upon'.

Naturally the spiritual welfare of prisoners – especially the condemned at Newgate – was considered to be of paramount importance. The repertories for 1562 contain a note. 'The Governors of the House of the Poor to take order with the vicar there for goodly advice to be given by him to the cast of men at Newgate when going to their deaths.' In 1595 it was directed that a Bible and a Prayer Book should be provided for each preacher in Newgate and subsequently that a pulpit and communion table should be placed in the chapel at the gaol. The first visiting clergyman had been appointed to Newgate in 1544 when it was arranged that one of the four chaplains at St Bartholomew's Hospital should undertake this extra duty. In 1546 the system was altered and from that year a member of the Clergy of Christ Church was nominated to be 'Visitor of Newgate' under the control of the aldermen and the Common Council. His duties, which were read over to him when he took up office commenced, 'Your charge is faithfully and diligently to visit all the poor and miserable captives within the prison of Newgate, and minister unto them such ordinary service at times convenient, as is appointed by the King's Majesty's book for ordinary prayer. Also that ye learn without book the most wholesome sentences of holy scripture, that may comfort a desperate man . . . ' He was further enjoined to persuade the prisoners to return any property they had stolen, and to 'disclose all such other persons as they know living, which by robbery or murder may hurt a common weal. And in all their extremes and sicknesses ye shall be diligent and ready to comfort them with the most pithy and fruitful sentences of God's most holy word.' In 1615 the Mayor suggested to the Governors of St Bartholomew's that the stipend of the Visitor might be increased; apart from preaching two or three times a week in the gaol, he said, the Visitor's functions included 'going with the condemned prisoners to the place of execution, to exhort them to prepare themselves to God' and 'adventuring daily the safety and health of his body in so contagious a place'. The Visitors of Newgate, who were more frequently referred to as the 'Ordinaries', continued to be part-time chaplains at the gaol until the appointment of Henry Goodcole in 1620 when the Court of Aldermen granted him five pounds a year in addition to the annual stipend of ten pounds which he was receiving from the Governors of St Bartholomew's. This extra payment became a permanent arrangement and it enabled the Ordinaries to devote themselves completely to their prison work. One of the stranger tasks they were expected to perform was the compilation of the case-histories of certain notorious prisoners; these accounts formed the basis of the two collections which were published at the beginning of the nineteenth century, both under the title of 'The Newgate Calendar'.

CHAPTER FIVE

THE CASTLE OF MISERY

DURING the reign of James I Newgate continued to be over-crowded with criminals, debtors and religious prisoners. The internal conditions in the City gaols showed no apparent improvement, as the repertories for the first few decades of the seventeenth century are filled with allusions to inefficiency, corruption and destitution. There were complaints against the keepers of both compters and the Bridewell alleging the 'taking of excessive fees' and other 'grievous exactions' from their prisoners; and there were numerous reports of abuses in Newgate where the poor prisoners were expressing an increasing dissatisfaction over both the inadequacy and the method of distribution of the meagre issues of free food. Simon Haughton, the keeper of Newgate at this time, incurred the anger of the king, not for his venality, but for allowing Masses to be said in his gaol and for showing reverence to priests who were confined there. In compliance with the royal wish that the keeper should be 'severely punished' for his laxity Haughton was replaced in 1611 – though the repertories note that the reason given for his dismissal was that he suffered 'Bartholomew Logate, an Arian, to go at large'. A year later he was prosecuted in the Star Chamber. In 1616 the keepers of all the City gaols were summoned before the Court of Aldermen for 'the reading of orders touching fees to be taken by them of prisoners', and shortly afterwards a committee was set up 'to examine the abuses of the keepers', in the City of London.

One of the earliest authentic glimpses into the interior of Newgate Gaol is provided by a mayoral proclamation in September 1617, an original copy of which is still preserved at the Corporation of London Records Office. It is headed 'A Proclamation for Reforming of Abuses in the Gaol of Newgate', and it reads:

Whereas of late, notorious mutinies and outrages have been commited by the prisoners within the gaol of Newgate, which is conceived to grow through the negligence of the keepers in suffering their prisoners to become drunk and disordered, permitting them wine, tobacco, excessive strong drink, and resort to women of lewd behaviour. By reason of which liberty, dissolute and lewd persons, who commit thefts and robberies, take a kind of comfort, and gather heart in the said gaol and are . . . intent to commit felonies, upon the hope of lewd company and such lewd comforts as they find in the said gaol.

Attached to the proclamation is a list of rules which had been drawn up, as it was stated, 'for reformation, to curb oppressions of gaolers, and to remove these shameful comforts'. The significance of this list is that it reveals by inference the nature of the 'abuses', so often referred to in the repertories and in other contemporary writings. The rules prescribed that the keeper must be 'attendant himself upon the said gaol and not farm it out'. The quantity of beer, ale and tobacco allowed into the gaol was to be restricted. The officers were to ensure 'that men prisoners and women prisoners be kept asunder, and not suffered to come together in any part of the said prison, except it be at the time of divine service, receiving the Sacrament, or hearing of sermons'. Further, the officers were not to permit 'any woman to be with any man prisoner alone in the prison, but only his wife, mother, sister, or near kind of woman to such prisoner, and so known to the keeper before she be admitted'. The levying of unofficial fees was forbidden and officers were not to accept gifts of 'meat, drink, or other needful provisions' from the prisoners; nor were they to demand any fees 'in respect of ease of irons', except those which they were lawfully entitled to charge. Prisoners who mutinied or showed insolence were to be 'loaded with more irons and put into the dungeon, or otherwise chastised in the discretion of the Master Keeper, so that such chastisement tend not to the loss of life or limb'. Finally, for the avoidance of quarrels amongst prisoners, the playing at cards, dice, or any other game whatsoever' was prohibited.

It was during the reign of James I that a new punishment crept into the British penal system which was to exercise a considerable influence on the future of prison development. The first reference to the wholesale penal banishment of criminals appears in a letter written by the king in 1619 when he mentioned that a hundred prisoners had been sent to the Colony of Virginia. Later in the seventeenth century an Act of Parliament provided that persons convicted of certain offences might be pardoned on condition that they agreed to be transported overseas; and since a sentence of transportation was usually an alternative to hanging there was little likelihood that any prisoners would refuse to give their consent. The normal periods of the sentence were seven or fourteen years, but it was sometimes ordered for life. The Webbs have stated in their authoritative history of imprisonment that during the Civil War transportation grew into the systematic disposal of felons and became, virtually, a branch of the slave-trade. The 'transports', as the prisoners were called, were handed over to contractors, who also received a bounty from the Government; the contractor then shipped out his transports to the plantations of Maryland or Virginia, and sold them in the regular slave-markets for the highest price obtainable. A parliamentary committee which in 1785 surveyed this early system of transportation found that 'it answered every good purpose that could be expected from it'; in addition to reclaiming the prisoners and rendering them good citizens, 'it was not attended with very much expense to the public, the convicts being carried out in vessels employ'd in the Jamaica or tobacco trade . . . for many years the Government paid five pounds a man and afterwards no premium at all, the contractor being indemnified by the price at which he sold their labour.'

There is little doubt that Newgate at this time was falling into a state of chronic disrepair; indeed, the gaol had not undergone any substantial restoration since it had been reconstructed by Richard Whittington's executors in 1423. In 1613 the Court of Aldermen had resolved that Newgate should be renovated, but little if any action was taken, for in 1627 the repertories record yet another decision that 'the decay in Newgate' was to be inspected. A year later a committee was formed 'to view the ruins of Newgate'; in due course they submitted an estimate that the replacement of stonework and other essential repairs would cost about three hundred and thirty-four pounds. Apparently the committee's recommendations were followed in whole or in part, as the repertories for 1629 mention the mending of the leads at the gaol and the provision of stone for the repairs in progress there. The renovations appear to have been extensive for in 1630 the keeper of Newgate in a petition to the king expressed a fear that prisoners might escape before the work was completed, 'because of the great ruins to the gaol'. He prayed that, to ease his problem, directions should be given to the Lord Mayor and the Recorder to certify 'how many are capable of His Majesty's mercy' and that the Attorney-General should prepare pardons for them accordingly. As a result forty-four prisoners were released. During the following years there are constant references in the repertories to inspections of the defects of Newgate; in 1643 there is a mention of further repairs to the gaol, and of an approach being made to the House of Lords for certain prisoners to be pardoned while the work was in hand.

The custom was still continued of releasing prisoners on condition that they joined the armed forces for service overseas. In 1619 the Lord Mayor certified to James I that certain inmates of Newgate were sufficiently able-bodied 'for service in foreign parts', and in 1622 the gaol became so overcrowded that sixty-three men were discharged upon their undertaking to enlist in the army. A year later a youth under sentence of death in Newgate for stealing a purse was released because, it was stated, he was 'an excellent drummer and fit to do the King's service'. In the summer of 1624 the Recorder of London sent to the Secretary of State a list of the names of thirty-one Newgate prisoners, with the comment, 'They pester the gaol this hot weather, and would do better service as soldiers than if pardoned, for they would not dare to run away.'

The state of Newgate Gaol in the seventeenth century, as revealed by the official, civic records is somewhat different from that which appears in the contemporary disclosures by some of the prisoners there. Although the repertories are full of allusions to complaints, abuses, and the misdeeds of various keepers, nevertheless they give the overall impression of a carefully supervised and comparatively well-ordered establishment. It would be only too easy to form a totally false impression from reading about the frequent inspections, the diligent inquiries and the administrative zeal of the aldermanic committees: it would be equally misleading to base an opinion solely upon the fragmentary recriminations which emanated from the pens and the lips of a handful of prisoners at the gaol. The two images must surely be complementary, the one providing the views of the authorities, and the other the impressions of the inmates regarding the state of the principal prison in London.

It is difficult to estimate how thorough a knowledge was possessed by the aldermen of the actual living conditions in Newgate. The majority of people shared an understandable reluctance to venture across the threshold of this or any other gaol owing to the infections, the stench and the general unpleasantness of the interiors, and it may well be that most of their information came indirectly from the representations of the prisoners and the keepers. The highest obligation of the civic authorities was to ensure that the gaols were functioning fairly adequately and to endeavour to curb all the more blatant excesses which came to their notice; nothing more was expected from them.

In 1572 an Act of Parliament had been passed requiring justices of the peace to levy a small parish rate for the purchase of bread, known as 'the county allowance', to be distributed in every county gaol to those in need. This was the earliest official scheme in Britain for supplying free food to indigent prisoners, but it was only designed to provide them with subsistence just above starvation level. Further, the county allowance was restricted to convicted felons; prisoners who had been sentenced for misdemeanours, and those who were detained for debt or were merely awaiting trial were not eligible to receive it; nor were felons who had finished their sentences but were remaining in custody because they could not afford to pay their discharge fees. The obligation upon creditors to provide the debtors they had imprisoned with a basic allowance of bread and water was consistently ignored. In the resulting situation the meagre and spasmodic allocations of money and food through philanthropic sources continued to be of vital importance to the welfare of the prisoners. The repertories for the seventeenth century disclose the Court of Aldermen's recurrent anxiety about the distribution of alms and the purchase of food in the prisons. In 1636 a committee was appointed 'to consider a supply of relief to the prisoners in Newgate'; two years later a sheriff was instructed to carry out an examination of butchers' and the bakers' accounts for the gaol. In 1650 the staff at Newgate were forbidden to share in the issues of free bread, and in 1653 the sheriffs were instructed to collect in all the relief money due to the gaol.

The allocation of charitable provisions in Newgate was largely in the hands of an official called the Steward. In 1630 the poor prisoners in the gaol protested that the holder of this office, a Henry Woodhouse, was responsible for extensive misappropriations. The Court of Aldermen set up a committee to investigate the allegations, and two years later a new code of rules was introduced 'for and concerning the good government of the Gaol of Newgate'. It was ordered that the sum of fifty-five pounds eight shillings and four pence 'given to the prisoners yearly by charitable gifts and legacies and other reliefs' was, from then on, to be handed direct to the aldermen who would organize a quarterly distribution at the gaol. Henry Woodhouse was to be replaced by another steward, 'nominated and chosen by the major part of the said prisoners in the Common Gaol from amongst themselves'; his term of service was to be limited to one year and he was only to receive 'his former accustomed allowance of twelve pence weekly in money and his double share of rations and his lodging in the Steward's room'. Naturally, it was too much to hope that a prisoner suddenly finding himself with the power and privileges of the steward would abstain from using them to his own advantage, and there were perpetual complaints against successive holders of this office.

The only penological principle at that time seems to have been that the criminal should be encouraged to feel a proper sense of repentance for his crime and a stoical resignation regarding his punishment. In this respect the Ordinary at Newgate played an important role, and in 1662 the aldermen decided that his salary should be increased by forty pounds per annum: the first incumbent to receive this addition was discharged a few years later for an unspecified offence. In 1657 it was resolved that the prisoners should be 'excited more devoutley to attend their Religious Duties'. During the same year the inmates of the City gaols petitioned that they should be allowed to beg in the street every Sunday morning during Divine Service; however, this proposal was rejected with the determination that, 'No further liberty could be given them than that which they use, which is to beg after five in the afternoon of that day.'

The idea that prisoners should be forced to undergo any sort of compulsory, organized work in place of their customary pastimes of drinking, gambling and fornication only commended itself to the legislature of a later age. Nevertheless, in 1658 the Court of Aldermen did set up a committee 'to consider how prisoners may be held to labour in the City prisons', but with no constructive results. An Act of Parliament in 1667 enabled Justices of the Peace to impose a rate of not more than sixpence per week in every parish for 'setting poor prisoners to work'; this statute was permissive rather than mandatory and it seems to have been generally disregarded.

Throughout this period the Court of Aldermen were encountering perennial complaints against their keepers for exacting illegal or excessive fees, although, oddly enough, in 1632 the keeper of Newgate was reprimanded for discharging prisoners without making them pay any fees at all. On several occasions the scale of fees in all the City prisons were examined by the aldermen, and sometimes a committee would be nominated by them to inquire into the fees which were being charged in some particular gaol. On one occasion the Lord Mayor and aldermen were obliged to demonstrate their authority over the sheriffs in the appointment of the Newgate keeper. This happened in 1638 when James Franklin died after holding the keepership for about two years. The sheriffs immediately appointed Henry Woolaston to succeed him, but the choice was unacceptable to the aldermen who had wished to settle the position upon a young man called Richard Johnson. The disagreement might well have been based on nepotism as it is significant that one of the sheriffs at the time bore the name of John Woolaston; on the other hand, Richard

C

Johnson was employed as clerk to the Recorder. Directly Henry Woolaston had taken up office the Lord Mayor and aldermen demanded that he should hand over all the keys of Newgate; this he refused to do without the permission of the sheriffs. Woolaston was thereupon arrested and Richard Johnson was installed in his place by the aldermen, the sheriffs being peremptorily directed to afford him 'quiet enjoyement' of the gaol. The sheriffs protested that the aldermen were usurping one of their ancient and undoubted privileges, and they pointed out that the direct responsibility for preventing escapes from the City gaols rested on them. The Court of Aldermen met to discuss an item which is referred to in the repertories as 'the question of the Pretended Right of the Sheriffs to the disposal of the Keepership of Newgate Gaol'. They decided that Richard Johnson should retain the office, but agreed to consider a petition from Henry Woolaston seeking financial compensation for his deprivation. This was not, in fact, the end of the matter for in 1642 Johnson was dismissed for misconduct, and Woolaston, with the joint approval of both the sheriffs and the aldermen, was officially appointed the keeper of Newgate.

It might be imagined that in any serious disputes between the prisoners and their keepers the aldermen would almost invariably have supported the latter, but this was by no means so. The affair of Walter Cowdery was a case in point. Cowdery became keeper of Newgate in 1664 and a year later the prisoners at the gaol submitted a petition to the Court of Aldermen complaining of his 'oppressions and cruelty'. The Court examined these grievances and were so well satisfied with their authenticity that they set up a committee to report on the advisability of 'prosecuting an indictment against the keeper'. Cowdery appeared before the committee, seeking to justify his behaviour; eventually he was dismissed from office and was apparently charged with some offence as there is a reference in 1668 to payment of the costs for his prosecution. Apart from his inhumanity to the prisoners there were other criticisms about conduct for the Recorder said of him, 'The keeper of Newgate hath at this day made his house the only nursery of rogues, prostitutes, pickpockets, and thieves in the world, where they were held and entertained, and the whole society met.' The sheriffs, the Recorder added, 'durst not this day commit him for fear of making him let out the prisoners, but were fain to go by artifice to deal with him.'

The best first-hand descriptions of Newgate in the seventeenth century come from the prisoners themselves and are mostly contained in their petitions for release; the grim brutality of the living conditions at the gaol emerges graphically from the phrases they employ. In 1620 some prisoners who had been recently transferred from the King's Bench prison spoke of Newgate as 'a place of infamy and great distress', and about the same period someone said of the inmates that 'lice seem to be their most constant companions'. Sir Nicholas Poyntz, who was imprisoned there in 1626 for killing a man in a street brawl, complained that he was kept in 'a dungeon without bed or light' and that he was forced to lie in a coffin; he petitioned the Privy Council to transfer him to another gaol instead of 'the loathsome prison of Newgate'. In 1630 a fishmonger wrote from the gaol that for the past five months he had been 'heavily laden with intolerable bolts and shackles'; he said he had become a lame, weak and aged man and was likely to perish. Another prisoner a few years later protested that he had 'lain in a dungeon for fourteen days without light or fire, living on a halfpenny worth of bread a day'. Thomas Reynolds, a fifty-eight year old priest who had been in Newgate for five years, petitioned for his release in 1634 pleading that, 'by the unwholesomeness of the air, the strictness of the imprisonment, and his great age he is fallen into dangerous infirmities'; he appended a certificate signed by three doctors stating that he was suffering from 'sciatica, defluxion of rheum and stone'.

It must be accepted that, for their part, most of the prisoners in Newgate, especially the felons, were neither docile nor obedient, and riots and disorders were habitual events in the gaol. Sometimes the trouble originated from totally unexpected causes. In 1642 six Jesuit priests, who were awaiting execution in the condemned hold, were granted an eleventh hour reprieve, 'whereupon did arise,' says an official report, 'a tumultuous mutiny among the other prisoners, who refused to die without the Jesuits, but afterwards they

[the mutineers] were mitigated into a kind of pacified tran-
quility.' Another revolt, in 1649, commenced in the chapel
where seventeen condemned prisoners were attending their
own funeral service. It had been arranged that a number of
their wives would infiltrate the congregation and that they
would be carrying an assortment of rapiers, daggers and
swords hidden beneath their cloaks. Directly the sermon
finished the women rushed forward and armed their husbands. During the ensuing mêlée several turnkeys were
wounded and fifteen of the prisoners managed to escape.

One of the more constant grievances amongst the inmates
of Newgate was the perpetual overcrowding at the gaol, in
the most unhygienic atmosphere imaginable. In 1642 the justices at the Sessions House reported that Newgate 'hath never
been more replenished with prisoners these many years than
now, there being very nigh three hundred prisoners committed to that infamous castle of misery'. A short while later, in
a petition, a prisoner pleaded for release from Newgate; 'this
place,' he said, 'being more full of horror than death.' There
seems to have been no improvement in the conditions under
the Commonwealth, the petitions addressed to Oliver Cromwell being couched in very similar terms to the ones employed
earlier; in 1655 a political prisoner described Newgate as 'a
place of so much horror and confusion'; and entreated the
Lord Protector not to let him 'perish in a loathsome dungeon
in the flower of my age'. It is not surprising that disease was
rampant and the mortality rate extremely high. One prisoner
lamented that he was suffering from the 'infectious, malignant
fever which sends many to their long home', and he added,
'The magistrates who think them unfit to breathe their native
air when living, bury them as brethren when dead.'

The condemned hold in Newgate at that time was probably
a large foetid dungeon below the gates. Colonel John Turner,
who was executed in 1662, described it as 'a most fearful, sad,
deplorable place'. There was, he said, 'neither bench, stool,
nor stick for any person there. They lie like swine upon the
ground, one upon another, howling and roaring – it was more
terrible to me than death. I would humbly beg that this hole
may be provided with some kind of boards . . . that a man may
lie down upon them in ease; for when they should be best pre-

pared for their ends they are most tormented; they had better take them and hang them as soon as they have their sentence.'

Throughout the Interregnum and during the first few years after the Restoration the Court of Aldermen were still discussing the repairs which had become so urgently necessary at Newgate. No extensive work had been commenced on the gaol when the City was devastated by the Great Fire in 1666. This conflagration broke out in a baker's shop in Pudding Lane in the early hours of the morning on 2 September. John Evelyn was in London at the time and the next day he wrote in his diary, 'The fire, conspiring with a fierce east wind in a very dry season, and having continued all this night – if I may call that night which was as liight as day for ten miles about.' A few hours later he visited the scene and watched the residents of the blazing streets 'running about like distracted creatures', but making no effort to fight the flames or to salvage their possessions. 'Such a strange consternation there was upon them that the fire burned, both in breadth and length, the churches, public halls, Exchange, hospitals, monuments and ornaments, leaping from house to house and street to street after a prodigious manner; for with a long spell of fair and warm weather, the heat had even ignited the air, and prepared the materials to conceive the fire, which, after an incredible manner, devoured houses, furniture, and everything.' On 4 September Evelyn returned to the scene and found the fire still raging. 'All of Fleet Street, Ludgate Hill, Warwick Lane, Newgate and the Old Bailey was now flaming,' he noted, 'and most of it reduced to ashes.'

No authentic account has ever come to light of the immediate effects of the Great Fire either on the inmates or upon the structure of Newgate; however, all the available evidence seems to indicate that both the gaol and the Sessions House were severely damaged if not completely destroyed. In the repertories for 1666 there occurs a mention of a 'Committee for Rebuilding the Sessions House and Gaol of Newgate', and there are further references to repairs in the volumes for 1669 and 1670. Amongst the documents at the Corporation of London Records Office are thirty accounts 'For Rebuilding the Gaol of Newgate and the Press Yard'; they are dated from

20 February 1670 to 2 August 1672 and are for amounts vary-
ing between ten pounds and two hundred and fifty pounds;
all have been paid by Sir Thomas Player, Chamberlain of
London. The new gaol was externally far more ornate than
the old. On the east side were statues representing Justice,
Fortitude and Prudence, and on the west, three ranges of
Tuscan pilasters with vertical recesses into which George
Dance, the architect, later erected the figures of Liberty,
Peace, Security and Plenty. A contemporary review of public
buildings passed the censorious comment, 'Newgate, considered as a prison, is a structure of more cost and beauty than
was necessary; because the sumptuousness of the outside but
aggravates the misery of the wretches within.'

CHAPTER SIX

NEWGATE REVEALED

DURING the latter part of the seventeenth century Newgate Gaol had already achieved an evil and a fearsome reputation throughout the whole of Britain. The Sessions House, too, at which eight separate sittings were held every year, was gaining a national and sinister renown under the familiar name of 'the Old Bailey'. Imprisonment at Newgate, trial at the Old Bailey and execution at Tyburn were becoming an accepted pattern for the nemesis of the unsuccessful felon.

Non-criminal offenders were still detained in Newgate as well. William Penn, the Quaker and later the founder of Pennsylvania, was committed to the gaol in the summer of 1670 at a time when the work of reconstruction was in progress after the Great Fire. Penn, together with his fellow Quaker, William Mead, was arrested for 'preaching seditiously and causing a great tumult of people on a royal street to be gathered together riotously and routously'. A warrant signed by the Lord Mayor and addressed to the keeper of Newgate ordered him 'to safely keep' the two prisoners until their lawful discharge from the gaol. The subsequent trial of Penn and Mead at the Old Bailey is one of the most disgraceful recorded episodes in the annals of British forensic history; if it typified the sort of justice which was meted out at the Sessions House it must have been a very sorry outlook for most of the untried inmates at Newgate.

The two Quakers were charged upon an indictment alleging that 'they had met together with force and arms to the terror and disturbance of His Majesty's liege subjects.' They appeared before a bench consisting of the Lord Mayor, the Recorder, five aldermen and the sheriffs. At the outset Penn and Mead, a little unwisely, declined to remove their hats while the indictment was being read and they were both peremptorily fined for contempt of court; thereafter they were

harassed, browbeaten, and insulted by various members of
the bench every time they endeavoured to develop their
defence. At one point the Lord Mayor upbraided Mead with
the words, 'You deserve to have your tongue cut out.' The
Recorder denounced Penn variously as, 'saucy fellow', 'imper-
tinent fellow' and 'troublesome fellow', and when Penn was
addressing the jury the Recorder shouted to the gaolers, 'Pull
that fellow down! Pull him down!' On another occasion, as
Penn was commencing a legal submission, the Lord Mayor
called out, 'Stop his mouth! Bring fetters and stake him to the
ground!'

Later in the trial a bitter dispute ensued between the bench
and the jury. After a retirement lasting for an hour and a
half Edmund Bushell, the jury foreman, announced that they
were unable to agree on their verdict; he was immediately
subjected to a barrage of vituperation and threats from the
bench, being told by one of the aldermen, 'You deserve to be
indicted more than any man that hath been brought to the
bar this day.' The jury were sent out again and came back for
the second time with a verdict that Penn had been guilty of
addressing the meeting but it had not been an unlawful
assembly. The Recorder informed them that this verdict was
unacceptable to the court. After a further retirement they
acquitted Mead and refused to alter their verdict regarding
Penn, whereupon they were told by the Recorder, 'You shall
not be dismissed till we have a verdict that the court will
accept; you will be locked up without meat, drink, fire or
tobacco. We will have a verdict by the Grace of God or you
shall starve for it.' The jury were then imprisoned for two
days and nights without, it is said, 'so much as a chamber
pot'. Eventually their endurance, fortitude and resolution
were triumphant and the court was compelled to abandon the
struggle of wills and to receive the verdict as it stood. But even
then the malice of the bench was not exhausted; the Recorder
fined each of the jurors the sum of forty marks and when they
refused to pay he committed them all to Newgate. Although
Penn and Mead had both been acquitted they, too, were sent
to Newgate in respect of the unpaid fines for their earlier
contempt. Bushell and three of his fellow jurors persisted in
the refusal to meet the fines, and they were finally freed on an

application for habeas corpus which established the lasting principle in British law that a jury should never be punished for returning a verdict which is true to their own consciences. Penn reluctantly agreed to allow his elderly father, who was mortally ill at the time, to pay his own and Mead's fines for contempt in order that he could get home before the old man's death.

The following year Penn was arrested again for addressing another Quaker meeting. This time he was convicted and sentenced to a term of six months in Newgate. If he had chosen to do so he could have served his time on the master's side of the gaol with its relative privileges and comforts, but instead he preferred to go to the common side where a number of other Quakers were already intermingled with the thieves, the highwaymen and the murderers. An associate of Penn's has left a description of the situation which they encountered there:

When we came to Newgate [he says] we found that side of the prison very full with Friends, who were prisoners there before us; as, indeed, were all the other parts of the prison and most of the other prisons in the town; and our addition caused a still greater throng on that side of Newgate. We had the liberty of the hall, which is on the story over the gate, and which in the daytime is common to all the prisoners on that side, felons as well as others. But in the night we all lodged in one room, which was large and round having in the middle of it a great pillar of oaken timber which bore the chapel which is over it. To this pillar we fastened our hammocks at one end, and at the opposite end, quite round the room, in three storeys, one over the other; so that they who lay in the upper and middle row of hammocks were obliged to go to bed first, because they were to climb up to the higher by getting into the lower ones. And under the lower range of hammocks, by the wall sides were laid beds upon the floor, in which the sick and weak prisoners lay. There were many sick and some very weak, and though we were not long there, one of our fellow prisoners died.

Newgate was used extensively for the imprisonment of the victims of Titus Oates' malignant allegations in 1678 and 1679. Oates invented a widespread Popish plot to murder

Charles II, massacre the protestants, and burn down the City of London. He succeeded in creating a panic, as a result of which large numbers of wholly innocent persons were convicted by biased juries and either condemned to the worst discomforts of the gaols or made to suffer the terrible incidents of a traitor's execution at Tyburn. Encouraged by the credulity of the nation Oates continued to cast his accusations at random. Two named Roman Catholic priests, he said, were conspiring to share the office of Ordinary at Newgate Gaol, 'in order to seduce the prisoners from their religion and their loyalty'. Even those in the highest places were not immune from his denouncements; in November 1678 John Evelyn recorded in his diary, 'Oates now grew so presumptuous as to accuse the Queen of intending to poison the King – which certainly that pious and virtuous lady abhorred the thought of, and Oates's circumstances made it utterly unlikely in my opinion.'

Amongst the prisoners detained in Newgate as a consequence of Titus Oates' accusations was Edward Coleman, the Duchess of York's secretary, who was convicted of selling state secrets to the Jesuits. He was drawn on a hurdle from the gaol to Tyburn where he was hanged, drawn and quartered with Oates as a spectator. Miles Prance, a silversmith who had often been employed by the queen, denounced by Oates for plotting with the Jesuits, was incarcerated in 'a certain underground hole in Newgate, without light, air or firing'. Here he was persistently tortured in an endeavour to make him confess. Five Roman Catholic priests were tied to hurdles outside Newgate and the condemned procession to Tyburn was led by a fife and drum band. Ironically enough Oates himself was to experience imprisonment in Newgate after he had been convicted of perjury at the Old Bailey in 1684. His sentence included being whipped from Aldgate to Newgate, and again two days later from Newgate to Tyburn. The first chastisement was mercilessly carried out and it is said that Oates 'made hideous bellowings, and swooned several times with the greatness of the anguish'. Of the second flogging Evelyn noted, 'Meanwhile, Oates, who had but two days before been pilloried at several places and whipped at the cart's tail from Aldgate to Newgate, was this day placed in a sledge

– not being able to walk by reason of his so late scourging – dragged from prison to Tyburn, and whipped again all the way. Some thought this to be very severe and extraordinary; but in case he were guilty of the perjuries, and so of the death of many innocents (as I fear he was) his punishment was but what he well deserved!'

The repertories for the period from the reconstruction of Newgate after the Great Fire to the beginning of the eighteenth century are fuller and more precise than the earlier volumes, but they follow a familiar pattern in content. A great many items in respect of prison administration are concerned with complaints against the staff and the regulation of scales of fees. On representations from the prisoners, one steward at Newgate was dismissed and another was called before the aldermen to answer allegations which had been made against him. There was an inquiry into the suggestion that the keeper of Ludgate was impounding money belonging to his prisoners and also that he was claiming 'exorbitant fees'; a few years later the Recorder and sheriffs were 'recommended to examine a complaint against the keeper of Newgate for demanding excessive fees'. In 1681 two of the yeomen were dismissed from the Wood Street compter, the first for 'exacting unreasonable fees', and the second for 'swearing and blaspheming'. The keepers of all the City prisons were ordered in 1689 to present to the Court of Aldermen a table of the fees they were charging and 'to show by what authority they demand them'; in 1691 an order was issued that 'Tables of fees are to be hung up in every City gaol'.

It is noticeable that during this era the aldermen were beginning to show concern about the perennial outbreaks of gaol fever and an appreciation, however slight, of the necessity of medical attention for the prisoners. In 1674 a Dr Hodges was paid ten pounds 'to inform himself of the gravity of the distemper of the prisoners in Wood Street compter', and approval was granted for settlement of an apothecary's bills for certain medicines used in treating the disease. The Poultry compter was also affected by this particular epidemic and instructions were given for apartments to be set aside there 'to separate the diseased prisoners from those in health'. Dr Hodges seems to have prolonged his association with Wood

Street as in 1680 he was paid a further sum of ten pounds 'for his care of the prisoners in the compter'. It may have been suspected at this stage that dirt and lack of hygiene were contributory factors to the dreaded infection which haunted the prisons. In 1675 it was decided to provide buckets and squirts for cleansing Newgate, but owing to lack of cooperation among the inmates these utensils were never effectively employed. Overcrowding was a constant problem at the gaol and in 1682 the Common Council considered a 'complaint of the keeper of Newgate touching the want of water for the prisoners'; the repertories contain no record of any steps being taken to increase the supply, although in 1692 there is a reference to the sheriffs investigating 'the deficiency of water at Newgate'. In the same year it was agreed that the governors of St Bartholomew's Hospital should arrange for a surgeon to be nominated to visit the gaol; this may well have been the first appointment of a prison medical officer in Britain, and it is apparent that the doctor began to carry out his duties very shortly afterwards, as there was an outbreak of gaol fever at Newgate the following year and the repertories record that 'a surgeon assisted by an apothecary' attended the sick prisoners.

It was only to be expected that the Court of Aldermen would also be preoccupied with the spiritual welfare of their prisoners, and especially that of the criminal population at Newgate. In 1667 it was decided that the Ordinary should hold a morning and an evening prayer service in the gaol every day, and a little later a grant was made for the provision of Bibles and Prayer Books for the prisoners. The Bishop of London consented in 1684 to appoint a clergyman to officiate at the weekly Sunday service in the Newgate chapel, and in 1694 he was asked by the aldermen to appoint 'some able Minister to preach to and instruct the condemned prisoners in Newgate' at the end of every sessions at the Old Bailey. Although they never went so far as abolishing the supply of intoxicating liquor to their prisoners – indeed, the profits from the taps were a well-recognized perquisite of the keepers – the aldermen in 1674 prohibited the sale of brandy in the City gaols; a few years later the question of prison labour was raised again when there was a half-hearted suggestion that the prisoners in Newgate should be kept at work inside the gaol.

Midway through the reign of Charles II a Bill came before Parliament the purpose of which was to establish a new and separate county gaol for Middlesex; however, this idea was abandoned in its infancy, and apart from a more rigorous enforcement of the provision that freemen of the City must be detained at Ludgate, the types of prisoner committed to Newgate remained much as before. Charitable issues of meat and bread continued to provide the staple diet for the common side at the gaol, and in 1674 a Mr Flower and a Mr Cressey each made a donation of books to the poor prisoners. That same year the inmates of Newgate were forbidden to beg, though whether this was due to a belief that charity supplies were sufficient for their needs or to some other reason is not disclosed. The practice of begging was still permitted at Ludgate, and in 1677 the Court of Aldermen acceded to a request from the prisoners there 'for leave to beg publicly through a grate to be made, as they were anciently wont to do before the fire'; a short while later they too were forbidden to beg. The security arrangements at neither Newgate nor Ludgate were very effective and the keepers of both gaols were perpetually harassed by actual and attempted escapes. This problem was particularly serious at Newgate with its large contingent of desperate criminals. Around this period the gaol contained an increasing number of highway robbers; according to Lord Macauley suspected highwaymen used to be paraded outside Newgate with their horses, and people who had been robbed were invited to come and identify them. Sometimes a keeper was offered inducements for helping a prisoner to get away; James Fell, keeper of Newgate, was convicted in 1696 of conniving at the escape of one of his prisoners in return for a financial reward. The offence does not seem to have been considered as especially grave for the sentence of the court was postponed indefinitely and Fell was allowed to retain the keepership.

The supervision of prisoners in Newgate was exceedingly lax; this applied even to the condemned, as is witnessed by an incident recounted in a letter to the Duke of Shrewsbury in 1699. 'All the talk of the town is about a tragic piece of gallantry in Newgate,' said the writer. 'I don't doubt but what your Grace has heard of a bastard son of Sir George Norton who was under sentence of death for killing a dancing master in the streets . . . It being signified to the young man, on Tuesday last in the afternoon, that he was to die the next day, his aunt, who was sister to his mother, brought two doses of opium and they took it between them. The Ordinary came soon after to perform his functions; but before he had done, he found so great alterations in both persons that it was no hard matter to find out the cause of it. The aunt frankly declared she could not survive her nephew, her life being so wrapped up in his; and he declared that the law having put a period on his life, he thought it no offence to choose the way he would go out of the world.' The Ordinary promptly summoned the keeper, and the keeper, an apothecary. Remedies were administered and the aunt recovered but the nephew lingered on until the following morning when he died at nine o'clock. The letter adds, 'He was fully resolved upon the business, for he had likewise a charged pistol in the room.'

A seemingly authentic impression of Newgate at the close of the seventeenth century was provided in a tract entitled *England's Calamities Discovered*. Of the general living conditions in the gaol the author says, 'If a thief or housebreaker would get unloaded of so many pounds of iron or purchase a sleeping-hole a little free from vermin, or with wholesome air enough to keep his lungs from being choked up, he must raise such extravagant sums to pay for it as can no ways be furnished but from theft and vice, supplied by his jades or brother rogues abroad, who must rob and whore to support him even with the necessaries of life. Nay, instead of employing their time in the amendment of life and a religious preparation for their trial, prisoners are forced to drink, riot and game to curry favour with the gaoler and support his luxury.' The prisoner for debt was in no better a position; 'As for the poor prisoner committed thither (for it is the county gaol) he receives the same treatment and hardships; for extorting and oppression, like the grave, make no distinction.' The tract continues with a comment on the depravity of the staff:

How commonly do under-officers, gaolers etc. excuse their barbarity and unreasonable exactions by alleging that they have no other way to make up the interest on their purchase-money? . . It is this alone that steels and case-hardens a gaoler's conscience against all pity and remorse, giving him the confidence to demand extraordinary fees and racked chamber-rent from his prisoners, or else to crowd them into holes, dungeons and common sides, designedly made more nasty to terrify the prisoner who, for the preservation of his life, is thereby forced to part with his money or be devoured by famine and diseases. This makes him let out his tap-houses at such prodigious rates that, where poor people should have the best and cheapest, they have the worst in quality and the smallest in quantity at excessive prices. Also he farms out his beds to mere harpies.

In 1699 the Society for the Promotion of Christian Knowledge appointed a small committe, led by Dr Thomas Bray, to visit and report upon the conditions in Newgate and other London prisons. The committee, the reliability and independence of whose members cannot be doubted, drew up a report which was never published at the time, but came to light unexpectedly many years later. The report is headed, 'An Essay towards ye reformation of Newgate and the other Prisons in and about London'. It commences with a list of 'the vices and immoralities' of the gaols, which are said to be:

1. The personal lewdness of the keepers and under-officers themselves, who make it their business to corrupt the prisoners, especially the women.
2. Their confederacy with prisoners in their vices, allowing the men to keep company with the women for money.
3. The unlimited use of wine, brandy and other strong liquors, even by condemned malefactors.
4. Swearing, cursing, blaspheming, and gaming.
5. Old criminals corrupting newcomers.
6. Neglect of religious worships.

The recommendations proposed by Dr Bray's committee were clear-sighted and, in parts, remarkably prophetic. Every prisoner should be confined in a separate cell, they suggested, and old criminals should not be allowed to converse with the others. All prison officers who were 'vicious and immoral' should be replaced; the Lord Mayor and sheriffs should use their authority for reforming the gaols and, in particular, they should ensure that all future prison appointments went to persons of 'virtue and morality'. Apart from charging for lodging and food prison officers should be forbidden to take money 'in consideration of their good usage towards the prisoners'. Wines and strong liquors should not be sold or bought in any gaol, 'unless in a case of necessity'. Habitual criminals should be made to do hard labour while they were in prison; when liberated they should be sent to workhouses, 'and not released until they can give security for entering into honest employment'. Women prisoners should be 'employed in such work as they have been bred to, and in the case of idleness or refusal, should be obliged to beat hemp, or to do any other hard labour'. With regard to the women prisoners who escaped sentence of death because they were pregnant – or, to use the official phrase, who were 'respited on account of their bellies' – the committee considered that they should not be permitted for ever to evade the rigour of the law, 'for this emboldens them in the commission of crimes which they would not probably be guilty of were they left without hopes of escaping.'

Daniel Defoe was imprisoned in Newgate for about six months in 1703 as a result of his publication of a religious tract, considered heretical by the authorities; twenty years later he set out his impressions of the gaol in one of his best known novels through the pen of Moll Flanders. The initial impact of Newgate on Moll Flanders must have been typical of that experienced by many prisoners. She says:

'Tis impossible to describe the terror of my mind, when I was first brought in, and when I looked round upon all the horrors of that dismal place. I looked on myself as lost and that I had nothing to think of but of going out of the world, and that with the utmost infamy: the hellish noise, the roaring, swearing and clamour, the stench and nastiness, and all the dreadful afflicting things that I saw there, joined to make the place seem an emblem of hell itself, and a kind of entrance into it.

Moll was visited by the Ordinary, 'but all his divinity ran upon confessing my crime,' she comments, adding that she received no manner of consolation from him; 'and then to observe the poor creature preaching confession and repentance to me in the morning, and find him drunk with brandy

by noon, this had something in it so shocking that I began
to nauseate the man, and his work too by degrees.'

Moll Flanders' description of the swift moral deterioration
of the Newgate prisoner must have been based on Defoe's personal observations:

Like the water in the hollows of mountains which petrifies and
turns into stone whatever they are suffered to drop upon; so the
continual conversing with such a crew of hell-hounds had the
same common operation upon me as upon other people. I degenerated into stone; I turned first stupid and senseless, and then
brutish and thoughtless, and at last raving mad as any of them;
in short, I became as naturally pleased and easy with the place
as if indeed I had been born there.

Later she says:

All my terrifying thoughts were past, the horrors of the place
were become familiar, and I felt no more uneasiness at the noise
and clamours of the prison, than they did who made that noise;
in a word, I was become a mere Newgate-bird, as wicked and as
outrageous as any of them; nay, I scarce retained the habit and
custom and good breeding and manners, which all along till now
ran through my conversation; so thorough a degeneracy had possessed me, that I was no more than the something that I had
been, than if I had never been otherwise than what I was now.

It was only on an execution day, apparently, that the embers
of humanity were rekindled at Newgate. She recollects:

The next morning there was a sad scene indeed in the prison.
The first thing I was saluted with in the morning was the tolling
of the great bell at St Sepulchre's, which ushered in the day. As
soon as it began to toll a dismal groaning and crying was heard
from the condemned hole . . . This was followed by a confused
clamour in the house, among the several prisoners, expressing
their awkward sorrows for the poor creatures that were to die,
but in a manner extremely differing one from another. Some
cried for them; some brutishly huzzaed, and wished them a good
journey; some damned and cursed those that had brought them
to it, many pitying them, and some few, but very few, praying
for them.

CHAPTER SEVEN

MORE REVELATIONS

IN the early eighteenth century three separate tracts were published in London, each of which contained a description of the interior of Newgate together with certain details about the lives of prisoners there. *The Memoirs of the Right Villainous John Hall* purported to be the prison reminiscences of the notorious housebreaker, footpad and pickpocket of that name who was hanged at Tyburn in 1707; probably the text had been sub-edited but despite the exaggerated irony of the style it bears the mark of authenticity and may well have been based either upon some notes compiled by John Hall himself, or by one of his contemporaries in the gaol. *The History of the Press Yard* was writen anonymously by one of the Jacobite prisoners who were detained in Newgate after the unsuccessful insurrection in 1715; it is a restrained and unembittered account of the prison experiences of an obviously well-educated man. And lastly, another anonymous publication which appeared in 1724 under the title of *An Accurate Description of Newgate with the Rights, Privileges, Allowances, Fees, Dues, and Customs thereof,* by B.L. of Twickenham; the author once again seems to have had an intimate knowledge of conditions at the gaol and was, presumably, a former inmate.

There was no reception ward at Newgate. Incoming prisoners entered the gaol through a lodge and either there or in an adjacent room they were generally placed in irons. The legality of indiscriminate ironing was being questioned by prominent jurists even at this period, and the consensus of opinion appeared to have been that a keeper was only permitted to iron a prisoner who was unruly, or one who had attempted to escape; nevertheless, in most gaols the matter was left to the complete discretion of the individual keeper. Debtors when first admitted to Newgate probably retained

their fetters until they had purchased their 'easement': the
majority of felons, especially those who had been convicted,
were ironed throughout their stay in the gaol. Newly admitted
felons were made to pass through an additional formality
before being allocated to their wards as, in the words of B.L.,
'It is customary when any felons are brought to the lodge in
Newgate to put them first in the condemned hold, wherein
they remain till they have paid two-and-sixpence, after which
they are admitted to the masters' or the common felons' side.'

The author of *The History of the Press Yard* has described
his initiation to Newgate in detail. When he had entered the
gaol, he says:

> I found myself in a lodge encompassed by a parcel of ill-looking
> fellows that eyed me as if they would look me through, and
> examined every part of me from head to toe, not as tailors to
> take measure of me, but as footpads that survey the goodness of
> the clothes first, before they grow intimate with the linings.

The group of practised extortioners who surrounded the
Jacobite was probably composed of turnkeys and wardsmen,
the latter being prisoners who were entrusted to assist the
staff. Their methods were blatant for he heard one man
remark, 'We shall have a hot supper tonight. The cull looks
as if he had the blunt, and I must come in for a share of it
after my few masters have done with him.' The speaker then
began to rattle a bunch of keys and called for a pint of brandy
to drink the newcomer's health. The bottle was immediately
brought in by 'a short protuberance of human flesh', who
turned out to be a convicted woman prisoner; she assured the
Jacobite that as he seemed to be 'a very civil gentleman' he
was certain to be placed in comfortable accommodation by
the gaolers responsible, 'who know how to distinguish persons
of worth from scoundrels'. Fortified, no doubt, by this information he ordered a flask of best claret and very soon, he says,
'all hands were at work in putting the glasses round for the
good of the house, as they put it, and six or seven flasks were
consumed.' Even while these people were drinking wine at his
expense they continued their intimidations by passing around
irons and fetters and whispering such remarks as, 'A pair of
forty pounds weight will be enough for him' and 'We ought

to send to the Governor to know whether he is to be handcuffed.' Eventually, in desperation he asked them how he
could avoid being ironed. They replied that this could be
arranged if he made it worth their while, and it was also in
their power to have him allocated to the most pleasant part
of the goal. By now he was in such a state of terror and depression that he willingly paid them all they demanded.

Having passed the new prisoner through the first phase of
their exactions, his tormentors proceeded to the second:

> Instead of the handsome apartment which I was made to hope
> for through their suggestions, I was conducted to the door lead-
> ing out of the lodge into the condemned hold, where they told
> me I must stay till their master's further pleasure should be
> known, for they could go no further than the easing me of irons,
> which they did not know but that they might have anger for by
> reason of the capitalness of the crime whereof I stood accused.

He says of the condemned hold that it was 'falsely supposed to be a noisome vault underground'; in fact, it lay
'between the top and bottom of the arch under Newgate,
from whence there dart in some glimmerings of light, though
very imperfect, by which you may know that you are in a
dark, opaque, wild room'. It was entered by a hatch, he states,
measuring about twenty feet in length and about fifteen feet
in breadth; other writers have reported that food was thrown
down to the prisoners through this opening. The floor and
walls of the hold were made of stone and it had an open sewer
running through the middle. The Jacobite continued:

> By the help of a candle, which you must pay through the nose
> for before it will be handed to you over the hatch, your eyes will
> lead you to boarded places, like those raised in barracks, where-
> upon you may repose yourself if your nose will suffer you to rest
> from the stench that diffuses its noisome particles of bad air
> from every corner.

Fixed into the stone floor were hooks, iron staples and
chains, 'to bring those to submission that are stubborn and
unruly'.

The condemned hold had the desired effect on the Jacobite,
for he says he was 'seized with a panic dread at the survey of
this, my new tenement and [I was] willing to change it for

another, almost upon any terms'. After half-an-hour a trap was opened in the ceiling above him and a man, whom he discovered later to be a fellow-prisoner employed as a waiter at the gaol, shouted down to him, 'Sir, I understand your name is – , and that you are a gentleman too well-educated to take up your abode in a vault set apart only for thieves, parricides, and murderers. From hence criminals after sentence of death are carried to the place of execution, and from thence you may be removed to a chamber equal to one in any private house, where you may be furnished with the best conversation and entertainment for a valuable consideration.' The speaker went on to say that he was acting solely from goodwill as he had suffered in the same manner himself until he had paid the admission fee for entrance to the Press Yard, since when he had lacked 'nothing that a gaol could afford him'. The Jacobite declared his willingness to produce any sum required, and a short while later the head turnkey, 'a gentleman-like man of very smiling aspect' visited him and apologized profusely for the way he had been treated, telling him 'that those who had used a gentleman like that should be well trounced for it'. The Jacobite was then conducted back to the lodge and over another glass of wine the head turnkey informed him that it would cost him twenty guineas to enter the Press Yard, and in addition he would have to pay a rent of eleven shillings a week there, adding that the keeper was obliged to charge these high prices since he had paid a £5,000 purchase fee for his appointment at the gaol. This figure might not have been an exaggeration; it was stated in 1696 that the keepership of Newgate had recently been sold for £3,500, and in a pamphlet on London, published in 1708, it was said that the keeper of the gaol 'holds that place of great trust under the Queen, giving £8,000 security'.

The memoirs of John Hall describe the method of extorting garnish on the common side of Newgate. One of the turnkeys used to accompany a new prisoner to the entrance of this part of the gaol and he would knock loudly on the gates three times:

No sooner are the three strokes given [says the tract] but out jump four truncheon officers from their hovel, and, with a sort of ill-manneredly reverence, receive him at the gate. Then, taking

him into their apartment, a couple of good-natured sparks hold
him while the other two pick his pockets, claiming sixpence as a
privilege belonging to their office. They then turn him out to
the convicts, who hover about him, like so many crows about a
piece of carrion, for garnish. This is six shillings and eight pence,
which they claim by prescription of time out of mind for entering this society. Otherwise they strip the poor wretch, if he has
not the wherewithal to pay it. Then the cook ruffian comes to
him for threepence for dressing the charity meat, which chari-
tably disposed persons send in every Thursday, when earthen
dishes, porringers, pans, wooden spoons and cabbage nets, are
stirring about against dinner time, as thick as burnt brandy and
brimstone possets in Lucifer's kitchen . . . But the caged person
is not clear of his dues, for next, two other officers, who have a
patent for swabbers, demand three halfpence more for cleaning
the gaol of its filth.

Garnish, or its equivalent, was collected in far less boorish
fashion on the masters' side. After the Jacobite had been
taken into the Press Yard he was 'cordially welcomed' by a
fellow prisoner who proceeded to instruct him in the local
conventions. 'You will according to custom, about seven or
eight of the clock this evening be called upon to pay your
entrance fee,' he was told, 'which was formerly only six
bottles of wine, and tobacco in proportion, but is now raised
to ten or twelve, which, if you are straitened for money will
be scored at the bar by the honest tapster, who, though he
has lost several hundred pounds by that method of proceeding, is not discouraged from going on with it in favour of
the unhappy gentleman.' That evening the Jacobite presided at the head of the table in the Press Yard taproom. He
found his new companions 'immensely civil', as indeed they
should have been since he was bearing all the expenses. 'I
continued whipping out sixpences to advance more bottles,'
he says, 'till our cheerfulness was turned into drowsiness, and
merriment became the subject of dispute with some of my
fellow prisoners, so it was thought high time by the most sober
of us to break up and retire to our chambers, with the ceremony of the turnkeys locking each of the two staircase doors
after us.' The following morning all the prisoners who had
been drunk the night before appeared before a mock court

organized by the turnkeys and were made to pay forfeits of various quantities of liquor.

Amidst the boredom and frustrations of existence in Newgate, hard drinking was the dominant preoccupation both for the prisoners and the staff. The principal taproom in the gaol was a large cellar adjoining the lodge; the barman was a prisoner, selected by the turnkeys, who was permitted to make a regulated profit on his sales. As the cellar was below street level and had no windows it always required artificial lighting. In here, John Hall's memoirs relate, the inmates sat around 'in the pleasant prospect of a range of butts and barrels, and the only grievance . . . is the paying for pipes and candles, which are placed in pyramidal candlesticks made of clay'. Both felons and debtors were permitted to use this cellar and to converse and drink together, 'by which means,' says B.L. of Twickenham, 'such wretchedness abounds therein, that the place has the exact aspect of hell itself, and by this means 'tis much to be questioned whether one debtor in ten who enters therein an honest man comes out the same, the wickedness of the place is so great.'

At that time where were three wards for male felons on the common side at Newgate. The least unpleasant of these was the Middle Ward on the first floor of the gaol, the entrance fee to which was one shilling 'civility money', as it was called. The Middle Ward contained no beds, but the floor was made of oak and the occupants usually kept the room in a clean and tidy condition. If a felon could not afford a shilling he had to go into the Lower Ward or the Stone Hold, both of which were virtually unlighted dungeons. 'In the Lower Ward,' according to John Hall's memoirs, 'the tight, slovenly dogs lie upon ragged blankets, amidst unutterable filth. Trampling on the floor, the lice crawling under their feet make such a noise as walking on shells which are strewn over garden walks.' The Stone Hold alongside seems to have been no better. 'This low dungeon,' says John Hall, 'is a real house of meagre looks and ill smells, for lice, drink and tobacco is all the compound.' B.L. of Twickenham's description is equally unfavourable. 'The Stone Hold,' he wrote, 'was a terrible, stinking, dark and dismal place, situate underground, into which no daylight can come. It was paved with stone; the prisoners had no beds, and lay on the pavement, whereby they endured great misery and hardship.'

Common side women felons either went into the Waterman's Hall on the second floor of the gaol, or the Women's Second Ward on the third floor. Perhaps the author of John Hall's memoirs was relying partly upon what he had seen and partly upon what he had been told for his account of the Waterman's Hall, where, he says, 'there are a troop of hell-cats lying head and tail together in a dismal, nasty, dark room, having no place to direct themselves but to the grate, adjoining the foot passage under Newgate, where passengers may, with some surprise and pity, hear them swear extempore, being so shamefully versed in that most odious profanation of Heaven that volleys of oaths are discharged through their detestable throats whilst asleep.' There were no beds in this hall, nor in the Women's Second Ward, but both had wooden floors with raised portions around the walls where the prisoners could lie down on their blankets. Most of the women in the Second Ward were awaiting transportation and, according to B.L., 'knowing their time to be short here, rather than bestow one minute towards cleaning the same, [they] suffer themselves to live rather worse than swine, for they are poisoned by their own filth, and their conversation is nothing but one continued course of swearing, cursing and debauchery.' B.L. declared that at Newgate the women prisoners in general were very much worse than the men, 'not only in respect to nastiness and indecency of living, but more especially as to their conversation, which, to their great shame, is as profane and wicked as hell itself can be'. The women had their own condemned hold. It was, said B.L., 'a small, dark, dismal dungeon, wherein is a barrack for prisoners to lie on, but no fireplace, and it is therefore cold at all times'.

On the common side of Newgate there were four wards for male debtors, Stone Hall, Tangier, Debtor's Hall and High Hall; the women debtors all lived in the Women's Ward. Common side debtors had to pay for their own heating; they had also to provide their own beds, but the sheriffs supplied sleeping boards to those who needed them. A free allocation of bread was made every day and a modest ration of charity

beef was issued once a week. B.L. found that the conversation
of these prisoners was 'generally very profligate', which he
attributed to their 'perpetually drinking and conversing with
the felons'. The Stone Hall was on the ground floor of the
gaol; it was a large, bleak room but it contained its own
water cistern and a fireplace. Tangier, likewise on the ground
floor, derived its name from the stuffiness of its atmosphere;
'the air in this ward,' said B.L., 'is very bad, occasioned by
the multitude of prisoners in it and the filthiness of their
lodging.' In contrast to Tangier, the Debtor's Hall on the
second floor had large windows facing out into Newgate
Street and was light and well ventilated; however, the bright-
ness of their room was not reflected in the demeanour of its
inmates, for John Hall says that in this ward 'every man
shows like so many wrecks upon the sea. Here the ribs of
£20; here the ruins of a good estate; doublets without but-
tons, and a gown without sleeves.' The High Hall on the
third floor was a spacious room which served both as a ward
for common side debtors and as a recreation space for common
side felons. The author of the John Hall memoirs used to
watch debtors and felons walking around the perimeter together and he would try to make out 'which was the gentleman, which the mechanic, and which the beggar; for they are
suited in the same form or kind of nasty poverty, which is a
spectacle of more pity than an execution. Only to be out at the
elbows is fashion here, and it is a great indecorum not to be
threadbare.' In the middle of the High Hall was an anvil
where condemned prisoners had their irons knocked off at
the outset of their journey to Tyburn. None of the three
tracts has described the Women's Ward, but it is known that
it was situated on the third floor of the gaol between the High
Hall and the Women's Second Ward for felons, so it should
have been reasonably light and airy.

Newgate had three wards for master's side felons; the First
Ward on the first floor, and the Second and Third Wards on
the second floor. All these rooms had adequate windows and
fireplaces, and flock beds were provided for the prisoners at
a fee of three shillings and sixpence per week. Superior and
more expensive accommodation was obtainable in the Press
Yard and in the Castle. The Press Yard at the eastern end

of the gaol was theoretically a portion of the keeper's house, although, in fact, there was no structural connection between the two. It was by far the most comfortable part of Newgate, consisting of 'divers large, spacious rooms' which were 'well supplied with light and air, free from smells and well equipped'. The inmates also had the use of a paved passage between the side of the prison and the boundary wall, where they could take their exercise in the open. Their domestic work was done for them by laundresses who cleaned the rooms and made up fires for a salary of a shilling a week from each prisoner. The Jacobite found himself in a room with three beds and a few old tables and chairs in it; the walls, he says, were of stone and were adorned with biblical scripts and scraps of verse written in charcoal by former tenants; and the bars across the window 'were as thick as my wrist and very numerous'. He was reminded by his room companion that on the master's side he would have had to pay eighteen pence per day 'for leave to associate myself with thieves and pickpockets'; after that, he adds, 'I neither minded the hardness of my bed nor the coarseness of the sheets.' The prisoners in the Press Yard idled away their days drinking and conversing about their former colleagues who had been taken to Tyburn and hanged – particular interest always being attached to the literary merits of their dying speeches. Outside visitors came and went almost as they pleased, and 'conviviality, was general,' said the Jacobite, 'liquor being freely called for, potations were deep, and the Press Yard of Newgate at night-time was like the taproom of a common inn.' The Castle consisted of two wards on the second floor at the western end of the gaol; although moderately comfortable, it was cheaper and less agreeable than the Press Yard.

There is comparatively little information available about the three wards for master's side debtors in Newgate, Hall Ward on the ground floor, and King's Bench Ward and Stone Ward on the first floor. The charges for all of these were similar, two shillings and sixpence a week for a bed, and an extra sixpence a week for clean sheets. Each had a fireplace and a scullery and all were furnished with long tables and wooden benches. Hall Ward was the largest of the three and B.L. has said that underneath its gallery was 'a very good place for prisoners therein to walk at their pleasure, which advantage the other wards are deficient of'. There was also a minute two-bedded ward on the first floor for master's side female debtors called 'My Lady's Hold'.

The Chapel was a lofty room on the third floor of the gaol; it had no heating and during the winter months the ill-clad prisoners suffered extreme discomfort from the cold. The male and female members of the congregation were allocated to different pews and there was also segregation between those who came from the master's and those who came from the common side. Church services were not compulsory except for the condemned who had to receive the Sacrament on the morning prior to their execution; as has been said these condemned services were generally attended by a number of outside visitors. The disorderly behaviour of the congregation during the regular Sunday services was notorious, the prisoners continuously talking, laughing and shouting to one another. Outside the doors of the Chapel at the head of the stairway was the main alarm bell for Newgate which was rung whenever there was an escape or an outbreak of violence.

On the second floor at Newgate there were three adjacent rooms, each of which was used for its own grim purpose. Bilbows was a punishment chamber where factious and insubordinate prisoners of both sexes were taken to be forcibly restrained, flogged or ironed. The Press Room next door was utilized for the same purpose when it was not needed for its primary function, the pressing to death of prisoners who had refused to plead at the Old Bailey. Across a passage was Jack Ketch's Kitchen where the hangman prepared for disposal the dismembered corpses of prisoners who had been executed for treason; as John Hall put it, it was a room in which 'in pitch, tar, and oil, he boils the quarters of those traitors who deserve to suffer for the several sorts of high treason'.

Looking at these three tracts in general it is clear that the lives of the prisoners in all parts of Newgate were degenerate and aimless, with little or no restrictions being placed upon communal drinking, gaming and fornication. It is said that the thieves kept in practice by stealing from each other and by picking the pockets of visitors to the gaol. The common side was perpetually cold and dark and had no proper ventilation; nor were the prisoners allowed any facilities for exercise. Water was always in short supply and was doled out in meagre rations both for drinking and washing. With the exception of those in the Press Yard and the Castle all the prisoners were locked up for the night at 9 p.m., when, says John Hall, 'they are hurried by their drivers like so many Turkish slaves, to their kennels, which are joined like so many huts, as though they took order from marital discipline.'

CHAPTER EIGHT

PRISONERS FOR DEBT

AT the beginning of the eighteenth century a substantial proportion of the gaol population in Britain were prisoners for debt. In his pamphlet *Thoughts on Trade and a Publick Spirit*, published in 1716, T. Baston commented, 'Tis reckoned there are about 60,000 miserable debtors perishing in the prisons of England and Wales.' Another writer about the same time said, 'The Marshalsea alone generally contains seven or eight hundred prisoners . . . two or three commonly perishing in one day in this miserable and wasting condition.' Many of these people had owed only trivial amounts and had been arrested through the sheer vindictiveness of their creditors; it was not unknown, too, for someone, prompted by malice, to swear a purely fictitious debt against an impecunious enemy or rival so as to have him locked up in gaol for an indefinite period. A lot of the small-debt prisoners were victims of the cupidity of the host of tallymen who, it was said, 'trust poor persons with twenty shillings worth of goods, or rather twelve or fourteen shillings worth instead of twenty, to pay them by six pence or twelve pence a week, wherein if they fail to pay, they hurry them into prison, with great charge for arrests and proceedings at law, which many times exceed the said debt'. Certain of the prisoners, of course, were people who had deliberately abstained from the settlement of their liabilities because they preferred to live in reasonable comfort on the master's sides of prisons, largely at their creditor's expense, rather than satisfying their lawful debts and impoverishing themselves in the process.

The two principal gaols in London for small-sum debtors were the Marshalsea and Whitechapel. Both were engaging hordes of officials for the execution of writs and processes and for making arrests; in 1729 it was estimated that the Marshalsea was employing 1,800 of these people whereas Whitechapel had over 500 of them, and the total in London was 'upwards of 3,000, a hopeful parcel to live upon the spoils of industry'. Thirteen years earlier T. Baston had stated that:

The tallyman generally keeps a rogue of a servant who he makes his bailiff, and for every arrest, if the debt is not eighteen-pence, exacts ten shillings besides other fees. Whitechapel Court is cramb'd full of these miserable creatures, at the suit of tally-men, and 'tis these rogues that chiefly support that court as well as the Marshalsea, and for the better encouragement of villainy . . the plaintiff, right or wrong, very rarely misses getting the day so that the whole number of insects, dependent on these wicked and barbarous courts, is on the bread, or rather the blood, of the poor.

Baston continued:

These miserable oppressions put men upon a kind of fatal necessity to turn knaves and wrack their wit to evade it all, which by the help of lawyers, if they have money, they may do. But where accrues the benefit of all this unchristian severity? To none but the very worst of rogues that tread on the face of the earth, viz, pettifoggers, jailers, keepers of spunging-houses, bailiffs and their followers.

Many of those who had fallen in debt absconded from their homes and went off into hiding or fled beyond the seas before their creditors could authorize their arrests. As a result, wives and families were left to starve, trades and crafts were abandoned, workmen suddenly found themselves without an employer and apprentices without a master. Faced with the awful prospect of indefinite imprisonment a debtor often fought savagely and desperately against the officials who were seeking to apprehend him. As was stated in a pamphlet published in 1714, 'if any man sees another coming to lay violent hands upon him, to attack his person and haul his body to prison, nature teaches him to take his assailor for his capital enemy and to act the best he may in his own defence.' The officials carrying out an arrest could be equally ruthless. In 1722 two sheriff's officers in Middlesex executed a warrant on a man named Lutterell for a debt of ten pounds; Lutterell placed a pair of pistols on a table and stood back telling the officers that 'he did not design to hurt [them] but he would not be abused.' Their immediate response was to draw their own pistols and to shoot him dead, for which act they were later convicted, not of murder but of manslaughter.

The only attempt to reform the system during the seventeenth century was made by a Member of Parliament called Pocklington who in 1696 drew the attention of the House of Commons to the condition of debtor prisoners in the Fleet. Although Pocklington succeeded in having the matter investigated by a select committee, his efforts brought about no radical improvements in the procedure of imprisonment for debt or of the treatment of debtors in the gaols. More than a quarter of a century was to elapse before the same cause was taken up by another Member, James Oglethorpe, the M.P. for Haslemere, later to become the founder of the American State of Georgia, of whom Boswell once said, 'This extraordinary person was as remarkable for his learning and taste as for his other eminent qualities.'

Before considering James Oglethorpe's work in this connection, mention should be made of a document which has come to light in the Corporation of London Records Office, entitled *Report of the Justices on the Abuses to Poor Debtors in Newgate Gaol*, 1702. The justices of the peace for the City of London were, of course, the aldermen, and this report was apparently made as a result of an investigation of the debtors' wards on the common side of the prison. The justices roundly condemned James Marshall, the keeper of Newgate, for 'divers great abuses committed on the debtors' – in particular for 'depriving them of their weekly allowance of beef and robbing them of the money which is allowed them quarterly'. There was also a criticism that the charity allowances were not being distributed equally amongst the prisoners. Garnish had recently been increased from nine shillings to seventeen shillings and the report stated that those 'not having the wherewithal to pay were stript, beaten, and abused in a most violent manner'. Sometimes their bedding was taken away from them and sold in order to satisfy a garnish fee which was still outstanding. The justices also commented adversely on the state of disrepair into which Newgate had been allowed to fall, and the lax state of morality which was permitted by the staff. 'Robinson, one of the turnkeys there,' they said, 'for his interest, did encourage lewd women, shop-lifters, pickpockets and common strumpets to come to the felons and lie all night.'

In 1728 Robert Castell, a writer on architecture and a close personal friend of James Oglethorpe, was arrested for debt and was committed to the Fleet. At that time the warden of this gaol was a ruthless tyrant named Thomas Bambridge, whose principal concern in his position was with the opportunities it afforded him for exacting illicit payments from his prisoners; one of his practices was to maintain a number of houses in the vicinity of the prison at which he would billet any debtors who still had the means to meet his exorbitant rents. For a short while Castell lived in moderate comfort at one of Bambridge's private lodgings, but when his money was almost exhausted he was notified that he was going to be transferred to a certain spunging-house in the Fleet where an epidemic of smallpox had just broken out amongst the inmates. Castell pleaded with Bambridge not to send him there as he had never had the disease before and he feared it greatly; in spite of his entreaties his removal took place and within a few days he contracted smallpox and died, cursing Bambridge as his murderer. Oglethorpe had visited Castell during his confinement at the Fleet and he was so shocked, not only at the fate of his friend but at the treatment accorded to the debtors generally, that he determined to raise the matter in Parliament.

In February 1729, largely on the instigation of James Oglethorpe, the Earl of Stafford drew the attention of the House of Lords to the hardships of insolvent debtors in the English prisons. He was supported by several other peers, Lord Townshend observing that 'the case of many debtors is, by the unmercifulness of their creditors, worse than that of galley slaves who are provided for and kept clean; whereas in England they are in a starving condition and rotting in gaol.' A few weeks later the House of Commons appointed a special committee, with Oglethorpe as its chairman, to enquire into the state of the gaols in Britain 'so far as it relates to the cruel usage of the prisoners'. The Committee presented their first report, concerning their investigations at the Fleet, on 20 March 1729; they confessed that the farther they had proceeded in their inquiries 'the more dismal and shocking was the scene of cruelty, barbarity and extortion' which had been revealed. The report commenced with a brief history of the Fleet. During the reign of Elizabeth a scale of fees was introduced, and this had been confirmed in the reign of Charles II, laying down the various payments which should be charged to such categories of people as archbishops, bishops, peers, baronets 'and others of lower degree' for the privilege of not being placed in irons. Bambridge's predecessor, John Huggins, had purchased the Fleet for the sum of £5,000 for his own and his son's lifetimes; however, in 1728 when Huggins wished to retire his son was disinclined to take over the wardenship so he had sold it jointly to Bambridge and a man named Cuthbert, again for £5,000. The high purchase price appears to have been amply justified by the income accruing from the gaol for, although the committee had been unable to ascertain the exact amount taken in fees and donations from the prisoners, they were satisfied that the annual gifts to the warden every Christmas alone amounted to over £2,800. There were no proper records maintained at the gaol; since Bambridge had been warden, said the committee, the books 'have been very negligently kept, and the discharges not duly entered, to the great prejudice of many of his Majesty's subjects; and he has not regularly taken charge of the prisoners, committed to his care by his patent, and hath not, as he himself confesseth, ever had any authentic list of the prisoners . . . delivered him; so that he cannot have executed the trust of keeping his prisoners in safe custody when he did not know who, or where, they were.' Bambridge was accused of conniving at escapes, and Huggins had 'owned to the committee, that so many prisoners had escaped during his time as warden, that it was impossible to enumerate them, he having kept no list of the persons so escaped'.

The committee had inspected the Fleet for themselves. There were three large wards on the common side, they said, in which the prisoners were 'obliged to lie on the floor if they cannot furnish themselves with bedding' — this was hired out at a cost of a shilling per week; also there were two smaller wards, one for women, which were 'very noisome and in very ill repair'. A number of rooms on the master's side were let out at indefinite charges and the occupants, 'who are uncertain what chamber rent they shall be obliged to pay, are at the mercy of the warden'. In general the living conditions were deplorable; 'In some rooms,' according to the report, 'persons who are sick of different distempers are obliged to lie together or on the floor; one, in particular, had the smallpox, and two women were ordered to lie with her; and they pay two shillings ten pence per week for such lodging.' Bambridge had used a special dungeon called the Strong Room as a place of punishment. The committee commented:

This place is a vault, like those in which the dead are interred, and wherein the bodies of persons dying in the said prison are usually deposited till the coroner's inquest hath passed upon them. It has no chimney, nor fire-place, nor any light but what comes over the door, or through a hole of about eight inches square. It is neither paved nor boarded, and the rough bricks appear both on the sides and top, being neither wainscoted nor plaistered. What adds to the dampness and stench of the place is its being built over the common shore, and adjoining to the sink and dunghill where all the nastiness of the prison is cast.

When taken into custody and sent to the Fleet every prisoner was expected to pay a total of five pounds, sixteen shillings and four pence in fees, which included two pounds, six shillings and eight pence for the warden, two pounds and six pence for the tipstaff, and one pound, two shillings and eight pence for the clerk of the judge who ordered the committal. If the prisoner appeared to have any means he was put, at first, in one of the spunging-houses where his remaining funds were rapidly whittled away; 'and when they can no longer bear the misery and expense of a spunging-house,' said the report, 'before they can obtain the privilege of being admitted to the prison, they are obliged to comply with such exorbitant fees, as the said Bambridge thinks fit to demand; which if they do not pay they are sure, under various pretences, of being turned down, if not put in irons and dungeons.'

The committee detailed various acts of cruelty which had been inflicted on prisoners in the Fleet. A Portuguese named Jacob Solas had been seized without warning, fettered and thrown into the Strong Room where he had remained for nearly two months, and had only been released when a friend of his had given Bambridge five guineas, 'and the unhappy man was prevailed upon by terror not only to labour gratis for the said Bambridge, but to swear also, at random, all that be required of him.' Captain John Mackpheadris, formerly a wealthy trader, had lived in a private room until he had protested about the rent. He had then been violently assaulted by the turnkeys and had been ordered by Bambridge to sleep in an open yard. Next he had been confined in the Strong Room, and irons had been fastened on his legs 'which were too little, so that in forcing them on, his legs were like to have been broken, and the torture was impossible to be endured; upon which the prisoner complaining of the grievous pain . . . Bambridge answered that he did it on purpose to torture him.' As a result of this treatment Mackpheadris was permanently lamed. Another of Bambridge's victims was an army officer, Captain Sinclair, whom he confined in the Strong Room until he lost the use of his limbs and his memory, 'neither of which,' said the report, 'is perfectly recovered to this day.' Even when Sinclair was on the point of death Bambridge felt no compunction, but moved him 'from that dungeon to a room where there was no bed or furniture', and kept him four days without food. After detailing several other atrocities the committee recommended that Bambridge, Huggins and four other members of the staff at the Fleet should all be committed to Newgate and should be prosecuted for their crimes.

On 14 May 1729 the Oglethorpe Committee presented to the House of Commons their second report, which was primarily concerned with the state of Marshalsea. The prison was nominally in charge of the Deputy Marshal, but early in 1727 this official had leased it to William Acton, a butcher, for a hundred and forty pounds a year; 'and by the same lease,' said the committee, 'did let the benefit of the lodging of the prisoners, and other advantages, for the further yearly rent of two hundred and sixty pounds.' They added the comment, 'To make the profits of the prison arise, to answer the said exorbitant rents, no kind of artifice or oppression hath been unpractised.' Here, as in other gaols, they found that excessive fees were exacted from the prisoners from the moment of their first admission; garnish was high too, sometimes amounting to as much as seven shillings and sixpence, 'the money from which is to be spent at the taphouse' where drinks were more expensive that at ordinary taverns and inns. The accommodation on the master's side varied from single or double chambers to rooms which were 'crowded to that degree, as even to make them unhealthy'; sometimes three prisoners were squeezed into one bed at a charge of two shillings and sixpence a week each. 'The gaoler of the said prison,' the report stated, 'out of view of gain, hath frequently refused to move sick persons, upon complaint of those who lay in the same bed with them.' A particularly unpleasant example was cited. A woman, who was sharing a bed with two others, fell ill and deteriorated slowly over a long period. Her companions 'frequently complained to the turnkeys and officers and desired to be removed; but all in vain. At length she smelt so strong that the turnkey himself could not bear to come into the room to hear the complaints of her bed-fellows, and they were forced to lie with her, or on the boards, till she died.' Prisoners on the common side of the gaol slept in wards, 'most of which are excessively crowded, thirty, forty, nay fifty persons having been locked up in some of them, not sixteen foot square'.

The report gave a grim portrayal of the fate of a destitute prisoner at the Marshalsea:

When the miserable wretch hath worn out the charity of his friends, and consumed the money which he hath raised upon his clothes and bedding, and hath eat his last allowance of provisions, he usually in a few days grows weak for want of food, with the symptoms of a hectic fever; and when he is no longer able to stand, if he can raise 3d to pay the fee of the common nurse of the prison, he obtains the liberty of being carried into the sick ward and lingers on for about a month or two [on charitable rations], and then dies.

The committee formed the opinion that relief in the prison from charity sources was 'notoriously and scandalously misapplied'. They also found innumerable instances of brutality and torture – Acton making habitual use of a thumbscrew and an iron collar which was sometimes screwed up so tight around a prisoner's neck that 'the blood gushed out of his ears and nose'. As formerly, they concluded their report with a recommendation that Acton and several members of his staff should be prosecuted.

The third and last report of the Oglethorpe Committee, dealing with the King's Bench Prison, was presented some time later. The members were critical of the rents and fees paid by the prisoners at the gaol, and although they found evidence of acts of great cruelty in the past they were satisfied that none had been committed by the keeper in office at the time, 'but on the contrary,' they said, 'he hath done many acts of compassion and charity to those on the common side by which . . . he hath rather entitled himself to favour than to blame.' As a result of the committee's earlier disclosures Bambridge and Huggins were separately tried at the Old Bailey for the murders of various prisoners at the Fleet, but they were both acquitted. Acton was charged with four murders committed in the Marshalsea; his trial took place at the Surrey Assizes and he was acquitted upon all four indictments.

Although the reports of the Oglethorpe Committee gave rise to a certain amount of disquiet they certainly did not create a grave public scandal. However, Parliament reacted swiftly to the situation by passing the Insolvent Debtors Relief Act, 1729, by the terms of which a table of fees was to be exhibited publicly in every debtors' prison; spunging-houses were to be abolished; prisoners were to have the right to send out for food and other necessaries; creditors were to contribute towards the upkeep of their gaoled debtors; and justices of the peace were to have increased powers of prison management. It cannot be said that all these provisions were faithfully observed for spunging-houses, although diminished in numbers, did not cease to exist, and creditors made no more effort than formerly to support the debtors whom they had imprisoned; even a later Act in 1759 which directed that a specific sum of four pence a day should be paid by every creditor for the maintenance of his debtor-prisoner was generally ignored. James Oglethorpe continued to press for the amelioration of the debtors' position. In 1732 he launched a new project for the establishment of a charitable fund to be used for paying off the debts of the most deserving prisoners and for sending them overseas to make a fresh start in North America; despite the opposition of Sir Robert Walpole, Oglethorpe succeeded in obtaining a royal charter for a board of trustees to supervise the settlement of the uninhabited country to the south of Carolina with pauper immigrants from England. A large sum was raised for this scheme and, in consequence, the Colony of Georgia came into being. After spending about ten years in Georgia, Oglethorpe returned to England in 1743 and subsequently enjoyed a long and successful career as a soldier, rising to the rank of General. He numbered amongst his friends such eminent figures as Doctor Johnson, Boswell, Goldsmith, Burke and the poet Alexander Pope, who paid tribute to him with the couplet:

> One, driven by strong benevolence of soul,
> Shall fly like Oglethorpe from pole to pole.

During the middle and latter parts of the eighteenth century several steps were taken to improve the predicament of debtors imprisoned for trivial amounts. From 1749 onwards the ancient county courts which had previously adjudicated on small debts were gradually replaced in some localities by Courts of Conscience* which were intended to give a more patient and sympathetic hearing to debtors appearing before them. In 1772 the Society for the Relief of Persons Imprisoned for Small Sums was founded; during its first twenty years this organization managed to secure the release from prison of about 700 debtors annually by arranging compositions with their creditors. A report published by the Society in 1785 drew attention to certain anomalies in the periods of imprisonment which were being imposed by various Courts of Conscience; for example, the court of the City of London had jurisdiction to send a small debtor to gaol for an indefinite period, whereas that for the County of Middlesex was restricted by law to a term of three months. In 1786 Parliament provided that the maximum terms of imprisonment which could be imposed by a Court of Conscience in England and Wales were twenty days for a debt of twenty shillings, and

---

* In general the jurisdiction of the Courts of Conscience was limited to debts of less than forty shillings. Sometimes the figure was increased to five pounds.

forty days for a debt of forty shillings; these periods might be increased to thirty and sixty days respectively if the debtor had acted fraudulently in concealing his assets.

CHAPTER NINE

EIGHTEENTH CENTURY LASSITUDE

BASIL Montagu, whose treatise *Hanging Not Punishment Enough* was published in 1701, was one of the earliest writers in Britain to analyse the purpose and effects of the penal system. His views, though draconian, were logical enough. Penalties should be more severe for serious than for lesser offences, he said; if an offender was to die for a moderate crime, it followed that for a graver one 'he should be made to feel himself die', for instance by being hanged in chains, slowly starved, broken on a wheel, or whipped to death. Montagu regarded gaols simply as places for the confinement of prisoners pending their trial and disposal, but he felt that executions should take place more speedly, 'for offenders may be in County Gaols three, four, five or six months sometimes before they are brought to trial', and during that period there were opportunities for escape or for interfering with the prosecution evidence. Prior to being tried, Montagu suggested, every prisoner should have a box or cell to himself, 'that they might not improve each other in wickedness. This would make their confinement more uneasy and in consequence more dreadful, and they would be better secured.' He was opposed to debtors being mingled in prison with felons as it merely laid them open to corruption. Montagu examined various suggested alternatives to execution. Offenders might be sold as slaves to Barbary in exchange for honest prisoners, or they might be condemned for life to the West Indian plantations; or else, he said, 'you might brand them in the forehead and condemn them to perpetual slavery at home, and employ them in the most painful and offensive works, and feeds them on bread and water.' However, he did not think any of these ideas would prove very effectual, and he concluded by regretting that some better method of punishing criminals could not be discovered than by taking away their lives; 'but what I have hitherto written,' he explained, 'is upon the supposition that none can be.'

The great difficulty for a humanitarian in the Britain of that age must have been how to devise any form of punitive confinement which would not have been an improvement on the general standard of living conditions in most of the urban areas. Writing in 1751 Henry Fielding described one of the poorer localities in London. 'If one considers the destruction of all morality, decency and modesty, the swearing, whoredom and drunkenness which is eternally carrying on in these houses on the one hand,' he wrote, 'and the excessive poverty and misery of most of the inhabitants on the other, it seems doubtful whether they are most the objects of detestation or compassion.' He said that some families only had a single loaf of bread as their entire food for a week, and 'if any of these creatures falls sick (and it is almost a miracle that stench, vermin, and want should ever suffer them to be well) they are turned out into the street by their merciless host or hostess, where, unless some parish officer of extraordinary charity relieves them, they are miserably sure to perish, with the addition of cold and hunger to their disease.' It was not surprising that few authoritative voices spoke up in favour of any radical reforms in the penal system, the cornerstone of which remained the deterrent qualities of the condemned procession and the hangman's rope. Instead of the criminal law being revised or penalties which had been prescribed in former centuries being repealed, there was, in fact a tendency towards increased severity. 'It was also the constant practice of Parliament in the eighteenth century,' said the historian W. E. H. Lecky, 'when new offences arose or when old offences assumed a new prominence, to pass special Acts making them capital. Hence an enormous and undigested multiplication of capital offences, which soon made the criminal code a mere sanguinary chaos.' On the accession of George II about fifty offences carried the penalty of death; during the thirty-three years of his reign sixty-three further offences were added to the list. By 1770 the number had increased to over one hundred and sixty and in the subsequent decades it still continued to rise. Lecky commented that 'the only difference in punishment by which the law of England distinguished the most atrocious murder from the theft of five shillings, was that in the first case, under a law of George II, the execution of the criminal was to take place within forty-eight hours of his conviction and his body was to be atomised.'

A certain mitigation of the so-called 'Bloody Code' was provided by the readiness of the judges to dismiss a case if there should be the smallest defect – even amounting to a mere technicality – in the indictment; also by the number of pardons granted under the royal prerogative of mercy. Condemned prisoners in London and Middlesex were usually returned to Newgate while the Recorder reported to the King in Council* either recommending a reprieve or an execution; it seems that approximately two-thirds of the total were pardoned during the early years of the eighteenth century, but Patrick Colquhoun, writing in 1785, said, 'Out of about a hundred who are upon an average every year doomed to suffer the punishment of death, four-fifths or more are generall pardoned, either on conditions of being transported, or of going into his Majesties' service.' The British ritual of execution did not impress the intelligent observers from overseas. 'So brutal and brutalizing a spectacle could be seen in no other capital in Europe,' remarked a Frenchman, 'nor could any be conceived more fitted to harden a dying criminal, to make him, if reckless and unrepentant, the hero of the mob, and to deprive his execution of every element of solemnity.'

Penal reform was a cause which attracted precious little support among British politicians and statesmen during the eighteenth century; in Parliament, according to Lecky, 'there were no debates which excited less interest, and were less attended or worse reported.' Edmund Burke stood out as one of the great exceptions to the prevalent mood of indifference; he constantly urged the necessity for a complete revision of the criminal code, which he described as 'radically defective and abominable', and he steadfastly opposed the continual additions to the list of capital offences. Another Member, William Hay, endeavoured to introduce a series of Acts in the

---

* The body which considered reprieves was the Cabinet Council; this frequently included such non-political persons as the Archbishop of Canterbury, the Lord Chief Justice and various court officials.

1730s to provide for the erection of new prisons and the appointment of special inspectors to supervise their management. The tenacious James Oglethorpe, too, consistently advocated penal reforms in the House of Commons and he was instrumental in having a parliamentary committee set up in 1754 to enquire into the state of the King's Bench prison. The committee subsequently reported that they had found 'a continuance of the well-known evils of promiscuity, extortions, drunkenness and every kind of irregularity'. As a result the existing King's Bench was demolished and a new gaol was erected on the same site. An Act of Parliament in 1759 required justices of the peace to prepare rules for the good government of all gaols within their counties, such rules to be submitted to the judges for their approval; in common with so much of the other penal legislation of the period this enactment, for the most part, was either ignored, overlooked or forgotten.

Despite the disclosures by the Oglethorpe Committee in 1729 and 1730 the British prisons continued in much the same state of depravity, disease, corruption and cruelty. Drinking remained the foremost activity in every gaol and tap was still a principal source of the keeper's income. In the King's Bench there were thirty different gin-shops at which an average 120 gallons of gin were sold each week, and it was said that at that prison there were 'few hours in the night without riots and drunkenness'. An Act of 1751 sought unsuccessfully to forbid the sale of spirits in the gaols, but even in the places where this law was enforced plentiful supplies of alcohol could be very easily smuggled in from outside. An Ordinary of Newgate writing about the difficulties of excluding spirits from a prison remarked that 'women who are chiefly the conveyors of them secrete them in such ways that it would be termed the grossest insult to search for them.' There were two half-hearted attempts during the century to abolish the garnish system. The first took place in 1752 when the sheriffs of London and Middlesex ordered that no debtors upon entering the gaols within their jurisdiction 'shall for the future pay any garnish, it having been found for many years a great oppression'; the second took place seven years later when the House of Commons passed an Act to put an end to garnish in the prisons generally. No effective measures were ever taken to implement either of these ordinances and the practice continued unabated. Garnish at that time was not peculiar to prison life; the custom, in various guises, also existed in many occupations and trades. For instance, a young man on obtaining his first employment in London as a hat-maker was expected by his felow-workers to contribute the sum of ten shillings as 'maiden garnish' to be spent in the purchase of alcohol; and a beginner, on his initiation as a journeyman cooper, was obliged to buy three gallons of beer for his colleagues and in addition another gallon for every piece of work he performed for the first time and for each different type of timber he used. It would be tempting to assume that the convention of exacting garnish derived from the tedium and frustrations of existence in prison or from the long hours and scant diversions of the lowly-paid workers in an urban district; however, the custom was also observed in more elevated spheres for the justices of the Middlesex Commission, on their initial appointment, were obliged to make a payment which was known as 'colt money' for the provision of drinks for the other magistrates.

It is difficult to discover a single abuse which was rife throughout the prison system during the sixteenth and seventeenth centuries and which did not persist into the eighteenth. The wholesale lasciviousness was encouraged by the fact that the gaol staffs were composed entirely of males; a contemporary writer said of the Clerkenwell Bridewell, 'The gatekeepers and other petty officers of the prison consider all the women prisoners as their seraglio, and indulge themselves in the promiscuous use of as many of them as they please. There are two wards called the "bawdy houses", in which the locker, for a shilling, will at any time lock up a man and woman together for the night.' The Gentleman's Magazine in 1759 described this particular gaol as 'a seminary of wickedness', and commented that a young prisoner who was sent there became 'the witness of the most horrid impiety and the most abandoned lewdness, and generally left whatever good quality he had brought in, together with his health'. The main reliance for security continued to be placed upon irons rather than supervision; and the running costs of the prisons, together with the remuneration of the turnkeys, were still met by fines, bribes and improvised extortion.

The wastage of human lives due to the unhealthy conditions in the gaols was accepted without question—except when an infection was carried outside the prison walls, as happened in London during the celebrated 'Black Assizes'. The prisoners from Newgate who were waiting for their cases to be called at the Old Bailey were confined in a small enclosure called the Bail Dock just outside the courtroom. In May 1750 the sessions calendar was excessively heavy and about a hundred prisoners were packed into this hold in appallingly insanitary and unhygienic conditions for several days. A sudden outbreak of gaol fever in Newgate spread rapidly from the Bail Dock to the court and resulted in the deaths of two judges, the Lord Mayor and over forty officials, barristers and jurymen. The Lord Chief Justice reacted by sending an urgent message to the Court of Aldermen apprising them of 'the necessity of some new regulations for Newgate Gaol, or it would be dangerous for persons to attend the business of the Session at the Old Bailey'. He enclosed a list of the people who had died 'from the noisome stench of the prisoners' and suggested that for the future Newgate and the Old Bailey should be 'cleansed and washed with vinegar'; also, that every prisoner should be scrubbed with vinegar before entering the court for his trial. The following October the Corporation of London set up a committee to enquire into 'the best means of procuring in Newgate such a purity of air, as might prevent the rise of those infectious distempers which not only have been destructive to the prisoners but dangerous to others'. On the recommendation of the committee the Court of Aldermen granted their approval for a completely new method of ventilation which had been designed by a Doctor Hales. This consisted of a series of tubes leading from various parts of the gaol and all connected with a large windmill on the roof which would extract the foetid air from the interior and replace it with fresh air from outside. The new system came into operation during the summer of 1752.

Out of the eleven labourers who installed Doctor Hales's ventilator at Newgate seven contracted gaol fever in the course of their work. There is an interesting document in the

Corporation of London Records Office headed, 'An Account of Several Persons seized with the Gaol Distemper working in Newgate, and of the Manner in which the Infection was communicated to one family'. It was written by John Pringle M.D., F.R.S.,* and dated 25 January 1753. The first person examined by Doctor Pringle was Clayton Hand, a journeyman, whom he saw at St Thomas's Hospital. Hand told the doctor that during the process of dismantling the old ventilator in Newgate he had had occasion to open one of the air tubes; an offensive smell had issued from it and immediately he had been 'seized with a nausea and sickness at his stomach'. The following night he had developed a fever and had become delirious. After eight days in that condition his friends had carried him to the hospital. He said that 'he recollected no other symptom succeeding these mentioned besides frequent retching to vomit, a trembling of his hands, and a constant headache.' A nurse at the hospital informed Doctor Pringle that Hand had remained in a fever for two or three weeks and had 'all along lain like one stupefied; after the fever had worn off he had continued for some time very dull of hearing.' Other of the workmen examined by Doctor Pringle had purple spots on their chests and backs. One fifteen-year-old boy had had to climb down the top of the old ventilator and had 'almost been suffocated with the stench before they could get him up'.

Doctor Pringle stated that as part of his investigation he followed up the after-effects of the disease on a workman called Thomas Wilmot who had appeared to have recovered, but who died soon afterwards. Wilmot did not return to Newgate but sought employment elsewhere, 'yet his strength would not permit him to continue at work above a day or two at a time, still complaining of an headache and pains across his breast, and a feebleness of his limbs, and a shaking of his hands, and a constant drought.' After a while he had become weaker and more feverish; 'at last he was seized with convulsions, having three fits in one day, he died in the last of them.' Wilmot's death was soon followed by that of his

---

* John Pringle (1707-82). Physician General to the Forces and physician to the King. An expert on the prevention of dysentery and hospital fever. He received a baronetcy in 1766.

mother who had contracted the disease through visiting him at his home; his four-year-old son was also infected but was fortunate enough to recover. Doctor Pringle concludes his account by saying, 'From all of which it appears how requisite it is that the public should take such measures as may prevent the like accidents arising from foul and crowded gaols; or indeed from any place wherein a multitude of people are long, closely and nastily kept.'

Although the new ventilator brought about a certain improvement in the atmosphere at Newgate, periodical outbreaks of gaol fever still continued to occur. In June 1755 the Court of Common Council set up a committee 'to enquire into the state and condition of the Gaol of Newgate and to consider how the same may be enlarged and rendered more healthy and commodious'. Among the witnesses heard by this committee was Richard Akerman, the keeper of Newgate. He told them that the gaol was 'very badly contrived'; air could not gain a free passage through it and the sun was invisible from several of the rooms. There were also difficulties with water supplies and lighting, and 'the privies are frequently stopped and overflow which may contribute to the distemper.' He added that Newgate was cleaned every week and a scavenger removed the dirt, 'but that if they attempt to wash the floors the prisoners oppose them, alleging they will give them cold'. In November 1755 the committee brought out their report. They considered that Newgate was far too small for the number of prisoners it contained, and that the water supply was insufficient to keep the prisoners 'in a clean and wholesome state'. The sanitary arrangements, too, were inadequate; 'several of the wards in the said gaol are destitute of privies and most of such as are there are generally choked up whereby a loathsome smell spreads itself throughout the gaol.' As a result, the report declared, people living in Newgate Street were unable to stand in their doorways and customers were reluctant to visit the shops in the vicinity 'for fear of infection'. They concluded by recommending that Newgate should be enlarged 'and rendered more healthy and commodious'.

Soon after receiving this report the Court of Common Council appointed another committee for the purpose of considering the best method of building a completely new prison in place of Newgate. The committee considered numerous schemes, but eventually decided that the best course would be the enlargement of the existing gaol and, in particular, the creation of an exercise yard for prisoners. Their recommendations were pigeon-holed by the Common Council; however, the matter of reconstruction once more came to the fore in 1757 when the residents in the neighbourhood of the gaol petitioned the Corporation of London, 'setting forth their apprehensions from their vicinity to Newgate, and from the stenches proceeding therefrom, of being subject to an infectious disease called the gaol distemper'. The Common Council were sympathetic to these complaints and acknowledged 'the immediate necessity for converting this seat of misery and disease, this dangerous source of contagion, into a secure and wholesome place of confinement'. George Dance, architect to the City of London, was instructed to draw up plans, and surveys and specifications were prepared. Dance's scheme entailed the demolition of a part of the gaol, the Old Bailey courthouse, and a number of houses in the locality. The reconstructed prison was to contain separate wards for male and female debtors and for the various categories of criminal prisoner; there would also be a chapel, a keeper's house, an infirmary, tap-houses, exercise yards, and a small, private reservoir to ensure an adequate supply of water. It was estimated that the whole project would cost about £40,000.

When the Court of Common Council first approached the House of Commons for a grant to finance George Dance's scheme they met with a sharp rebuff, being told that no money was available; but in 1766 an Act of Parliament authorized the City to raise a loan of £50,000 specificially for the rebuilding of Newgate Gaol and the Sessions House. On 31 May 1770 the Lord Mayor laid the first stone of the project and presented all the workmen present with a gift of twenty pounds to mark the occasion. It was soon apparent that the preliminary specifications were a considerable underestimate, and by 1778, although the work was still unfinished, the Corporation had already spent over £52,000; in consequence, Parliament had to authorize the raising of a second loan of a further £40,000.

Doctor William Smith visited some of the completed buildings in 1776, not through idle curiosity, but 'from a charitable desire to afford medical assistance to the sick'. He found the prison 'filled with nasty, ragged inhabitants, swarming with vermin'. The wards, though over-crowded, were large, high and airy; they were kept 'as clean as will be supposed where such a motley crew are lodged'. Doctor Smith did not consider that the reconstructed gaol was worth the money which was being spent on it; he thought the site unsuitable and he would have preferred to see the new prison 'high and dry in an open field and at a distance from the town'. He was also of the opinion that partitions should have been erected in the wards to prevent the prisoners from associating. Richard Akerman, the keeper, was more satisfied with the improvements. Giving evidence before a House of Commons committee in 1779 he said that the old gaol had been very unhealthy, but the new one was 'far more commodious and airy', and very few of the inmates were suffering from any illnesses; however, he had observed 'a dejection of spirits among the prisoners in Newgate which had the effect of a disease, and many of them had died broken-hearted'. On the subject of personal cleanliness he told the committee that all prisoners were supposed to wash themselves, 'but it was very difficult to compel them'. The male prisoners accused of felonies were now separated from those accused of misdemeanours during the night-time, he said, although they associated by day; debtors were segregated from felons the whole time, and men from women. When he was asked about the possibility of employment he replied that as yet there was no place in which the prisoners could work, 'but he fancied it was meant to build one: the gaol was not yet finished'. He had, in fact, allowed some of the inmates to continue with their trades at their own request. Akerman doubted if he would have been able to maintain discipline if the 'young and robust' had not been removed to the hulks; as it was, the prisoners 'frequently stole from strangers who came to see them, and robbed one another'. When they were unruly, he said, he locked them up and put irons on their legs; and then he added a comment which is of particular significance in view of the penal policies devised in the following century – 'They seem to dread solitary confinement.'

CHAPTER TEN

JOHN HOWARD'S PILGRIMAGE

IF John Howard had lived a hundred – or even fifty – years earlier it is extremely doubtful whether he would have exerted any appreciable stimulus to the cause of penal reform; as it was, his views and disclosures gained an added significance because they were formulated during an era which was characterized by a growth of social compassion and the gradual development of a sense of civic responsibility. For the latter part of the eighteenth century, Lecky observed, was marked in Britain by 'a great wave of philanthropic enthusiasm which proceeded from the Evangelical movement'.

Howard was neither an exciting nor a romantic figure; he was aptly described by Thomas Carlyle as 'a man full of English accuracy, English veracity, solidity and simplicity'. Perhaps if the style of his writing had been more vigorous or more emotional the impact of his condemnations would have been less persuasive and less abiding; in fact, the conviction of his words was derived from his fixity of intent and his singleness of purpose, the qualities to which the Webbs have referred as his 'ever-present impulse to remove human suffering'. Howard had no pretensions to being anything but ordinary. He was born in 1726, the son of a comparatively wealthy London upholsterer, and from his infancy he was afflicted with physical frailty and recurrent bouts of ill health. In appearance he was described as being 'short, thin and sallow' – essentially nondescript apart from a penetrating eye and a benevolent smile. 'There was an animation in his manner and a quickness in his gait,' someone said, 'which corresponded with the activity of his mental powers. In his address he was dignified, kind, and condescending, always adapting himself to the persons with whom he conversed; as free from a cringing servility amongst his superiors in station as he was from arrogancy towards those of lower rank.' His letters and

diaries show that his deeply-felt religious beliefs were the compelling force throughout his life.

After completing his education Howard was apprenticed
to a firm of grocers in the City of London. His father died
when he was sixteen leaving him a comfortable income and a
property in Bedfordshire, and Howard decided to leave the
world of commerce and to spend the next few years in foreign
travel. On coming back to England he settled in Stoke Newington and at the age of twenty-six he married his landlady
who was then in her middle fifties; when she died three years
later, in 1755, he resumed his wanderings abroad. Eventually
he returned once more, remarried and settled down on his
estate in Bedfordshire. For the next nine years until 1765 he
lived the secluded life of a model philanthropic landlord, de-
voting his time to improving the housing and the welfare of
his tenants. His second wife died in 1765 whilst giving birth
to their first child, a son. After spending another long period
travelling in Europe Howard resumed the management of his
estate and in 1773, when he was forty-seven, he was appointed
High Sheriff of Bedfordshire. Part of his duty in that office
was to attend the judge at the Bedford Assizes and one day,
not being content merely to act as a spectator at the muted
drama of a succession of criminal trials, he decided to inspect
the local gaol. It is a striking example of the general ignorance
which prevailed at the time concerning prison conditions
that even a well-informed humanitarian such as Howard was
surprised and appalled by what he saw. The two of the factors
which made the deepest impresion on him were, first that
the gaolers and turnkeys were paid no regular salaries but
were obliged to exact their living from the prisoners; and
secondly, that large numbers of persons who had been discharged by the grand jury or acquitted at their trials were
still detained owing to the fact that they had been unable to
pay their discharge fees. Howard immediately suggested to
the Bedfordshire county justices that they should commence
paying regular wages to their gaolers and should abolish the
whole system of prisoner's fees. In reply the justices asked him
if he knew of any precedent for his proposal. As he did not
know of one he decided to tour the prisons throughout

England and Wales to discover whether or not such a precedent existed.

In 1773 Alexander Popham, M.P. for Taunton, endeavoured to get a bill through Parliament with the object of paying fixed salaries to gaolers out of county rates. His measure met with an apathetic response in the House of Commons and was withdrawn after its second reading. At this stage Howard was still engaged on his preliminary survey of the prisons and through the influence of Popham and a handful of other supporters he was invited in March 1774 to appear before a committee of the House to report on his findings. His views made a deep impression on the members present who passed a resolution acquainting him 'that the House are very sensible of the humanity and zeal which had led him to visit the several gaols in this kingdom, and to communicate to the House the interesting observations which he has made on that subject'. Within the next few months Popham was able to pilot two bills through Parliament both of which were based on Howard's recommendations. The first provided that all prisoners who were acquitted should be immediately set at liberty in open court without having to pay any discharge fees. The second required justices of the peace to ensure that the walls and ceilings of all prisons within their jurisdiction were scraped and whitewashed at least once a year, that the wards were properly ventilated and regularly cleaned, that adequate provision was made for sick prisoners, that clothes should be issued to the naked, and that underground dungeons should be used as little as possible.

Howard's detailed acount of his observations entitled *The State of the Prisons in England and Wales* was first published in book form in 1777; a second and a third edition, both revised as a result of subsequent tours of inspection, appeared in 1780 and 1784 respectively. His book was widely read and extensively discussed; it brought home to the general public for the first time the true conditions of prisoners in the British gaols. Howard's purpose in writing the work can best be summed up in his own words; 'I was called to the first part of my task by my office as sheriff. To the pursuit of it I was prompted by the sorrows of the sufferers, and love of my country. The work grew upon me insensibly.'

There are prisons [said Howard], into which whoever looks will, at first sight of the people, be convinced that there is some great error in the management of them: their sallow, meagre countenances declare, without words, that they are very miserable. Many who went in healthy are in a few months changed to emaciated, dejected objects. Some are seen pining under diseases, sick and in prison; expiring on floors, in loathsome cells, of pestilential fevers and the confluent smallpox; victims, I must not say of cruelty, but I will say to the inattention of sheriffs and gentlemen in the commission of the peace. The cause of all this distress is that many prisons are scantily supplied, and some are totally destitute, of the necessaries of life.

Gaol fever added to the torments, he said, 'prevailing to the destruction of multitudes, not only of felons in their dungeons, but of debtors also'. Howard himself ran grave risks in carrying out his investigations. 'It was not, I own, without some apprehensions of danger,' he confessed, 'that I first visited the prisons: and I guarded myself by smelling vinegar while I was in these places, and changing my apparel afterwards.' But gradually he relaxed these precautions and after a while he began to rely solely on the 'Divine Providence'.

Entering the gaols from the outside Howard had found the atmosphere almose unendurable:

Air which has been breathed is made poisonous to a more intense degree by the effluvia of the sick and what else in prisons is offensive. My reader will judge of its malignity when I assure him that my clothes were in my first journeys so offensive that in a post-chaise I could not bear the windows drawn up; and was therefore obliged to travel commonly on horseback. The leaves of my memorandum book were often so tainted that I could not use it till after spreading it an hour or two before the fire: and even my antidote, a vial of vinegar, has, after using it in a few prisons, became intolerably disagreeable. I do not wonder that in those journeys many gaolers made excuses and did not want to go with me into the felons' wards.

He had seen prisoners packed into small rooms, cells, and underground dungeons; sometimes their straw or bedding was laid in an inch or two of water; often there was no exercise yard, and if there was one the prisoners were not allowed to use it because the walls were too low or too dilapidated for proper security, or because the gaoler had taken it over for his own purposes. 'Some gaols,' he added, 'have no sewers or vaults; and those that have, if they be not properly attended to, they are, even to a visitant, offensive beyond expression: how noxious then to the people constantly confined in these prisons.' Howard alleged that one of the contributing factors to the appalling atmosphere inside the gaols was that the gaolers had to pay window-tax and were tempted 'to stop up the windows and stifle the prisoners'. This invidious levy, assessed in proportion to the number and size of a house-holder's windows, was first introduced in 1696 and was gra-dually increased until its abolition in 1851; apart from its effects on prisons, it caused the poorer classes generally to block up their windows in order to curtail their liability.

With regard to food Howard discovered that in some gaols the felons were receiving no free allowances at all; in others the daily ration varied between a pennyworth and twopenny worth of bread a day. 'It is not uncommon,' he said, 'to see the whole purchase, especially of the smaller sums, eaten at break-fast, which is sometimes the case when they receive their pit-tance but once in two days: and on the following days they must fast.' In about half the prisons he had visited the debtors received no free bread at all; 'although,' he commented, 'it is granted to the highwayman, the house-breaker and the mur-derer.' Likewise he found that in some Houses of Correction there was no food allowance and in others the rations were only minimal. The provision of water was also grossly inade-quate. 'Many prisons,' he said, 'have no water. This defect is frequent in bridewells and town gaols. In the felons' courts in some county gaols there is no water: in some places where there is water the prisoners are always locked up within doors and have no more than the keeper or his servants think fit to bring them.'

Howard gave a grim account of the daily lives of the prisoners. Few gaols provided any form of bedding, or even straw, on which they could lie down, 'and if by any means they get a little,' he added, 'it is not changed for months to-gether, so that it is offensive and almost worn to dust. Some lie upon rags, others upon the bare floors.' Frequently they were not allowed any eating utensils through a fear that these might be employed 'for escape or other mischief'. All types of prisoner were mixed up, said Howard, 'debtors and felons, men and women, the young beginner and the old offender. Few prisons separate men and women in the daytime.' Furthermore, a number of county gaols were combined with Houses of Correction, and there 'the petty offender is committed for instruction to the most profligate. In some gaols you see (and who can see it without sorrow) boys of twelve, or fourteen eagerly listening to the stories of practised and experienced criminals, of their adventures, successes, stratagems, and escapes.' Howard condemned the widespread practice of confining idiots and lunatics side-by-side with ordinary prisoners; this custom was particularly rife in Houses of Correction:

Many of the bridewells are crowded and offensive because the rooms which were designed for prisoners are occupied by the insane. Where they are not kept separate, they disturb and terrify other prisoners. No care is taken of them, although it is probable that by medicines and proper regimen some of them might be restored to their senses and to usefulness in life.

Despite the half-hearted efforts which had been made in former years to prevent the indiscriminate ironing of prisoners this procedure continued without diminution. Howard declared:

Loading prisoners with heavy irons, which make their walking, and even lying down to sleep, difficult and painful, is another custom which I cannot but condemn. In some country gaols and even bridewells the women do not escape this severity: but in London they do: and therefore it is not necessary in the country. The practice must be mere tyranny – unless it proceed from avarice, which I rather suspect, because some country gaolers do sometimes grant dispensations and indulge their prisoners, men as well as women, with what they call 'choice of irons', if they will pay for it.

The prisoners from certain gaols were obliged to walk, still wearing their fetters, for distances of ten or fifteen miles to attend their trials. If the town in which the assizes or quarter sessions were being held had no local prison, said Howard,

'numbers of both sexes are shut up together for many days
and nights in one room. This occasions much confusion and
distress, and shrieks and outcrys as can be better conceived
than described.' A lot of prisoners were in custody for twelve
months before they were even tried; the scarcity of gaol deliveries in some places was ascribed to 'the expense of enter-
taining the judges and their retinue'. Howard cited a case of
a man named Peacock who had been charged with murder
and who was kept in prison for three years before eventually
being tried and acquitted.

The exaction of garnish-money amongst prisoners was also
denounced by Howard. 'A cruel custom obtains in most of our
gaols,' he wrote, 'which is that of prisoners demanding of a
newcomer garnish, footing, or (as it is called in some London
gaols) chummage. "Pay or strip" are the fatal words.' Persons
without means were forced to hand over their clothing, 'and
then if they have no bedding or straw to sleep on, contract
diseases which I have known to prove fatal. In many gaols, to
the garnish paid by the newcomer, those who were there
before make an addition, and a great part of the following
night is often spent in riot and drunkenness. The gaoler or
tapster finding his account in this practice, generally
answers questions concerning it with reluctance.' The
garnish ritual, in common with so much of the mischief
perpetrated by the prisoners, was attributable to the idleness
of their lives. Howard discovered no organized prison-labour;
even in the Houses of Correction, which were supposed
to be teaching the habits of honest toil, no work was
possible because there were neither tools nor materials of any
kind. 'The prisoners spend their time,' said Howard, 'in
sloth, profaneness and debauchery to a degree which, in some
of these houses, is extremely shocking.' One could seldom
enter a prison, he added, without seeing gaming in progress,
especially cards, dice or skittles, and the play usually ended
in obscenities, brawls and riots.

The conditions of debtor-prisoners were especially criticized
by Howard:

Debtors crowd the gaols (especially those in London) with their
wives and children. There are often by this means ten or twelve
people in a middle-sized room, increasing the danger of infection

and corrupting the morals of the children . . . The number of men in the same room, and of lewd women admitted under the name of wives, prove that this affair needs some regulation.

He had come across nearly six hundred prisoners who were being detained for debts of less than twenty pounds, and in the whole of England and Wales, apart from the counties of Middlesex and Surrey, he had discovered only twelve debtors who were receiving the authorized allowance of four pence a day from their creditors. He was opposed on principle to the imprisonment of debtors for any sums, however large; 'their destruction is not only unjust,' he said, 'it is inconsistent with prudence and sound policy.'

A most important section of John Howard's book was devoted to his proposals for improvements 'in the structure and management of prisons'. At this time Howard was rightly regarded as the foremost expert on British prison conditions; since he was also the first penal reformer to set out in detail a design for humanizing imprisonment, his ideas and suggestions exerted a considerable influence both on his own and on subsequent generations. He was never an expressed opponent of the prison system as such, nor was he interested in the efficacy of imprisonment as a punishment. He declared on more than one occasion that he was no advocate of luxury in prisons: he was only concerned as a philanthropist and a Christian in ameliorating the cruelties and the hardships which he had witnessed during his extensive tours of the gaols.

Howard believed that prisoners should sleep alone in small rooms. 'Solitude and silence are favourable to reflection,' he said, 'and may possibly lead to repentance. Privacy and hours of thoughtfulness are necessary for those who may soon leave the world.' He stressed the necessity for segregation. 'The women-felons' wards should be quite distant from the men; and the young criminals from the old and hardened offenders. Debtors and felons should have wards totally separate.' Better hygiene was imperative; in every gaol each court should have a pump or a water-pipe.

In a room or shed near the pump or pipe there should be a commodious bath with steps to wash the prisoners that come in dirty and to induce them afterwards to the frequent use of it. It should be filled every morning and let off in the evening through the sewers and the drains. There should also be a copper in the shed to heat a quantity of water sufficient to warm that in the bath for washing those that are sickly. There should likewise be an oven: nothing so effectually destroys vermin in clothes and bedding, nor purifies so thoroughly when tainted with infection, as being a few hours in an oven moderately heated.

For the preservation of the prisoners' health an experienced surgeon or apothecary should be appointed to every gaol; his primary duty would be 'to order the immediate removal of the sick to the infirmary and to see that they have proper bedding and attendance. Their irons should be taken off; and they should have, not only medicines, but diet suitable to their condition.' In Howard's opinion every prison should have its own infirmary or sick wards situated 'in the airy part of the court, quite detached from the rest of the gaol. These rooms should never be without crib beds and bedding.'

Howard was vehemently opposed to a prison-keeper having any connection with the sales of liquor:

Gaolers who hold or let the tap, find their account in not only conniving at, but in promoting midnight revels so that most of our gaols are riotous alehouses and brothels. What profligate and debauched company of both sexes do we see let into our gaols that the tap may be kept running! Even condemned criminals are sometimes heated with liquor till they become outrageous.

In certain gaols, he alleged, open favouritism was shown to prisoners who spent a lot of money in the tap. He had questioned two gaolers, whom he had found 'most candid and intelligent', about the most likely way of effecting a thorough reformation in the prisons. 'The answer I had from both,' he said, 'was to this purpose: "let no licences be granted for selling beer or wine in gaols; let it be made some other way worth our while to keep them".' A number of gaolers had declined to accompany Howard when he was visiting the felons' wards at their prisons, presumably through fear of infection. In censuring this indifference to the responsibilities of their office, he commented, 'It is the gaoler's duty to inspect the wards himself every day, that he may see they are clean and not leave this to his servants.' Howard also deprecated the habit amongst gaolers of employing prisoners to act as unpaid turn-keys in order to reduce their own expenses.

The rest of Howard's recommendations may be summarized briefly. He thought that all the gaols should hold church services every Sunday and that the prisoners should be encouraged to attend them. He advocated the adoption of 'a kind of prison uniform', in part because an escaped prisoner would then become more noticeable. 'On the other hand,' he added, 'they should be tried in their own clothes, for the obvious reason that they may be more easily identified by witnesses.' Further, he proposed that the system for issuing free food to destitute prisoners should be completely over-hauled. And lastly, there should be a special inspector appointed to each prison by the local magistracy or by Parliament. He said that he had enquired of many gaolers whether the sheriffs or justices of the peace ever inspected their prisons; 'many of the oldest have answered, "None of these gentlemen ever looked into the dungeons, or even the wards of my gaol": others have said, "Those gentlemen think that if they came into my gaol they would soon be in their graves".' In Howard's opinion the attitude of the officials responsible for the proper administration of the prisons was epitomized in the words of Telemachus: 'The prosperous turn away their eyes from the miserable, not through insensibility, but because the sight is an interruption of their gaiety.'

In the later editions of his book John Howard gave his further impressions of the prisons and the changes he had noticed on his subsequent visits. In 1779 he found Newgate 'clean and free from offensive smells'. Although the new gaol was a considerable improvement on the old one, he thought that the prisoners were still in great danger of contracting gaol fever. He was critical of the women's wards where, he said, in three of four rooms almost one hundred and fifty prisoners were crowded together, 'many young creatures with the old and hardened'. In the men's wards he saw a number of boys of twelve or fourteen, some of whom were almost naked. The condemned cells of the old Newgate building were still in use; there were fifteen of these, situated on three floors, all measuring approximately nine feet by six feet and being about nine feet high:

In the upper part of each cell is a window double-grated, near three feet by one and a half. The doors are four inches thick. The strong stone wall is lined all round each cell with planks studded with broad-headed nails. I was told by those who attended them, that criminals who had an air of boldness during their trial and appeared quite unconcerned at the pronouncing of sentence upon them, were struck with horror and shed tears when brought to these darksome, solitary abodes.

John Howard's opinions, together with those of Cesare Beccaria and Jeremy Bentham, were to form the basis for the majority of the rational and progressive penological theories for more than a century.

CHAPTER ELEVEN

THE MYSTIQUE OF NEWGATE

DURING the early years of the eighteenth century a perceptible change took place in the attitude towards Newgate of the people of London. The huge, grey walls, although still recognized as concealing from view an enclave of horror, brutality, disease and death, had assumed an air of mystery – a compulsive allurement. It might have been due to the mesmerism of depravity, or the morbid fascination of the gibbet, or perhaps to an illogical veneration of the more spectacular members of the criminal fraternity, especially amongst the murderers, the robbers, and the highwaymen. Throngs of sightseers began to assemble daily outside the massive entrance gates, just watching and waiting and seeping themselves in the malevolent atmosphere of the gaol. And Newgate was constantly in the news; sometimes there had been a daring escape, sometimes a notable execution, sometimes an outbreak of violence, an epidemic, or the startling revelations of a committee of inquiry.

The most sensational escapes in that era were those of Jack Sheppard who was eventually hanged at Tyburn in November 1724, and about whom the Newgate Calendar declared that 'no public robber had ever obtained more notoriety.' Very early in his life Sheppard became a pickpocket and a housebreaker. The first time he was captured he managed to break out through the roof of the St Giles's Roundhouse where he was being held in custody awaiting his trial. On his second apprehension, soon afterwards, he was committed to Newgate with his mistress Elizabeth Lion, better known as Edgworth Bess; as the two were passing as husband and wife they were allowed to share a room in the master's side of the gaol. They had only been in Newgate for a few days when Sheppard had a file smuggled in to him by a visiting friend. A night or two later Edgworth Bess helped him to free himself from his fetters and after they had wrenched a few bars from the window, they scrambled down a line of knotted sheets into the yard some twenty-five feet below. From there they scaled the twenty-two foot perimeter wall and made off into the unlit streets outside the gaol before their disappearance had been noticed.

Jack Sheppard then continued his career as a robber, achieving a considerable reputation for ruthlessness and daring. He was recaptured in the summer of 1724 when he was sentenced to death at the Old Bailey. Just before the day fixed for his execution he was visited in the condemned hold at Newgate by Edgworth Bess and another of his female admirers. Visitors to condemned prisoners could speak to them through an open hatch which was completely covered by large iron spikes. Sheppard had again obtained some instrument with which he succeeded in breaking away sufficient spikes for the girls to lift him through the hatch, and the three of them strolled casually out of the main gates of the gaol without being either recognized or challenged. This time he did not remain at liberty for more than a few months and directly on his apprehension he was returned to Newgate where stringent precautions were taken to prevent him from escaping for the third time. Not only was he confined by himself in a special strong room, but he was kept permanently handcuffed and shackled to a staple embedded in the floor. His exploits had aroused such an interest that he was visited, according to the Newgate Calendar, by 'a great number of people of all ranks, scarce any of whom left him without making him a present in money, though he would have more gladly received a file, a hammer, or a chisel, but the utmost care was taken that none of his visitors should furnish him with such implements'.

Sheppard's last escape from Newgate was the most dramatic of all. In his room he found a small nail and after he had been locked up for the night he used it to release himself from his handcuffs and to pick the padlock connecting his shackles to the staple in the floor. Then, with the shackles still attached to his legs, he attempted to climb up the chimney stack but he was held up at first by a thick iron bar which had been wedged firmly across the whole width of the flue.

After a hard struggle he managed to dislodge this obstacle and to break through to an empty room above his own. From there he crept down a passage and entered the chapel. He appears to have known what route he should follow, for after forcing two doors and climbing a wall he reached the upper leads of the gaol. He then worked his way along to the edge of the roof and lowered himself down on to the leads of a neighbouring house. Even when he had climbed through an open garret window his difficulties were by no means finished, for on several occasions he was almost discovered as he was trying to descend the staircase as noiselessly as his clanking chains would allow. Finally, he managed to leave the house unnoticed, and in the early hours of the morning he took shelter in a disused cowhouse in a field near Tottenham Court Road. Despite the pleas of his mother and his friends that he should flee the country, Sheppard insisted on staying in London, and only a few days later he was recaptured at an alehouse almost insensible with liquor. Once again he received a perpetual stream of visitors in Newgate; 'he endeavoured to divert them,' says the Newgate Calendar, 'by a recital of the particulars of many robberies in which he had been concerned; and when any noblemen came to see him he never failed to beg that they would intercede with the king for a pardon, to which he thought his singular dexterity gave him some pretensions.' Sheppard was only twenty-two when he was hanged; 'he died with difficulty,' commented the writer of the account in the Newgate Calendar, 'and he was much pitied by the surrounding multitude.'

Although the more daring prisoners were perpetually attempting to escape from Newgate, only a very small proportion were actually successful in doing so. The methods which they employed varied considerably. One obvious way, with so many visitors passing in and out of the gaol, was to walk boldly through the gates in the hope of getting past the turnkeys on duty there without being recognized. A prisoner in 1663 changed clothes with his wife in a dark corner of his ward and left the gaol unnoticed, only to be recaptured in the vicinity on the following day. Another prisoner escaped in the disguise of a footman. Alexander Scott, the highwayman, dressed up as an oyster-girl, but he aroused the suspicion of the gate-keepers who chased and overpowered him just out-side the gaol. In 1679 seven prisoners managed, under cover of darkness, to knock a hole in the perimeter wall sufficiently large for all of them to climb through, and their absence was not discovered until the following morning. Sometimes a mass attempt occurred, as in 1692 when the inmates of one of the felons' wards started a fire in a yard and in the ensuing com-motion they made a concerted attack on the gates which, how-ever, was repulsed by a detachment of turnkeys armed with cutlasses. The common sewers passing under Newgate were also regarded as a possible way out, but only by the most intrepid because of the natural risks involved. In 1731 six prisoners hacked their way through a dungeon floor and entered the principal sewer below. After crawling and wading for a long period four of them managed to get up into a shop in Fleet Lane, though one was subsequently recaptured; the remaining two were either suffocated or drowned soon after they set out, their skeletons being discovered some years later. A similar escape occurred in 1737 when Daniel Malden, a street robber, though shackled with heavy irons, broke out of the condemned hold and entered the main sewer by way of a subterranean vault and a long narrow tunnel running under-neath. After spending forty-eight hours in the sewer he climbed through an open manhole and made his way to the house of a friend who arranged for a blacksmith to knock off his irons. Malden then fled to the continent, but he was un-wise enough to return to England shortly afterwards, and being recognized and apprehended he was hanged at Tyburn.

An interesting sidelight on the security arrangements at Newgate was disclosed in a document signed by William Pitt, the keeper, on 16 November 1730, which set out his answers to certain complaints which had been made against him by the debtor prisoners. Amongst their other grievances the debtors had alleged that the taps in the gaol were managed dishonestly by wives of the turnkeys. Pitt replied that the turnkeys' wives in charge of the three taps were 'sober, indus-trious and honest people', who provided good measure for fair prices. He added, 'And as escapes are often contrived in the Gaol of Newgate, the turnkeys' wives, being constantly

508.—Newgate. (Eighteenth Century.)

Top) The rebuilt and enlarged gaol which had just been completed in
1780 when it was burned down by the mob during the Gordon Riots.
The keeper's house can be seen in the centre.

(Above) A prisoners' yard inside Newgate. It is uncertain whether this
sketch was made in the gaol which was destroyed in 1780 or in the
building which was erected after the Gordon Riots.

(Top) A view of Newgate Gaol at the corner of Newgate Street and the Old Bailey in about 1800.

(Above) A service for the condemned in the Chapel of Newgate Gaol in 1808. The prisoners about to be executed are seated in an enclosure around a symbolic coffin.

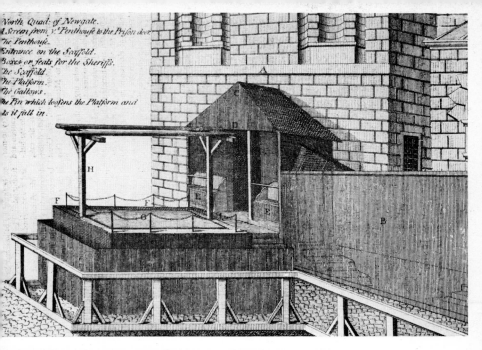

(Top) The last hanging took place at Tyburn in 1783. From that time onward executions were performed on a portable gallows erected outside the debtors' entrance to Newgate. This sketch was printed in 1794, when 'the drop' – a method of hanging by the use of a collapsible platform – was still a recent innovation.

(Above) Elizabeth Fry reading to the prisoners in the women's section of Newgate.

(*Top*) The tread wheel and exercise yards at Coldbath Fields in about 1870. Coldbath Fields, the Middlesex House of Correction, was set up in the reign of James I. A vagrants' ward was opened in 1830 and four years later the silent system was adopted in the whole prison.

(*Above*) A prisoner picking oakum in his cell at Newgate. This useless occupation consisted of unravelling lengths of old rope.

A school-class in the Chapel of the Surrey House of Correction at Wandsworth, which was opened in 1851. Under the separate system, as applied at this and a number of other prisons, the prisoners were not allowed to see or to communicate with each other during lessons and services.

A condemned cell at Newgate in 1873. The warder watches attentively while the prisoner under sentence of death reads his Bible.

PRISONERS AT EXERCISE.

(Top) Prisoners at exercise in Pentonville. This prison, completed in 1842, was specially designed to operate the separate system and when prisoners left their cells their faces had always to be covered with masks.

(Above) Prisoners at exercise in a yard at Newgate during the latter part of the nineteenth century. These are men who have not yet been tried so they are still wearing their own clothing.

A photograph of Newgate taken from the corner of Newgate Street and the Old Bailey during the last few years before the demolition of the gaol. The dome of St. Paul's can be seen in the background.

there, do often prevent their villainous designs by giving timely notice to their husbands.'

The macabre inquisitiveness which centred around the condemned felons at Newgate was almost insatiable. In the course of William Pitt's apologia, just referred to, he replied to complaints that the debtors were sometimes prevented from attending services in the chapel and that the keeper was making money out of exhibiting his prisoners there:

The debtors, their wives and friends are never hindered from going to Divine Service on the Lord's Day, except when great numbers of criminals are under sentence of death, and then, as the curiosity of many gentlemen and others brings them to see these unfortunate people, the turnkeys have a small advantage which was always allowed them, of which the keeper receives no part.

Horace Walpole, in a comment on James Maclane, the twenty-six-year old Irish highwayman who was hanged in October 1750, wrote:

The first Sunday after his trial three thousand people went to see him. He fainted away twice with the heat of his cell. You can't conceive the ridiculous rage there is of going to Newgate and the prints that are published of the malefactors, and the memoirs of their lives.

The mystique of Newgate was further engendered during that period by an emotional absorption in crime and punishment amongst the literary and artistic circles. This was exemplified in the setting and theme of John Gay's musical satire *The Beggar's Opera*. Samuel Johnson, quoting an account given by Pope, wrote:

Dr Swift had been observing once to Mr Gay, what an odd pretty sort of a thing a Newgate Pastoral might make. Gay was inclined to try at such a thing for some time; but afterwards thought it would be better to write a comedy on the same plan.

Gay wished to create an authentic atmosphere, as he informed Swift before he started the play that he was going to revisit Newgate in order to refresh his memory of the criminal background. The first performance of *The Beggar's Opera* took place at the Theatre Royal, Lincoln's Inn Fields in

E

January 1728 with the enchanting nineteen-year-old actress
Lavinia Fenton in the part of the heroine, Polly; the play was
attended, according to one report, by 'a prodigious concourse
of nobility and gentry', and the final curtain was greeted
'with greater applause than was ever known'. The play was
produced in subsequent years at other theatres throughout
Britain with comparable success. *The Beggar's Opera* mani-
fests the adulation of the daring villain by the masses and the
forlorn glory of the final procession from Newgate to Tyburn.
'The youth in his cart,' someone says, 'hath the air of a lord,
and we cry, "There dies an Adonis".' And in Polly's soliloquy
on the highwayman Macheath she exclaims:

Methinks I see him already in the cart, sweeter and more
lovely than the nosegay in his hand. I hear the crowd extolling
his resolution and intrepidity. What vollies of sighs are sent from
the windows of Holborn!

It is said that William Hogarth saw *The Beggar's Opera*
several times during its initial run and that it made a strong
appeal to his imagination. Hogarth himself was immensely
interested in the criminal fraternity. In the spring of 1733
he visited Newgate to draw a portrait of Sarah Malcolm two
days before she was hanged; he was accompanied by his
father-in-law Sir James Thornhill, who nine years earlier had
sketched Jack Sheppard as he lay in the condemned hold for
the last time. Sarah Malcolm had been convicted of three
vicious murders. Her expression as depicted by Hogarth was
both merciless and unrepentant; indeed, he said of her afterwards, 'This woman, by her features is capable of any wickedness.' It is probable that Hogarth was inside Newgate on a
number of other occasions; Peter Quennell in a recent, per-
ceptive study of Hogarth's work has said that his knowledge
of the London underworld was founded on the gaol. The
grim horror of an execution-day was featured in a couple of
Hogarth's well known picture-cycles. Plate XI of 'Industry
and Idleness' shows Tom Idle arriving at Tyburn in the condemned cart with his back resting against his own coffin; and
in plate IV of 'The Four Stages of Cruelty' Tom Nero's
corpse, the rope still about its neck, is being dissected in
Surgeons' Hall with a dog sniffing about at the entrails.

James Boswell also experienced the sinister lure of New-gate. On his first visit to London, just after his coming-of-age, he paid a visit to the gaol, apparently to the condemned cells, which he briefly described in his journal for 3 May 1763:

I stepped into a sort of court before the cells. They are surely most dismal places. There are three rows of 'em, four in a row, all above each other. They have double iron windows, and within these, strong iron rails; and in these dark mansions are the un-happy criminals confined. I did not go in, but stood in the court, where were a number of strange blackguard beings with sad countenances, most of them being friends and acquaintances of those under sentence of death.

On the following day Boswell decided to attend a hanging:

My curiosity to see the melancholy spectacle of the executions was so strong, that I could not resist it, although I was sensible that I would suffer much from it. In my younger days I had read in the 'Lives of the Convicts' so much about Tyburn that I had a sort of horrid eagerness to be there.

Accompanied by a friend Boswell took up his position very close to the scaffold. 'There was a most prodigious crowd of spectators,' he continued. 'I was most terribly shocked and thrown into a very deep melancholy.' Later in his life Boswell overcame his initial sensitivity and witnessed a number of other executions; he also became a fairly frequent visitor to Newgate and in the course of time he was able to refer to the keeper there as 'my esteemed friend Mr Akerman'.

Richard Akerman, the keeper of Newgate, was a remark-able person and most unlike the majority of his notorious predecessors. In a graceful tribute written just after the Gor-don riots, Boswell said that Akerman had long discharged a very important trust with an uniform intrepid firmness, and at the same time a tenderness and a liberal charity, which entitled him to be recorded with distinguished honour. Doctor Johnson, who knew Akerman too, once remarked that in spite of his continuous contact with the worst of mankind he was 'yet eminent for the humanity of his disposition'. The same trait of compassion was praised by several others. Doctor William Smith, after inspecting Newgate in 1776 remarked, 'Mr Akerman the keeper is extremely humane in keeping the place as wholesome as possible;' and John Howard noted on his visit to the gaol in 1779 that there were ninety-one prisoners who would have had to subsist on the charitable ration of a penny loaf each a day, but that 'Mr Akerman generously contributed to their relief.' Boswell recounts a story which illustrates Akerman's courage as well as his compassionate, though resolute method of controlling his prisoners. A fire had broken out in a section of Newgate – Boswell does not mention the date but it may well have been the Press Yard fire of 1762 when two of the inmates were burnt to death – and a number of prisoners panicked and endeavoured to break out through the gates. Akerman soon appeared on the scene and personally took charge of the situation. He persuaded the prisoners to fall back from the gates, assured they would come to no harm, and invited them to let him lead them to a place of safety. 'The prisoners peaceably followed him,' says Boswell, 'while he conducted them through passages, of which he had the keys, to the extremity of the gaol which was most distant from the fire.'

Perhaps it was inevitable in view of the emotional significance attaching to Newgate that the gaol should be one of the first official buildings to be stormed by the mob during the Gordon Riots. On the evening of the 6 June 1780 a frenzied horde rampaged along Holborn into Newgate Street and Old Bailey. Ostensibly they came to demand the liberation of three prisoners who had been committed from the Bow Street Office on the previous day; but for a great many the sacking of Newgate Gaol must have appeared as a symbolic act of anarchical fervour, for it signified the destruction of the seemingly impregnable: the desecration of a timeless tradition.

Initially the crowd converged on the keeper's house, only to find the doors bolted and chained and locked shutters drawn across the windows. The ringleaders ordered Akerman to release the three prisoners and were met with a categorical refusal. The assault on the house then began with battering rams, cudgels and crowbars; very soon the mob had burst in and were flinging pictures, books, clothes and furniture into the street, while Akerman and his servants made their escape, some of them by clambering along the rooftops. Akerman went straightaway to the sheriffs and asked them to summon military assistance. But the sheriffs were tremulous and indecisive and in the end they did nothing. Boswell said later that if the keeper had been sent proper aid initially it would have enabled him to save both his house and his prison; as it was, the systematic devastation proceeded virtually without hindrance, and Akerman returned home an hour or two later to find his house pillaged and in flames.

It is not necessary to turn to Dickens's fictional, though authentic, description of the storming of Newgate in *Barnaby Rudge*, as there are several reliable eye-witnesses and contemporary reports of what occurred. Thomas Holcroft has recounted the demolition of Akerman's house:

> What contributed more than anything to the spreading of the flames was the great quantity of household furniture, which they threw out of the windows, piled up against the doors, and set fire to; the force of which presently communicated to the house, from the house to the Chapel, and from thence, by the assistance of the mob, all through the prison. A party of constables to the amount of a hundred, came to the assistance of the keeper; these the mob made a lane for, and suffered to pass till they were entirely encircled, when they attacked them with great fury, broke their staffs, and converted them into brands, which they hurled wherever the fire, which was spreading very fast, had not caught.

The Reverend George Crabbe mingled with the frenzied crowd outside and surveyed the scene in amazement.

> By eight o'clock Akerman's house was in flames [he wrote later], I went close to it and never saw anything so dreadful. The prison, as I have said, was a remarkably strong building, but, determined to force it, they broke the gates with crows and other instruments, and climbed up the outside of the cell part, which joins the two great wings of the building where felons are confined; and I stood where I plainly saw their operations. They broke the roof, tore away the rafters, and having got ladders they descended. Not Orpheus himself had more courage or better luck; flames all around them, and a body of soldiers expected, they defied and laughed at all opposition.

Frederick Reynolds' report of the attack on Newgate is equally vivid:

The mob fired the gaol in many places before they were enabled to force their way through the massive bars and gates which guarded the entrance. The wild gestures of the mob without, and the shrieks of the prisoners within, expecting instantaneous death from the flames, the thundering descent of huge pieces of building, the deafening clangour of red-hot iron bars striking in terrible concussion on the pavement below, and the loud, triumphant yells and shouts of the demoniac assailants on each new success, formed an awful and terrific scene.

By then the three prisoners who had formed the original pretext for the assault had been forgotten and the rioters were determined, amongst their other objectives, to release every inmate of Newgate. From his point of vantage Holcroft was able to watch their efforts. He recalled:

The activity of the mob was amazing. They dragged out the prisoners by the hair of the head, by arms or legs, or whatever part they could lay hold of. They broke the doors of the different entrances as easily as if they had all their lives been acquainted with the intricacies of the place, to let the confined escape. Great numbers were let out at the door that leads to the Sessions House, and so well planned were the manoeuvres of these desperate ruffians that they had placed sentinels at all the avenues to prevent any of the prisoners being conveyed to other gaols.

Crabbe saw a party of about eight men and twelve women, some of whom were under sentence of death, 'ascend from their confinement to the open air'; they were still in chains as they were led from the gaol. Meanwhile Henry Angelo, who had taken cover in a building in Newgate Street, decided to come out and investigate what was happening. 'Leaving my place of safety,' he wrote in his reminiscences, 'I got to the lane with difficulty as it was crowded with felons, and in many of the houses I heard them knocking off their fetters. While listening to the noise of the hammers at one house, I narrowly escaped being knocked down for my curiosity.' Frederick Reynolds remained in the vicinity of the gaol throughout, until at length, he said, 'the work of ruin was accomplished, and while the gaolers and turnkeys were either flying or begging for their lives, forth came the prisoners, blaspheming and jumping in their chains. The convicts being taken to different blacksmiths in the neighbourhood, I followed one of them who was to have been hanged on the following Monday.' Crabbe who had been away for a while, returned to the scene at eleven o'clock that night. 'Newgate was at this time open to all,' he declared, 'anyone might get in and, what was never the case before, anyone might get out. I did both.'

What dumbfounded the general public was not merely that a building with a structure as sturdy as Newgate Gaol should have been sacked so easily, but that it should have been sacked at all. The *Gentleman's Magazine* expressed the national sentiment, when it declared:

It is scarce to be credited with what celerity a gaol, which to the common observer appeared to be built with nothing that would burn, was destroyed by the flames; nor is it less astonishing that from a prison thus in flames a miserable crew of felons in irons and a company of debtors to the number, in the whole, of more than 300, could all be liberated as it were by magic, amidst flames and fire-brands, without the loss of a single life.

Crabbe added his own comment:

Thus was the strongest and most durable prison in England, in the building on which the nation had expended immense sums, demolished, the bare walls excepted, which were too thick and strong to yield to the force of the fire, in the space of a few hours.

On the following day the smouldering shell of Newgate Gaol was visited by large numbers of curious sightseers; they included Doctor Samuel Johnson who later told Mrs Thrale in a letter:

On Wednesday I walked with Dr Scot to look at Newgate, and found it in ruins, with the fire yet glowing. As I went by, the Protestants were plundering the Sessions-house at the Old Bailey. There were not, I believe, a hundred; but they did their work at leisure, in full security, without sentinels, without trepidation, as men lawfully employed, in full day.

Oddly enough, many of the escaped prisoners returned to

loiter aimlessly amongst the embers of the gaol and were re-captured without difficulty; others, homeless and destitute, surrendered themselves during the next few weeks and were sent to rejoin their former associates, who were temporarily confined in the compters. No time was wasted in the pre-paration of plans for the complete reconstruction of New-gate and the repair of the extensively damaged Sessions House.

CHAPTER TWELVE

THE UTILITARIANS

THE humanitarian influence of the utilitarian school of philosophers has been emphasized so often that it would be all too easy to imagine the benevolent aspect of their theories as being the predominant feature of their penal doctrine. It is true, of course, that Beccaria's radical concepts had a profound effect in mitigating the severity of sentences in many of the advancing nations of the world; also, that the views of Jeremy Bentham attracted considerable contemporary attention and transformed the nature of imprisonment in Britain and America during the nineteenth century. Yet the fact remains that the utilitarians were principally concerned, not with the amelioration of penalties, but with the reasons for punishing criminals and the efficacy of the methods of punishment which were then in general use.

Cesare Beccaria, an Italian writer on moral and political economy, was born at Milan in 1734. He first published his celebrated treatise *An Essay on Crimes and Punishments* in 1764; within eighteen months it had been reproduced in six further editions, and during the next decade the translated versions were being studied with interest all over Europe. For his theory as to the origin of government Beccaria accepted the postulate known as 'the social contract', which greatly affected his opinions on the treatment of criminals. The social contract, as expounded by Locke, rejected the alternative seventeenth century belief that power was bestowed on rulers by divine right – which necessarily involved the fundamental, inherited servility of the masses – and maintained that civil government was the outcome of a real or imaginary compact between the rulers and ruled. 'In a republic where every man is a citizen,' wrote Beccaria, 'subordination is not the effect of compulsion, but of contract.' And elsewhere he says:

Laws are the conditions under which men, naturally independent, united themselves in society. Weary of living in a continual state of war, and of enjoying a liberty which became of little value from the uncertainty of its duration, they sacrificed one part of it, to enjoy the rest in peace and security.

Another tenet of utilitarian philosophy which influenced Beccaria's views on penal reform was the belief that the morality of human actions must be judged by a simple yard-stick, those which promote happiness being good and those which cause pain being bad; hence the distinction between right and wrong must be measured by the balance of happiness over pain.

Beccaria did not believe that a community could ever free itself from crime. 'In every human society,' he said, 'there is an effort continually tending to confer on one part the height of power and happiness, and to reduce the other to the extreme of weakness and misery.' There would always be conflicts of interest and emotional dissensions and it was the purpose of good laws to reconcile them. 'It is not only the common interest of mankind that crimes should not be committed,' he declared, 'but that crimes of every kind should be less frequent, in proportion to the evil they produce to society.' It was the duty of the ruler to punish criminal acts because his people had bartered a portion of their individual liberty in return for his undertaking to protect them. But an infliction of punishment which could be avoided became wrongful. He said:

Every act of authority of one man over another for which there is not an absolute necessity is tyrannical. It is upon this then, that the sovereign's right to punish crimes is founded; that is, upon the necessity of defending the public liberty entrusted to his care, from the usurpation of individuals, and punishments are just in proportion, as the liberty, preserved by the sovereign, is sacred and valuable.

The utilitarians totally repudiated the proposition that society was ever justified in punishing its criminals for the purpose of retribution. A similar view had been put forward several times during former ages, particularly by the celebrated Dutch jurist Hugo Grotius (1583-1645) who wrote, 'It is clear that man cannot rightly be punished by man simply for the sake of punishing him.' Nevertheless, retribution had remained a dominant feature of penal systems throughout the world. Beccaria stated clearly and categorically that both from a moral and a logical viewpoint the sole purpose of punishing should be deterrence. The end of punishment, he said, 'is no other than to prevent others from committing the like offence. Such punishments, therefore, and such a mode of inflicting them, ought to be chosen as will make the strongest and most lasting impressions on the minds of others, with the least torment to the body of the criminal.' When a criminal act had been performed it could not be undone and it was useless and tyrannical to treat the culprit with cruelty. 'Can the groans of a tortured wretch,' he asked, 're-call the past or reverse the crime he has committed?'

According to Beccaria, you could only assess the seriousness of crimes by the extent of the injury they inflicted to society as a whole. 'Every crime, even of the most private nature, injures society,' he said, 'but every crime does not threaten its immediate destruction.' It followed that the most heinous offences were those which harmed the basic structure of the community; less grave were those which affected the life, pro-perty or honour of private individuals; and the least serious of all consisted of actions which were merely contrary to laws enacted for the general good of the populace. He drew a sharp distinction between crime and sin. The concept of sin involved the intention of the sinner and depended upon 'the malignity of the heart which is impenetrable to finite being'. In any event, the sinner was punished by God in due course according to the notions of divine justice.

Beccaria laid down certain principles of punishment. First of all, trial and sentence should take place with the mimimum delay:

The more immediately after the commission of a crime a punishment is inflicted, the more just and useful it will be. It will be just because it spares the criminal the cruel and super-fluous torment of uncertainty . . . and because the privation of liberty, being a punishment, ought to be inflicted before con-demnation for as short a time as possible. Imprisonment, I say, being the only means of securing the person of the accused until he be tried, condemned or acquitted, ought not only to be of as short duration, but attended with as little severity as possible.

He laid great stress on the necessity for an efficient system
of law enforcement:

Crimes are most effectually prevented by the certainty, than the
severity, of punishment. The certainty of a small punishment will
make a stronger impression than the fear of one more severe if
attended with the hope of escaping.

Beccaria considered that within the limits of practicality a
penalty should be analogous to the offence for which it was
imposed; in every case the severity of the sentence should be
proportionate to the gravity of the crime:

If equal punishment be ordained for two crimes that injure
society in different degree, there is nothing to deter men from
committing the greater, as often as it is attended with greater
advantage.

He deprecated the use of cruelty in punishing, for if punishments were too barabarous criminals were naturally
tempted to commit further crimes in order to avoid being
sentenced for their earlier ones:

That a punishment may produce the effect required it is sufficient that the evil it occasions should exceed the good expected
from the crime. All severity beyond this is superfluous and therefore tyrannical.

The most novel and forceful arguments which Beccaria
advanced in his treatise occurred in his criticisms of the death
penalty:

The useless profusion of punishments, which have never made
men better induces me to inquire whether the punishment of
death be really just or useless in a well-governed state? What
right, I ask, have men to cut the throats of their fellow-creatures?

His answers to those questions formed an unequivocal de-
nunciation of penal execution. Morally, the punishment of
death was pernicious to society from the example of barbarity which it afforded. Further, the public were filled with
contempt for the cruelty of the judges, magistrates and everyone else who took part in the execution ceremony; the inevitable reflection of the onlookers was, 'Murder, which they
would represent to us as a horrible crime, we see practised

by them without repugnance or remorse.' Beccaria also thought than an execution had no real value as a deterrent:

Experience of all ages has proved that the death penalty has never prevented men from injuring society. The death of a criminal is a terrible but momentary spectacle and therefore a less efficacious method of deterring others than the continued example of a man deprived of his liberty, condemned as a beast of burden to repair by his labour the injury he has done to society. 'If I commit a crime,' says the spectator to himself, 'I shall be reduced to that miserable condition for the rest of my life.' The terrors of death make so slight an impression that it has not force enough to withstand the forgetfulness natural to mankind.

Quite apart from the evanescent impressions of a public execution Beccaria held that instead of inspiring an exemplary terror amongst the observers it was apt to arouse in them a compassion for the victim.

Since the entire object of punishment was to deter the commission of crimes Beccaria thought it should always be administered with the utmost publicity. Even though he was more concerned with the philosophy of punishment than with its practical application, he did suggest as the ultimate deterrent a penalty he called 'perpetual slavery', by which society became the absolute master of the criminal while the latter atoned for his wrongfulness and for his violation of the social contract. He commented:

I shall be told that perpetual slavery is as painful a punishment as death and therefore as cruel. I answer that if all the miserable moments in the life of the slave were collected into one point it would be a more cruel punishment than any other; but they are scattered through the whole of his life, while the pain of death exerts all its force in a moment. There is also another advantage in the punishment of slavery, which is that it is more terrible to the spectator than to the sufferer himself; for the spectator considers the sum of all his wretched moments, whilst the sufferer, by the misery of the present, is prevented from thinking about the future.

Although Beccaria did not discuss the matter of a sentencing policy in any detail it is apparent that he conceived the penalty of slavery should be applied for various periods according to the gravity of the crime. He favoured corporal punishment for offences against the person; and on the analogy principle he thought a flogging combined with a period of slavery was the appropriate penalty for robbery with violence. He had his doubts about the usefulness of fines because they tended to swell the numbers of the poor, and he felt that sentences of imprisonment, or of transportation to distant countries, served no effective purpose as the misery of the convicted criminal should be on constant view to his fellow-citizens throughout the whole period of his punishment.

Whereas Cesare Beccaria contented himself with propounding the penal theories of utilitarianism Jeremy Bentham endeavoured to put them into practice. Bentham was born in London in 1748 so he was only sixteen when Beccaria's treatise was first published, but from an early age he was determined to discover some solid foundation for what he believed to be the precepts of morality and law. Having graduated at Oxford he was called to the Bar by Lincoln's Inn in 1772, and during the years that followed he gained a considerable international reputation as a writer on law and political economy. Bentham maintained, like Beccaria, that good and happiness were synonymous terms; in the natural process, he thought, every person was perpetually seeking his own pleasure and the purpose of the criminal code was to reconcile the interests of the individual with the welfare of the community.

Fundamentally, the penal principles of Bentham and Beccaria were identical, but in the development of their theories they reached a number of dissimilar conclusions. The main purpose of punishment, Bentham wrote, was to prevent the commission of like offences:

> In many cases it will be impossible to redress the evil that is done, but it is always possible to take away the will to repeat it; for however great may be the advantage of the offence, the evil of the punishment may be always made to outweigh it.

All penalties should be unpleasant because if they were not dreaded they would not effect their purpose. 'The amount of punishment,' he said, 'should not be greater in amount, nor should it be lesser than is necessary to deter men from committing crimes.' He argued that a fine of a shilling would be an adequate penalty for murder provided it evoked as much fear as a sentence of death; punishment which was unnecessarily severe became unjustifiable cruelty. Bentham was not opposed to executions which he thought should be presented to the public in the form of a solemn tragedy; 'the tribunal, the scaffold, the dresses of the officers of justice, the religious service, the processions ought to bear a grave and melancholy character. The executioners might be veiled in black that the terror of the scene might be heightened.' On the other hand, he believed that expiation should be followed by forgiveness:

It ought not to be forgotten that the delinquent is a member of the community as well as any other individual and that there is just as much reason to consult his interest as that of any other. It may be right that the interest of the offender should in part be sacrificed to that of the rest of the community, but it can never be right that it should be totally disregarded.

Jeremy Bentham's views on imprisonment were dominated from an early stage by his ardent belief in the efficacy of solitary confinement. A number of authoritative writers have attributed a similar conviction to John Howard. However, Howard did not advocate such a system; it is true that in his opinion segregation was necessary in order to prevent moral and physical contamination, and he once suggested that silence might lead to repentance, but nowhere in his writings did he recommend a deliberate process of isolation. In fact, the theory that solitary confinement should be one of the central features of imprisonment seems to have originated in America where it was applied in the early Quaker prisons of Pennysylvania. Jonas Hanway, the philanthropist, gave the idea his unqualified support when he said in 1766:

Everyone has a plan, and a favourite system: mine is solitude in imprisonment, with a proper profitable labour and a spare diet, as the most humane and effectual means of bringing malefactors . . . to a right sense of their condition.

Bentham first disclosed his support for this principle in 1778 when he set out his comments on a proposed Hard Labour Bill. He declared:

When I had read Mr. Howard's book on prisons, one fruit of it was a wish, still more earnest than what I had been led to entertain from theory, to see some general plan of punishment adopted, in which solitary confinement might be combined with labour.

At that time reformation does not seem to have been uppermost in Bentham's mind, but rather the deterrent effect produced on the mind of the prisoner himself, for as he explains, 'The circumstances of secrecy and seclusion give an air of mystery to the scene which contributes greatly to enhance the terrors it is intended to impress.' At the same time he did not consider it advisable 'to rest the whole of the punishment altogether on the ground of terror'; since terror was obliterated in due course by familiarity. There should be other factors of unpleasantness, such as the drabness of the diet, so that it would be less necessary to incur 'any inconvenient expense in screwing the sentiment of terror to the highest pitch.' In accordance with Beccaria's confidence in the beneficial example of perpetual slavery, Bentham suggested that outside the gates of every prison should be a notice reading, 'Had they been industrious when free, they need not have drudged here like slaves'.

In 1791 Bentham published the details of his purposeful and radical scheme for a completely new type of imprisonment, under the title of *The Panopticon or Inspection House*. He summed up the former system with the aphorism, 'The gallows was always ready with open arms to receive as many as the jail-fever should have refused.' The panopticon was based on an idea conceived by Jeremy's brother, the naval architect Sir Samuel Bentham; it was devised, Jeremy said, to provide safe custody, confinement, solitude, forced labour, and instruction. He recommended its use for 'punishing the incorrigible, reforming the vicious, confining the suspected and employing the idle'. It is noticeable that by then Bentham had abandoned the emphasis which he had placed eleven years previously upon the necessity of terror and had incorporated into his scheme the element of reformatory toil. Beccaria, in defining the objects of punishment, had never ever alluded to the possibility of reformation.

The panopticon was to be a circular building, with the

prisoner's cells side-by-side all round the circumference. The inspector's lodge, separated from the cells if possible by an empty space, was positioned at the centre. The cells were completely divided from one another so that no prisoner could either see or communicate with his neighbours; each cell had a window in its outer wall and the place of the fourth wall, facing towards the centre, was entirely filled by a large iron grill containing a door. The lighting was to be arranged so that the inspector could watch all the prisoners from his lodge, but would himself remain invisible to them; it was important, according to Bentham, that the prisoners 'should always feel themselves as if under inspection'. Bentham never shared that obsessive belief in the mystical reformative qualities of solitude which was to dominate the penal thinking of a later age both in England and America. That the inmates of gaols should feel themselves to be 'solitary and sequestered beings' seemed to him an essential component of their punishment; indeed, when discussing the treatment of prisoners befor trial he said, 'But as there can be no ground for punishing them any otherwise than in so far as the restraint necessary for safe custody has the effect of punishment, there can be little ground for subjecting them to solitude, unless where that circumstance should also appear necessary.'

Of the many advantages claimed by Bentham for the panopticon, not the least was the complete security of the scheme;

Overpowering the guard requires a union of hands and a concert of minds. But what union, or what concert can there be among persons no one of whom will have set eyes on any other from the moment of his entrance? Undermining walls, forcing iron bars, requires commonly a concert, always a length of time exempt from interruptions . . . Upon all plans hitherto pursued the thickest walls have been found occasionally unavailing: upon this plan, the thinnest would be sufficient.

Also, it would render unnecessary the use of irons:

Confined in one of these cells every motion of the limbs and every muscle of the face exposed to view, what pretence could there be for exposing to this hardship the most boisterous malefactor? Indulged with perfect liberty within the space allotted to him, in what worse way could he vent his rage than by beating his head against the walls? And who but himself would be the sufferer by such folly? Noise, the only offence by which a man thus engaged could render himself troublesome (an offence, by the by, against which irons themselves afford no security) might, if found otherwise incorrigible, be subdued by gagging – a most natural and efficacious mode of prevention,' as well as punishment, the prospect of which would probably be for ever sufficient to render the infliction of it unnecessary.

The principal medium for reformation in the panopticon was to be the constant employment of the prisoners in profitable labour. A contractor would be engaged to manage the prison as a commercial venture, paying out wages* to the inmates and making his profit by selling their produce. The prisoners were to receive a basic ration of cheap bread and water. Bentham wrote:

If a man won't work, nothing has he to do from morning to night but eat his bad bread and drink his water, without a soul to speak to. If he will work his time is occupied and he has his meat and his beer or whatever his earnings may afford him . . . It is necessary every exertion he makes should be sure of its reward; but it is not necessary that such reward be so great, or anything near so great, as he might have had, had he worked elsewhere. The confinement which is his punishment, preventing him carrying the work to another market, subjects him to a monopoly; which the contractor, his master, like any other monopolist makes, of course, as much of as he can.

Prisoners awaiting trial would receive a subsistence allowance; they would not be compelled to work, but would be allowed to do so if they wished to increase their incomes.

Bentham did not particularize the type of productive labour which would be performed in the panopticon; he merely stated it must be 'some sort of business that was easy to learn'. The contractor was solely concerned with the commercial function of the prison. He would not be allowed to beat or to punish the prisoners; indeed, to keep him conscious of their physical welfare he would have to pay a fine for every inmate who died. 'I would make him pay,' said

* Bentham made the farsighted proposal that a part of each prisoner's wages should be deducted to pay for his keep, and a part should be put aside and given to him on his release.

Bentham, 'without troubling myself whether any care of his could have kept the man alive'. The keepers and inspectors were to be responsible for the maintenance of discipline. He suggested :

A correction-book might be kept in which every instance of chastisement, with the cause for which it is administered, might be entered upon record. If these checks be not enough, the presence of one or more persons besides him by whom the correction was actually administered might be required as witnesses of the mode and quantum of correction and of the alleged cause.

During the course of his outline of the panopticon scheme Bentham commented on the disinclination of judges and magistrates to visit the gaols. He said :

Amongst other causes of this reluctance, none at present is so forcible, none so unhappily well-grounded, none which affords so natural an excuse, nor so strong a reason against accepting any excuse, as the danger of infection – a circumstance which carries death, in one of its most tremendous forms, involving in one common catastrophe the violator and the upholder of the laws.

However, the panopticon would be virtually immune from outbreaks of gaol-fever and would be quick, safe and simple to inspect. 'Were Newgate upon this plan,' he asserted, 'all Newgate might be inspected by a quarter of an hour's visit to Mr Akerman.'

CHAPTER THIRTEEN

NEWGATE RESTORED

As soon as the Gordon Riots had subsided George Dance, the architect of the City of London, was once again called in to re-design and to restore Newgate Gaol. He adopted a very similar internal scheme to the one he had used before, but with the provision of increased accommodation and with larger spaces for exercise. The ground-plan of the post-1780 prison shows as its essential features a row of three quadrangles each surrounded by wards and other buildings. The quadrangle to the north was reserved for debtors, the women's section and the men's being separated by a fifteen-feet-high wall. The men felons' quadrangle, the largest of the three, was in the centre; and that to the south was kept for the women felons. There were various taps for the sale of beer, and a chapel, described as 'plain and neat', in which the debtors were kept apart from the felons and the pew in the most central position was again reserved for the condemned. Two rooms were set aside as infirmaries, one for males, and the other for females. A further innovation was a private passage connecting the gaol with the Sessions House so that the prisoners would no longer have to pass down the street in fetters through crowds of curious spectators. The condemned block had been one of the few parts of the inside of the gaol to withstand the fire and the fifteen cells, five on each of three floors, were retained for their original purpose.

The reconstructed Newgate was completed in 1783. For the most part contemporary observers were well-pleased with the external appearance which, for all its gauntness and its lack of feature, was described as 'impressive' and even as 'noble'. But the atmosphere of the gaol was not altered. Writing in 1850, Hepworth Dixon commented, 'In spite of the rebuilding – in spite of the reforms suggested by Howard – Newgate

continued and continues down to our day, one of the worst
hot-beds of vice and moral disease in London.'

The total number of prisoners at Newgate at any one time,
and the proportion of debtors to felons, varied enormously.
Richard Akerman had given a House of Commons committee
the figures for the years from 1756 to 1764. During that
period, he said, there were always between 31 and 139 debtors
in the gaol, and between 101 and 724 felons; the complete
population had ranged from a minimum of 132 to a maximum of 840. Howard obtained the figures between 1775 and
1780 which showed that in those five years the total number
of inmates was invariably less than 300. The rebuilding of
Newgate was sufficiently advanced by 1782 to allow for a
fresh intake of prisoners, and 3 debtors together with 291
felons were admitted. It is impossible to tell what sort of records were maintained at Newgate during the eighteenth
century, but there are two printed broadsheets in the Corporation of London Records Office, one for the period between 28 September 1785 and 28 September 1786: the other
covering the period from 28 September 1786 to 28 September
1787. These documents, which contain a number of interesting details concerning classification and disposal, are headed,
'The State of the Gaol as to the Number of Prisoners, the
Number of Sick, and the Deaths'. The first broadsheet shows
that during the period covered a total of 1325 prisoners on
criminal charges had passed through the gaol; of these 294
were eventually transported, 176 were whipped, 61 were
hanged and one burnt, 16 died in prison and 613 were
acquitted at their trials. The corresponding figures on the
second broadsheet disclose that out of 1454 criminal prisoners, 364 were transported, 63 were whipped, 87 were
hanged, 56 died in prison and 615 were acquitted. The
majority of the felons had been sent to Newgate for theft,
burglary and highway robbery. There were 13 murderers in
the gaol during the first period and 17 during the second.

It was ironical that Lord George Gordon, the man who
was indirectly responsible for the burning down of Newgate,
should have ended up as a prisoner there himself. After the
riots had ended he was confined for some months at the
Tower of London. In February 1781 he stood his trial before

the Court of King's Bench on a charge of traitorously levying an insurrection against the king, 'by assembling together a great crowd of persons, armed and arrayed in a warlike manner, with colours flying, and with swords, clubs, bludgeons, stones and other weapons'. Although his guilt on this indictment must have been manifest beyond a shadow of doubt, he was unaccountably acquitted and discharged. A few years later Gordon had started to visit the prisoners in Newgate who had been condemned to death or were awaiting transportation, and in an effort to assist the latter he drafted a provocative document entitled, 'The Prisoners' Petition to the Right Honourable Lord George Gordon to preserve their lives and liberties and prevent their Banishment to Botany Bay'. In the course of the petition he imprudently alleged that 'the everlasting law of the statutes of the Almighty is changed and his true record is falsified and erased by the lawyers and judges'. As though this were not enough he wrote two letters to the *Public Advertiser,* attacking Marie Antoinette, the French queen. In 1786 he was arrested and charged with the publication of two seditious libels, the first 'calculated to incite insurrection, discontent and sedition among the prisoners confined under sentence of death or transportation'; and the second, an attempt 'to asperse the character of Her Most Christian Majesty, the Queen of France'. He was convicted of both these charges but estreated his bail and fled to Holland before he had received his sentence. After six months of freedom Gordon returned to England where he was recaptured, and in January 1788 he was sentenced to a total of five years imprisonment in Newgate and fined five hundred pounds. In addition, it was ordered that on his release from prison he should enter into a recognizance in the sum of £10,000 to be of good behaviour for fourteen years, with two sureties of £2,500 each.

Initially Gordon was sent to the felons' section on the common side of Newgate where he was confined in an underground dungeon the stone walls of which were said to have been continually covered with a green mould. After a few months, however, he was transferred to a private room on the masters' side; John Wesley, who visited him there, described it as being 'more like the study of a recluse in a private house than a prison'. The surviving accounts of Gordon's subsequent years of imprisonment at Newgate provide extraordinary reading. His great friend and admirer, Dr Watson, who went to see him almost every day, has told how Gordon used to spend the morning reading, and writing letters to various journals on political topics. At midday he would start to receive his guests, who were sometimes so numerous that there were not sufficient seats to go round; he himself once remarked, 'I am become one of the shows of London for strangers and foreigners to stare at.' He dined in his room at two o'clock, usually sitting down at table with at least half-a-dozen guests. 'They were composed of all ranks,' Watson wrote, 'and ranged as chance directed, the Jew and the Gentile, the legislator and the labouring mechanic, the officer and the soldier; all shared alike, liberty and equality were enjoyed to their full extent as far as Newgate would allow.' The meal was usually plain and simple and afterwards 'the conversation generally turned to politics.' Every fortnight Gordon gave a formal dinner-party, sometimes followed by music or dancing. His guests, said Dr Watson, included the Dukes of York, Clarence and Sussex, and members of the Court, 'who it is not safe to name. They came sometimes in uniform and sometimes in disguise, but on all occasions I have remarked them to deliver their sentiments on the present administration with great freedom.'

During his confinement at Newgate Lord Gordon was attended by two personal maids and it has been suggested that one of them, a beautiful Jewish girl named Polly Levi, was also his mistress. Certainly Horace Walpole has referred to Gordon as a man of 'loose morals', and a woman who knew him well once described him as being 'entirely debauched'. Gordon completed his official sentence in January 1793, but owing to an iniquitous system then prevailing he was recommitted to Newgate for an indefinite term because he was unable to comply with the stipulation requiring him to find two sureties for his good behaviour. He died of gaol fever on the 1 November 1793.

At that time entertainment by the wealthier prisoners in Newgate may not have been such a rarity. It is recorded that Renwick Williams celebrated his reprieve from a sentence of transportation by holding a ball in the gaol to which he invited twenty guests. The festivities commenced at four o'clock in the afternoon with dancing to two violins and a flute. According to an account:

At eight o'clock the company partook of a cold supper and a variety of wines, such as would not have discredited the most sumptuous gala, and at nine o'clock departed, that being the usual hour for locking the doors of the prison.

Although the Newgate Gaol which reopened in 1782 did not embody any radical developments in prison planning it was probably a considerable improvement on the average British gaol of the period in several important respects. The segregation of male and female prisoners had not by then been accepted as a necessary principle; in 1757 the *Gentleman's Magazine* described the situation which usually existed:

The men and women prisoners are all put together till they are locked up at night, and have perpetual opportunties of retiring to the dark cells as much as they please; the women, indeed, are generally such as do not need much solicitation to this commerce . . . as many of them are totally destitute of both money and friends they would have no alternative but to become prostitutes or to perish with hunger.

Howard had discovered at St Alban's Gaol in 1779 that a young girl was locked up every day in a room with two soldiers, and at Swansea during the same year he had found that two men and two women had shared the same cell for nearly a week. The new Newgate was also better supplied with water and washing facilities than most county gaols, of which the *Gentleman's Magazine* had written in July 1767, 'The felons of this country lie worse than dogs or swine, and are kept much more uncleanly than those animals are in kennels and sties.' Houses of Correction were allowed to persist in a similar grossly unhygienic condition, being crowded, it was said in 1776, with 'vagrants and disorderly women of the lowest and most wretched class of human being, almost naked, with only a few filthy rags almost alive and in motion with vermin, their bodies rotting with bad distemper, covered with itch, and with scorbutic and venereal ulcers'. The utter disregard for the conditions under which prisoners were allowed to exist at this time was, no doubt, a reflection of the attitude of Archdeacon William Paley, who wrote in his *Moral and Political Philosophy,* published in 1785:

In the reformation of criminals, little has ever been effected and little, I fear, is practicable. From every species of punishment that has hitherto been devised, from imprisonment and exile, from pain and infamy . . . malefactors return more hardened in their crimes and more instructed.

The shipment of British felons to the colonies of Maryland and Virginia was terminated in 1776 following the outbreak of the American War of Independence. Even when the transportation system had been operating on a fairly large scale the prisons in Britain had remained hopelessly overcrowded, and the Government were now faced with the sudden problem of disposing of all their criminals at home. An Act was hurried through Parliament to provide that instead of being transported, convicts might in the future be sentenced to terms of imprisonment with hard labour in Britain; at the start they were to be put to work on the clearance of soil and gravel from beds of the Thames and of other navigable rivers. It was arranged that until more prisons could be built the prisoners would be accommodated on special convict-ships – later known as 'the hulks'. Two vessels were put into use immediately; an old East Indiaman called the *Justitia,* and a frigate called the *Censor.* Both of these ships were moored at Woolwich and each of them was fitted to receive a full complement of a governor, 20 warders and 120 prisoners.

Meanwhile the Government appointed a Special Commission consisting of John Howard, Sir William Blackstone the jurist, and William Eden a radical politician, to make recommendations for the disposal of prisoners in these altered circumstances. The result of their labours was an Act in 1779 for the establishment of one or more penitentiary houses. The members of the Commission conceived these new establishments as being prisons to which offenders would be sent for specific periods of reformatory confinement. The regimen would alternate between spells of solitary confinement and of organized hard labour; the former were to accustom the prisoners to serious reflection, and the latter were devised as work 'of the hardest and most servile kind, in which drudgery is chiefly required, and where the work is little liable to be spoiled by ignorance, neglect or obstinacy, and where the materials or tools are not easily stolen or embezzled, such as treading a wheel, or drawing in a capstan for turning a mill or other machine or engine'. Whilst they were serving their sentences the inmates of a penitentiary house would receive proper medical attention and would be taught the habits of cleanliness and industry; above all, they would have instilled into them the principles and practice of their moral and Christian duties.

As a prelude to the setting up of the first penitentiary house the Government appointed a Commission of three supervisors, including Howard, to select and acquire a suitable site. Unfortunately these three found it impossible to reach agreement, Howard wanting to erect the prison in Islington and one of his colleagues being equally decided on a location in Limehouse. Eventually Howard resigned from the Commission and another supervisor was appointed in his place. It has been surmised that Howard was influenced in this action by a desire to resume his travels in order to keep abreast of prison conditions in other countries; this theory is supported by the opinion of one of his friends who described him as appearing 'to think himself supported in his particular pursuit by Divine Providence', and never allowing any other occupation or amusement to interfere with it.

In September 1786 William Pitt, who had formed his first administration three years before, wrote to William Wilberforce saying, 'The multitude of things depending, has made the Penitentiary House long in deciding upon. But I still think a beginning will be made in it before the season for building is over.' In fact the Penitentiary House scheme receded in importance when it was decided to commence a massive transportation project to the newly- discovered continent of Australia. In the spring of 1787 a fleet of nine convict transports accompanied by two men-of-war set sail from Portsmouth on the eight months voyage to Botany Bay in New South Wales. Many of the prisoners died at sea and many more were desperately ill with scurvy, dysentery and syphilis when they eventually reached their destination. From that time onward convoy after convoy was to discharge its cargo of conscripted immigrants into the barren and hostile settlement. The conditions in the ships were appalling. A chaplain who went aboard a newly arrived transport at Port Jackson in 1790 said:

I beheld a sight truly shocking to the feelings of humanity, a great number of [prisoners] lying, some half and others nearly quite naked, without either bed or bedding, unable to turn or help themselves. Spoke to them as I passed along, but the smell was so offensive, I could scarcely bear it.

He added: .

Sometimes for days, nay, for a considerable time together, they had been up to the middle in water, chained together hand and leg – even the sick not exempted – nay, many died with the chains still on them.

During the early years of the project a woman was only ineligible for transportation if she was over fifty years of age, and mothers with small children or babies were callously separated from them to undergo their sentences.* The women prisoners were locked in the holds of the ships at night, but were allowed on deck during the daytime. Directly the transports laid anchor in Botany Bay a number of officers and troops from the settlement used to come on board to inspect the women and to choose their concubines. And yet Lecky, who wrote his massive history of the eighteenth century about a hundred years later, felt able to say:

There were great abuses in the early convict system in Australia, and especially in the treatment of the female convicts; but on the whole, transportation to this distant and unknown country was probably a more deterrent punishment than imprisonment at home, and the fate of transported convicts was in most respects superior.

In July 1789 John Howard set out from England on what was destined to be the final journey of his life. On 20 January 1790 he died of camp fever in the south of Russia. 'Give me no monument', he had written, 'but lay me quietly in the

---

* Later on women were allowed to take their children with them provided they were less than seven years old.

earth; place a sundial over my grave, and let me be forgotten.'
A year after Howard's death Parliament passed the well-
intentioned Prison Act, 1791, the preamble of which described it as a statute 'for the better regulating of gaols and
other places of confinement'. The Act provided that pending
the erection of national penitentiary houses all local gaols and
houses of correction were to be treated as penitentiaries and
prisoners might serve sentences of hard labour in them instead of being transported. It also placed upon justices of the
peace far more stringent responsibilities in inspecting and
repairing prison buildings and in supervising the management of the gaols within their jurisdiction. However, nearly
all the clauses in the statute were permissive rather than mandatory, and in consequence its reformatory provisions were
almost entirely disregarded. The publication of Bentham's
Panopticon in 1791 rekindled the interest of the Government
in the creation of a new style of prison. A year later Bentham
formally proposed that he should be allowed to establish a
penitentiary house which would be built and managed
according to his plan. Pitt was enthusiastic about the suggestion but it is believed that it was bitterly opposed by George
III who distrusted Bentham's radical opinions. As a result
there was a delay of two years before a contract was agreed
between Bentham and the treasury, by the terms of which
he undertook, for the sum of £19,000, to erect a penitentiary
large enough to hold a thousand convicts. He did, in fact,
acquire a suitable site in the vicinity of Tothill Fields; but
by this time the Anglo-French war was gathering momentum
with its consequent drain on the national resources and the
treasury declined to advance the money which was necessary
to fulfil the project. In the meanwhile the increasing emphasis
on fixed-term sentences in Britain was causing a major problem in view of the complete absence of facilities for after-care.
Patrick Colquhoun, a London magistrate, writing in 1797,
estimated that a total of 11,934 prisoners had been released
from the prisons in the Metropolis during the previous four
years. He said:

Without friends, without character, and without the means of
subsistence, what are these unhappy mortals to do? They are no
sooner known or suspected than they are avoided. No person will

employ them, even if they were disposed to return to the paths of honesty; unless they make use of fraud or deception, by concealing that they have been inhabitants of a prison or the hulks. At large upon the world, without food or raiment, and with the constant calls of nature upon them for both, without a home or any other asylum to shelter them from the inclemency of the weather, what is to become of them?

At the end of the eighteenth century the ritual of execution underwent a procedural alteration. In 1783 the sheriffs of the City of London issued a pamphlet in which they denounced the condemned procession from Newgate to Tyburn as a hideous mockery of the law. The final scene had lost all its terrors, they declared; it taught no lesson of morality to the spectators, but rather it served as an encouragement to vice. An execution day was treated as a public holiday. They continued:

If the only defect were the want of ceremony, the minds of the spectators might be supposed to be left in a state of indifference; but when they view the meanness of the apparatus, the dirty cart and ragged harness, surrounded by a sordid assemblage of the lowest among the vulgar, their sentiments are inclined more to ridicule than pity. The whole progress is attended with the same effect. Numbers soon thicken into a crowd of followers, and then an indecent levity is heard.

The fatal tree was surrounded by a riotous mob, swearing, jesting and blaspheming. 'Thus are all the ends of public justice defeated; all the effects of example, the terrors of death, and the shame of punishment are all lost.' The pamphlet went on to state that the sheriffs had doubted their power to alter the arrangements for executions and had consulted the judges who had affirmed their ability to do so. 'With this sanction, therefore, we have proceeded,' they said, 'and instead of carting the criminals through the streets to Tyburn', the sentence of death would in future be carried out in front of Newgate on a temporary scaffold hung with black. They hoped that the new system would be beneficial because the crowd would be smaller and easier to control; also people could be kept at a greater distance from the gibbet. An atmosphere of solemnity would be created by the tolling of the funeral bell in Newgate throughout the execution. Thus the spirits of a doomed prisoner 'will be composed by the decorum of the place and he may prepare his soul for its dissolution by calm meditation'.

The first executions took place in front of Newgate Gaol on the morning of 3 December 1783 when ten prisoners were hanged. Immediately afterwards the inhabitants in the area petitioned the sheriffs requesting them to reinstate the gallows at Tyburn, but in spite of these objections the new arrangements were continued. It was during the year 1783 that a new method of hanging known as 'the drop' came into general use in Britain, the object of which was to hasten the process of strangulation. The drop was a substitution for the old hangman's cart and suspended the victim by suddenly opening a trap on which he had been standing. A portable gallows was erected whenever necessary outside the debtors' door of Newgate. A contemporary description stated, 'The last part of the stage, or that next to the gaol, is enclosed by a temporary roof, under which are placed two seats for the reception of the sheriffs, one on each side of the stairs leading to the scaffold.' On three sides were galleries for officials and privileged spectators and the whole structure was enclosed by a strong set of railings to hold back the mob. In the middle of the central platform, below the gibbet, was a trap-door measuring approximately ten feet by eight feet; this was held in position by several bolts which, at the appropriate moment, could be simultaneously withdrawn by the operation of a hand-lever. The burning to death of women was finally abolished in 1790, but from 1783 until then, this punishment was also inflicted outside the debtors' door at Newgate. A broadsheet in 1788 described the burning of Phoebe Harris which was attended by 'a great concourse of people'. As she came out of Newgate, according to this account, 'she appeared languid and terrified, and trembled greatly as she advanced to the stake.' Mrs Harris was hanged for half-an-hour before two cart-loads of faggots were piled about her and lighted. 'The fire had not quite burnt out four hours later.'

It soon became obvious that the elimination of the condemned procession had neither imparted a dignity nor a solemnity to the execution ritual, for the crowds attending at Newgate were almost as large and just as disorderly as those which had gathered at Tyburn in the past. Various opinions were expressed about the new arrangements at the time, Doctor Johnson making a forthright, if a somewhat odd criticism:

It is not an improvement. They object that the old method drew together a number of spectators. If they do not draw spectators, they don't answer their purpose. The old method was satisfactory to all parties; the public was gratified by a procession; the criminal was supported by it. Why is all this to be swept away?

CHAPTER FOURTEEN

ELIZABETH FRY

WHEN people have acquired legendary reputations for their altruistic works it becomes all too easy to embellish their memories with a personal saintliness which they never possessed. It is not unfair to say that this has happened to Elizabeth Fry, who devised and inspired so many improvements that she completely transformed the conditions of women's imprisonment in Britain. Like many other educated ladies of her time, Mrs Fry maintained a frank and intimate journal, and it is from her own self-revelations that her apparent shortcomings have come to light. For instance, the undoubted strength of her religious beliefs tended to lead her into the snares of bigotry and intolerance; her philanthropy was prompted, in part, by an obsessive craving for spiritual purification; and in her later life some of her entries betrayed more pleasure than distate for the adulation which was so frequently lavished upon her. But despite her very human frailties she was one of the most far-sighted and effective reformers in penal history who, once she had adopted her cause, pursued it with courage, tenacity, and with great tactical skill. Perhaps her most notable achievement was that she persuaded a predominantly unresponsive, masculine oligarchy that the imprisonment of women created certain totally different problems from the imprisonment of men.

Elizabeth Gurney was born on 21 May 1780, just over two weeks before the burning down of Newgate in the Gordon Riots. Her father was a wealthy, Quaker merchant-banker and most of her childhood was spent at his country estate at Earlham in Norfolk. Looking back on those early years from her middle age she wrote, 'The impressions then made remain vivid in my recollection; the delight in the beauty and wild scenery in parts of the common; the trees, the flowers and the little rills that abounded on it; the farm houses, the village school and the different poor people in their cottages.' It was indeed a setting of family affection, peace and plenty, but it was marred for Elizabeth by recurrent bouts of nervous debility; and also, even in her extreme youth, by the solemnity of her character and her tendency to indulge in spiritual introspection. 'My remembrance is of the pleasure of my childhood being almost spoiled through fear,' she recalled, 'and my religious impressions, such as I had, were accompanied by gloom.' But she was sufficiently assured in her faith at the age of seventeen to enter in her journal, 'My idea of religion is not for it to unfit us for the duties of life, like a nun who leaves them for prayer and thanksgiving; but I think it should stimulate and capacitate us to perform those duties properly.' A short while later her parents decided to send her to London to introduce her to the social life of the capital. She was described at that period as being tall and graceful with a profusion of soft, flaxen hair; 'in countenance', it was said, she was 'very sweet and pleasing'. Many girls of her age and with her background might have been dazzled and enraptured by the endless round of parties, balls, and operas, but not Elizabeth Gurney; in fact, after a few months in London she recorded in her journal:

I felt the vanity and folly of what are called the pleasures of this life, of which the tendency is not to satisfy, but eventually to enervate and injure the heart and mind . . . I was in my judgement much confirmed in the infinite importance of religion, as the only real stay, guide, help and comfort in this life, and the only means of our having a hope of partaking of a better.

Having returned from London to Earlham just before her eighteenth birthday, Elizabeth Gurney adopted a way of living which accorded more closely with her convictions. She laid aside all her bright and fashionable clothes and started to dress with quiet simplicity; she spent her time visiting the poor and the sick in her neighbourhood and reading the Bible to them; and she opened a school for poor children at a disused laundry in which, at the start, she herself did the teaching. Her journal at this time discloses the anguish of self-critical humility conflicting with a certainty of her own

F

predestination. One day she could write, 'Let me once more try and pray that the many evil roots in my own mind may be eradicated;' and on another, 'I have great reason to believe Almighty God is directing my mind to a haven of peace; at least, I feel that I am guided by a Power not my own.' Yet she was subject, too, to the nomal emotions of youth as appears from an entry made just after she had attended a ball:

If I could make a rule never to give way to vanity, excitement or flirting, I do not think I should object to dancing; but it always leads me into some of these faults — indeed, if not a little of all three.

On 19 August 1800, at the age of twenty, Elizabeth Gurney was maried to Joseph Fry, a rich Quaker businessman, at the Friends Meeting House in Norwich. She confessed in her journal that she awoke that morning 'in a sort of terror' at the prospect before her. During the wedding ceremony, she says, she wept a good part of the time, 'and my beloved father seemed nearly as much overcome as I was.' Although her entries around that period betray no deep affection for Joseph Fry, she always referred to him in the future with fondness and respect. During the first twelve years of their married life the Frys had three sons and five daughters. At their house in London Elizabeth was fully occupied with her ever-increasing family and her husband's social activities, but she managed to find the time to interest herself in a charity school and to become a visitor to a workhouse at Islington which was managed by the Quakers. It is difficult to know if she found this limited amount of philanthropic work sufficient, or whether she was waiting for some further and more exacting opportunities. In July 1805 she wrote, 'It appears to me that we who desire to be the servants of Christ, must expect to do a part of our Master's work.' And almost exactly a year later she was declaring, 'How much I desire that above all things, I may have a life in doing the will of my Creator'. In 1809, on the death of Joseph's father, the Frys took over the family residence at Plashet in Essex. In her new home Elizabeth busied herself in looking after her poorer neighbours and establishing a school for their children. In 1811 she was appointed a minister in the Quaker community, and she wrote in her journal:

Oh Lord, if it be thy will to preserve my life yet a little longer and continue me in this service, preserve me through chastisement from ever hurting thy great and holy cause, and enable me to walk worthy of thy vocation wherever I am called.

This was her frame of mind when Elizabeth Fry's attention was first drawn to the conditions of the women prisoners at Newgate.

Two of Mrs Fry's daughters, writing soon after her death, described how in January 1813, during a particularly severe winter, a few members of the Society of Friends paid a visit to some prisoners in Newgate who were awaiting execution. Afterwards, according to this account, one of the Quakers named William Forster persuaded Elizabeth Fry 'to inspect the state of the women with the view of alleviating their sufferings occasioned by the inclemency of the season'. This version of her initial visit to Newgate differs slightly from the one given by Stephen Grellet, an American Quaker. Grellet came to London in 1812 'travelling in the ministry'. During January 1813 he applied to Mr Newman, the keeper of Newgate, for permission to look around the gaol.

The first visit to that part of Newgate which is occupied by the women prisoners had very nearly been frustrated [he relates]. The gaoler endeavoured to prevent my going there, representing them as so unruly and desperate a set that they would surely do me some mischief; he had endeavoured in vain to reduce them to order, and said he could not be responsible for what they might do to me, concluding that the very least I might expect was to have my clothes torn off.

However, in spite of this ominous warning Grellet insisted on going inside. At that time the women at Newgate were accommodated in two wards and two cells. The main part of the quadrangle which had originally been intended for their use had been divided off and allocated to state prisoners, but the partition wall was low enough to afford the men a clear view of the women's narrow yard and of the uncovered windows of their wards and cells. Into this restricted space close on three hundred women and girls, some convicted and some untried, were confined with their numerous children. They were, said Mrs Fry's daughters, 'destitute of sufficient clothing, for which there was no provision; in rags and dirt, without bedding, they slept on the floor, the boards of which were in part raised to supply a pillow. In the same room they lived, cooked and washed.' Although armed soldiers were posted on the roof above them there were only two turnkeys, a man and his son, on duty in the whole section, and they remained in sole charge of the prisoners by day and by night. Stephen Grellet described his visits to the wards. He differs from Mrs Fry's daughters inasmuch as he said that some of the prisoners slept in hammocks. 'When I first entered,' he wrote, 'the foulness of the air was almost insupportable; and everything that is base and depraved was so strongly depicted on the faces of the women who stood crowded before me with looks of effrontery, boldness and wantonness of expression that for a while my soul was greatly dismayed.' He also entered the women's infirmary; there, he said, 'I was astonished beyond description at the mass of woe and misery I beheld. I saw many sick lying on the bare floor or on some old straw, having very scanty covering over them, though it was quite cold; and there were several children born in the prison there, almost naked.'

According to Stephen Grellet, directly after visiting Newgate he called on Elizabeth Fry who was staying at her house in London. He said:

I described out of the fullness of my heart what I had just beheld, stating also that something must be done immediately for these poor suffering children. The appeal was not in vain. She immediately sent for several pieces of flannel, and had speedily collected a number of our young women Friends, who went to work with such diligence that on the very next day she repaired to the prison with a bundle of made-up garments for the naked children.

When Mrs Fry went to Newgate with these clothes she was accompanied by Anna Buxton, a sister of the Quaker philanthropist Sir Thomas Fowell Buxton who was married to one of Elizabeth's younger sisters. The two ladies insisted on entering the women's section, against the wishes of the keeper who made them leave their watches with him for safety. Sir

Thomas Buxton has recorded Mrs Fry's first impressions of
the women's section with which she acquainted him later.
'All I tell thee is a faint picture of the reality,' she declared;
'the filth, the closeness of the rooms, the ferocious manners
and expressions of the women towards each other, and the
abandoned wickedness which everything bespoke are quite
indescribable.' Mrs Fry had seen them openly drinking
spirits, 'and her ears were offended by the most terrible im-
precations. Everything was filthy to excess and the smell was
quite disgusting. Everyone, even the governor, was reluctant
to go amongst them.'

It is believed that Elizabeth Fry only visited Newgate three
times during that winter. Her daughters have said that 'on
this occasion nothing more was done than to supply the most
destitute with clothes.' On 15 February 1813 Mrs Fry wrote
in her journal:

My fear for myself the last few days is, that I shall be exalted
by the evident unity of my dear friends whom I greatly value by
being, as I feel I am, in some degree looked up to, by those less
experienced than myself in the gift (small as my own is) . . . Oh
how deeply I fear the temptation of ever being exalted.

The following day in company with Anna Buxton she paid
the last of her three visits to the gaol to distribute clothing.
Afterwards she made another entry:

Yesterday we were some hours at Newgate with the poor female
felons, attending to their outward necessities. We had been twice
previously. Before we went away dear Anna Buxton uttered a
few words in supplication, and very unexpectedly to myself I did
also. I heard weeping and I thought they appeared much ten-
dered; a solemn quiet was observed; it was a striking scene, the
poor people on their knees around us, in their deplorable condition.

Elizabeth Fry did not re-enter Newgate Gaol for nearly four
years. During the intervening period she gave birth to her
ninth and tenth children and spent most of her time at
Plashet. Her journals show that she was perpetually afflicted
with depression, nervous instability, and a hunger for spiritual salvation. 'None know but those who suffer from them,'
she once wrote, 'the deep humiliations such disorders create

as those I have lately had: I mean great bodily weakness accompanied by nervous lowness of spirits and mental fear.' On another occasion she stated, 'The craving of my soul for preservation is almost past expression.' If the women of New-gate were ever in her thoughts during those years she certainly does not reveal the fact in her journals. However, the Frys decided to return .to London for the winter of 1816–17, when Elizabeth was thirty-six years of age; and just after Christmas she paid another visit to the gaol. The only improvements since her former acquaintance with the women's section were that the prisoners had now been supplied with mats to sleep upon and they were allowed the use of the whole of their quadrangle; otherwise they existed in much the same con-ditions as before. Mrs Fry's initial purpose in re-visiting New-gate is not clear. It is known that she spent several hours alone with the women, reading the Bible to them and telling them about the mercy of Jesus Christ. She was warned not to ven-ture inside alone but once again no harm befell her, possibly because the prisoners were so impressed by her courage and by the obvious sincerity of her faith.

Both Buxton and Mrs Fry's own daughters are agreed that it was at the time of the Christmas 1816 visit to Newgate that she conceived the notion of setting up a school in the gaol for the children of the female prisoners there. When she asked the women for their opinion of the scheme, according to Buxton, 'the proposal was received, even by the most aban-doned, with tears of joy.' Mrs Fry immediately arranged a meeting with the sheriffs and the Ordinary; and these three officials, Buxton says, 'approved her idea with cordial approba-tion; but, at the same time, unreservedly confessed their apprehension that her labours would be fruitless'. Conse-quently an unoccupied cell was converted into a school-room and an educated prisoner named Mary Connor was appointed as the mistress in charge. The cell was too small to accom-modate the vast number who wished to enrol as pupils, but eventually thirty were selected, ranging in age from children of seven to girls of about twenty-five. Elizabeth Fry accom-panied by one of her friends, Mary Sanderson, attended at the school on the opening morning. Miss Sanderson told Thomas Buxton afterwards that the cell had been crowded with half-naked women struggling together to get to the front of the class. At first, she said, she had felt as though she was entering a den of wild beasts and she recollected shuddering when the door closed behind her, 'and she was locked in with such a herd of desperate companions'. On subsequent days Mrs Fry, Miss Sanderson and several other Quaker ladies took turns in visiting Newgate to supervise the school, which proved to be an immediate success. This work brought them into contact with all the less pleasant sides of prison existence, as Mrs Fry was to disclose a few year later:

We were witnesses of the dreadful proceedings that went forward on the female side of the prison; the begging, swearing, fighting, gaming, singing, dancing, dressing up in men's clothes – the scenes too bad to be described.

For herself though, Elizabeth Fry had now discovered her mission in life. She stated in a letter in February 1817:

I have lately been much occupied in forming a school in Newgate for the children of the poor prisoners, as well as the young criminals, which has brought much peace and satisfaction with it.

The following month in another letter, she wrote:

My heart and mind and time are very much engaged in various ways – Newgate is a principal object, and I think until I make some attempt at amendment in the plans for the women, I shall not feel easy but if such efforts should prove unsuccessful I think that I should then have tried to do my part and be easy.

It soon became clear to Elizabeth Fry and her helpers that if the conditions in the women's section of Newgate were to be improved some sort of work would have to be provided for the prisoners, and that there would have to be a voluntary acceptance by them of a fairly strict code or regulations. When Mrs Fry began to formulate a plan to introduce industry and order to the section she met with the almost universal response that her ideas were altogether too visionary. She was reminded, says Buxton, 'that a regular London female thief, who has passed through every stage and every scene of guilt; who has spent her youth in prostitution, and her maturer age in theft and knavery, whose every friend and connection are accomplices and criminal associates, is of all characters, the most irreclaimable.' But Mrs Fry thought otherwise. She gradually gained the confidence of the prisoners until she was able to record in her journal, 'Already, from being like wild beasts, they appear harmless and kind.' In April 1817 she formed a group of twelve ladies who shared her aspirations into The Association for the Improvement of Female Prisoners in Newgate, all the members of which with one exception were Quakers. Again, the keeper and both the sheriffs, in spite of their personal misgivings, promised to give the scheme their full support, and one Sunday afternoon the three of them together with the Ordinary and the Ladies Committee (as it was called), assembled all the women prisoners to obtain their approval for a proposed code of rules. The rules, which were passed unanimously, laid down that the prisoners were to be engaged in needlework, knitting or other suitable employment; that there was to be no begging, swearing, gaming, card-playing, quarrelling or immoral conversation; that the women should elect from their number a yard-keeper to generally supervise their behaviour; that the prisoners should be divided into small classes, each of which would elect its own monitor; and that at nine o'clock in the morning and at six o'clock in the evening all the women should collect in one ward to hear a reading from the Bible. Before the meeting dispersed Mrs Fry was able to inform the prisoners that the sheriffs had agreed to the appointment of a matron to look after them.

Elizabeth Fry was determined to provide useful and productive work for the women in Newgate. She arranged with a firm in the City that they would buy any articles of clothing made in the gaol and then sell them later to the transported convicts at Botany Bay. Initially the project was financed by several of Mrs Fry's relations with the support of the sheriffs; a number of Quaker merchants also assisted by donating quantities of material. The women were paid for their work but some of their money was withheld to be given to them on the day of their release or, if they were less fortunate, on the day they set out for their long, hard and comfortless journey to New South Wales. Mrs Fry did not share the view that the general development of prison industry might be prejudicial to the free manufacturing trades. She once stated:

The benefit which society derives from the employment of criminals greatly outweighs the inconvenience which can possibly arise to the mass of our labouring population from the small proportion of work done in our prisons.

As a result of the efforts of Elizabeth Fry and her committee, the women's section of Newgate was very soon altered beyond belief. A man who visited the wards a few weeks after the introduction of the new routine has described their condition:

On my approach no loud or dissonant sounds or angry voices indicated that I was about to enter a place, which I was credibly assured, had long had for one of its titles that of 'Hell above ground'. The courtyard into which I was admitted, instead of being peopled with beings scarcely human, blaspheming, fighting, tearing each others' hair, or gaming with a filthy pack of cards for the very clothes they wore, which often did not suffice even for decency, presented a scene where stillness and propriety reigned. I was conducted by a decently-dressed person, the newly appointed yards-woman, to the door of a ward where, at the head of a long table sat a lady belonging to the Society of Friends. She was reading aloud to about sixteen women prisoners who were engaged in needle-work around it. Each wore a clean looking blue apron and bib, with a ticket having a number on it suspended from her neck by a red tape. They all rose on my entrance, curtsied respectfully and then at a signal resumed their seats and employments.

In the spring of 1817 Elizabeth Fry wrote in her journal, 'I have found in my late attention to Newgate, a peace and prosperity in that undertaking that I seldom, if ever, remember to have done before.' A great deal of attention was now being paid to her work at the gaol; she was receiving letters from all over the country enquiring about her methods and hardly a day passed without the women's section being inspected by some distinguished visitor. Her sudden advent to fame caused a revival of her old forebodings. She entered in her journal in August 1817, 'My having been brought publicly forward in the newspapers, respecting what I have been instrumental in doing at Newgate, has brought some anxiety with it.' And three weeks later she was writing, 'I have felt of late fears whether my being made so much of; so much respect paid to me by the people in power in the City, and also being so publicly brought forward, may not prove a temptation and lead to something of self-exaltation or worldly pride.'

Mrs Fry was paid the signal honour in February 1818 of being invited to give evidence before a House of Commons Committee on prisons. After she had explained in detail the changes she had introduced in the women's section at Newgate she went on to express some personal views on the future treatment of women prisoners. She shared John Howard's opinion that prisoners should work in association by day, but should be confined in single cells by night. She was insistent that women prisoners should be looked after solely by women wardresses and that the only men who need attend them at all should be physicians and ministers of religion; indeed, she told the committee that she would like to see the establishment of entirely separate women's prisons. In general, she stated, prisoners ought to be properly fed and properly clothed, and she urged the necessity for efficient systems of classification and segregation. At present all types of prisoner were mixed up together, she said, 'old and young, hardened offenders with those who have committed only a minor offence, or their first crime; the lowest of women with respectable married women and maid-servants. It is more injurious than can be described in its effects and its consequences.'

The beneficial influence of the Ladies' Committee affected many different aspects of life in the women's section at Newgate. Hitherto, on the night before a party of prisoners was to leave the gaol to embark for transportation the women concerned used to run amok, shouting, screaming and smashing windows and furniture. This disorderly behaviour had continued on the following morning while the prisoners were being loaded into open wagons outside the gaol, before a crowd of inquisitive onlookers, for the journey to Deptford where the transport vessels were moored. Mrs Fry persuaded the keeper to allow the women to make the journey from Newgate to Deptford in closed hackney coaches accompanied by turnkeys and by members of her committee, in return for their undertaking not to stage a riot on the evening before they left. She frequently accompanied the coaches herself and with all the prisoners assembled on the deck of the transport ship she would read a passage from the Bible and lead them in prayers before they sailed. The Ladies' Committee also formed the women prisoners into groups when they were aboard and organized sewing and patchwork for them to work at during the voyage. Mrs Fry continually pressed for them to be placed in the charge of a matron on board instead of being under the care of the sailors until they reached Botany Bay. The other activities of the Ladies' Committee included the setting up of a small shop inside Newgate where the women could buy tea, sugar and small items of clothing, and the institution of stringent regulations to curtail the supplies of alcohol which were being introduced to the women's section of the gaol.

By now Elizabeth Fry had become a national celebrity. She recorded in her journal, with evident pleasure, that on one occasion Lady Harcourt had taken her to a reception at the Mansion House:

Amongst the rest the Queen was there. Much public respect was paid me, and except the Royal family themselves, I think no one received more attention. There was quite a buzzing when I went into the Egyptian Hall, where one to two thousand people were collected: and when the Queen came to speak to me, which she did very kindly, there was, I am told, a general clap.

Sometimes this personal glorification filled her with anxiety, as when she questioned, 'Am I separated in heart more from my Lord? Have my public engagements diverted me from the life of self-denial of daily taking up my cross?' And yet she was certain that she had been especially chosen to fulfil her work of prison reform. 'I have a secret feeling which wonderfully upholds me under the difficulties that may arise,' she declared. 'In the first place, I believe I have been providentially brought into it, not of my own seeking.' During November 1822 Mrs Fry had her eleventh and last child at her home in Plashet. The following month she visited Newgate again; 'I felt peaceful there,' she wrote, 'and afresh sensible that the work was not ours.' Although she was called upon increasingly at this stage to attend at various public functions she maintained her close connection with the gaol and in the spring of 1823 she played an active part in organizing a sale of the women prisoners' work.

Until the end of her life Elizabeth Fry continued to urge the total reform of the conditions under which women were confined in British gaols. In 1824 she achieved one of her principal aims when an Act of Parliament made possible the appointment of wardresses to look after them. She gave evidence before another parliamentary committee in 1828 and renewed her pleas for better classification, the provision of regular work, separation of prisoners at night, the superintendence of women solely by female officers, and the expansion of compulsory religious instruction. The improvements for which Elizabeth Fry was responsible permeated to many other gaols besides Newgate, and in 1845, during the last years of her life, according to her two daughters, 'she had the happiness of knowing that Newgate, Bridewell, the Millbank Prison, the Giltspur Street Compter, White Cross Street Prison, Tothill Fields Prison and Cold Bath Fields Prison were all in a state of comparative order; some exceedingly well arranged, and female convicts in all more or less visited and cared for by ladies – varying according to their circumstances and requirings. The prisons generally throughout England much improved, and in the greater number, ladies encouraged to visit female convicts.'

CHAPTER FIFTEEN

THE MOVEMENT TOWARDS REFORM

AT the beginning of the nineteenth century two sharply divergent opinions were being expressed in Britain concerning the fundamental purpose of imprisonment. The first, which was stated by the Reverend Thomas Bowen, Chaplain of the City of London Bridewell, stemmed from the hypothesis that, 'in inflicting punishment, true policy has regard to the reformation of the offender, and his restoration as a useful member of society'. The second, as put forward by the Reverend Sidney Smith, was that prisons were solely intended 'to keep the multitude in order and to be a terror to evil doers'. The commencement of a prison sentence, in Bowen's view, was a moment of crisis in the life of an offender. 'Sharp calamity,' he said, 'is an instrument which the grace of God uses to awaken sinners to a sense of their condition; and, when they are left to their own hearts in silence and in solitude, they are then placed in a situation best calculated to dispose their minds for the reception of religious truths.' Sidney Smith, however, considered that prisons could not fulfil their object unless they were made as unpleasant as possible. 'There must be a great deal of solitude,' he wrote, 'coarse food; a dress of shame; hard, incessant, irksome, eternal labour; a planned and regulated and unrelenting exclusion of happiness and comfort.' The City authorities apparently acceded to the same philosophy for in 1815 the aldermen declared that 'their prisoners had all they ought to have, unless gentlemen thought they ought to be indulged with Turkish carpets'.

Perhaps the most degrading and the harshest aspect of prison existence during this period was the continued reliance on irons. 'Very rarely is a man ironed for his misdeeds,' said Sir Thomas Buxton, 'but frequently for those of others; additional irons on his person are cheaper than additional elevation to the walls. Thus we cover our own negligence by

increased severity to our captives.' Women prisoners travelling to Deptford to join their ships for transporation were
brutally ironed, sometimes for very lengthy journeys. Mrs
Pryor, a member of the Ladies' Committee, watched a party
embarking in 1822. 'The prisoners from Lancaster Castle
arrived,' she stated, 'not merely handcuffed, but with heavy
irons on their legs which had occasioned considerable swelling
and in one instance, serious inflammation.' A year later Elizabeth Fry described how she witnessed a group of women
arriving at the docks from Lancaster, 'iron-hooped round
their legs and arms, and chained together'. Their complaints,
she said, were very mournful. 'They were not allowed to get
up or go down the coach without the whole lot being dragged
together: some of them had children to carry, they received
no help or alleviation to their suffering.' At that time there
were no prison vans and the humiliation of an offender, or an
alleged offender, commenced at the moment when a magistrate had examined the evidence against him and decided to
commit him to gaol. In London, Buxton said:

The prisoner, after his commitment is made out, is handcuffed
to a file of perhaps a dozen wretched persons in a similar situation and marched through the streets, sometimes a considerable
distance, followed by a crowd of impudent and insulting boys,
exposed to the gaze and to the stare of every passenger. The
moment he enters prison irons are hammered on him; then he is
cast into the midst of a compound of all that is disgusting and
depraved. At night, he is locked up in a narrow cell, with perhaps half-a-dozen of the worst thieves in London, or as many
vagrants, whose rags are alive and in actual motion with vermin.
He may find himself in bed and in bodily contact between a
robber and a murderer or between a man with a foul disease
on one side and one with an infectious disorder on the other.

In the ensuing months, Buxton continued, the prisoner
could be deprived of food, air and exercise whilst he awaited
his trial and eventually, if he was acquitted, 'he may be dismissed from the gaol without a shilling in his pocket and
without the means of returning home.' The chances of a
verdict of 'not guilty' were by no means unfavourable; Colquhoun has given the figures for trials at the Old Bailey
during a twelve-month period at the close of the eighteenth

century, when out of a total of 1,060 prisoners, 493 were convicted and 567 were acquitted; he does not allude to these
proportions as being in any way unusual.

In the years following the turn of the century the Bloody
Code was operating in all its rigour, but the expansion of
transportation to New South Wales had resulted in a considerable diminution of the number of prisoners who were
actually hanged. The fact that the gallows at Newgate was
less frequently in use tended to heighten its morbid attrac-
tions. At the execution of the murderers Holloway and
Haggerty in 1807 there was a stampede in the vast panic-
stricken crowd, in which twenty-eight persons were killed and
nearly seventy injured. 'This dreadful scene continued for
some time,' said the Annual Register. 'The shrieks of the
dying men, women, and children were terrific beyond description, and could only be equalled by the horror of the event.'
The spectators at a hanging were sometimes treated to an
additional unedifying spectacle when a condemned prisoner,
crazed and desperate, put up a last-minute resistance on the
scaffold. In 1823 Charles White, who had been sentenced to
death for arson, jumped forward at the exact moment the
lever was pulled and balanced himself with a precarious foot-
hold just above the open trap; the crowd roared their encouragement as he struggled furiously with the executioner and
his assistants. Eventually he was hurled down the drop with
the hangman swinging on his legs. Others managed, after
being suspended, to pull themselves back and to wedge their
feet against the sides of the trap. One murderer managed to
perform this feat four times, being beaten back on each
occasion. After the eleven Cato Street conspirators had been
hanged at Newgate in 1820 there was a revolting scene when
a masked executioner mounted the gallows with an ampu-
tation knife and in full view of the crowd proceeded to
decapitate each of the bodies in turn.

Out of sight of the onlookers at an execution certain
regular formalities were being enacted inside Newgate. It
was customary for the keeper to entertain a dozen or so distinguished guests to breakfast directly a hanging was over;
sometimes his party re-emerged from the gaol after the meal
to witness the cutting down. The condemned prisoner him-

self was not exempted from a share in the ceremonial. John Thomas Smith, the biographer of Nollekens the sculptor, was determined to see what befell a malefactor on the morning of his execution. With this object in view he approached Doctor Forde, the Ordinary of Newgate, on the day before the hanging of Governor Wall in 1802, and the doctor agreed to admit him to the gaol at the appropriate time. Wall had been a notoriously severe governor of the colony of Goree in West Africa. Eight years previously he had ordered that a soldier of the garrison named Armstrong should be tied to a gun-carriage and should be given eight hundred lashes with a cat-o'-nine-tails. Armstrong had died as a result of this chastisement and, in due course, Wall had been charged with his murder. After living in France for seven years Wall voluntarily returned to England and surrendered himself for his trial, at which he was convicted and sentenced to death. John Thomas Smith, in accordance with Doctor Forde's instructions, reported to the felons' door at Newgate very early on the morning of the execution. He was let in by a turnkey and introduced to 'a most diabolical-looking little wretch denominated "the Yeoman of the Halter", Jack Ketch's head man'. Presently Doctor Forde arrived, dressed in full canonicals with an enormous nosegay under his chin, to take him to see the condemned malefactor. 'As we crossed the Press Yard', Smith wrote, 'a cock crew; and the solitary clanking of a restless chain was dreadfully horrible. The prisoners had not risen.' Doctor Forde led him into a stone-cold room, filled with 'a most sickly stench of green twigs with which an old, round-shouldered, goggle-eyed man was endeavouring to kindle a fire'. After a while Governor Wall was brought in. Smith said:

He was death's counterfeit, tall, shrivelled, and pale and his soul shot so piercingly through the port-holes of his head that the first glance of him nearly petrified me. After the yeoman had requested him to stand up, he pinioned him, as the Newgate phrase is, and tied the cord with so little feeling that the Governor, who had not given the wretch his accustomed fee observed, 'You have tied me very tight', upon which Doctor Forde ordered him to slacken the cord, which he did, but not without much muttering. 'Thank you sir,' said the Governor to the Doctor, 'it is of little moment.'

From Smith's description it is easy to imagine the nervous tension of the atmosphere in the waiting room: the brittle periods of silence and the awkward lunging into conversation. When a servant entered with a large shovel of coals Wall remarked inattentively, 'Ay, in one hour that will be a blazing fire.' Then suddenly turning to Doctor Forde he asked, 'Sir, I am informed that I shall go down with great force. Is that so?' The Ordinary proceeded to explain the mechanism of the gallows to him, and then they joined together in a few moments of prayer. Eventually, Smith continued:

the sheriff arrived, attended by his officers, to receive the prisoner from the keeper. A new hat was partly flattened on [Wall's] head; for, owing to its being too small in the crown, it stood many inches too high behind. As we were crossing the Press Yard the dreadful execrations of some of the felons so shook his frame that he observed 'The clock has struck,' and quickening his pace he soon arrived at the room where the sheriff was ready to give a receipt for his body.

When John Thomas Smith left Newgate after the execution was over he saw the yeoman of the halter standing outside the gaol selling pieces of the rope 'with which the malefactor had been suspended' for the price of a shilling an inch. Further down Newgate Street another man and a prostitute were each conducting their own sales with lengths of what was also supposed to be rope from the scaffold.

During the early years of the nineteenth century convicted criminals were being shipped off to Australia as frequently as the transport fleets could be assembled. In 1810 the infant colony of New South Wales had a total population of just over ten thousand people, the great majority of whom were transported convicts: by 1821 this figure had grown to about thirty thousand, made up in the approximate proportions of two-thirds convicts to one-third free settlers. The prisoners were either put to work on development projects in the coastal areas or were assigned to the settlers in the hinterland, virtually as slave labour. A House of Commons Committee reported that assigned women-convicts were 'received rather as prostitutes than as servants'. Throughout the colony living conditions were primitive and discipline was harsh, with flogging and hanging as the customary penalties for all but the most trivial offences. Social conventions were almost non-existent; thieving, drunkenness and sexual promiscuity abounded; and the relationship of marriage was a rarity as, indeed, was the birth of a legitimate child. By and large, the public in Britain was kept in complete ignorance of this situation since convicts seldom wrote home and few official reports on the colony were ever published. However, Elizabeth Fry continually pressed for information on what was happening to the women prisoners. In 1819 she received a letter from the Reverend Samuel Marsden, a chaplain in New South Wales, who told her:

To this day there has never been a place to put female convicts in when they land from the ships. For the last five-and-twenty years many of the convict women have been driven to vice to obtain a loaf of bread or a bed to lie upon. Many of these have told me with tears, their distress of mind on this account; some would have been glad to have returned to the paths of virtue if they could have found a hut to live in without forming improper connections . . . When I am called on to visit them upon their dying beds, my mind is greatly pained, my mouth is shut, I know not what to say to them. To tell them of their crimes is to upbraid them with misfortunes. They will say, 'Sir, you know how I was situated. I did not wish to live the life I have done. I could not help myself; I must have starved if I had not done as I have done.'

Marsden concluded by saying:

It was the custom for some years, when a ship with female convicts arrived, for soldiers, convicts and settlers to go on board and make their choice. This custom is no longer pursued openly, but the lack of provision for women convicts makes the real situation just as bad as ever. And so it will remain till they have been provided with a barrack.

Mrs Fry took up this matter with her usual vigour and a few years later a women's barracks was built just outside Sydney.

At this time the causes both of penal reform and of the reformation of the criminal law were led in the House of Commons by Sir Samuel Romilly who had become Solicitor-General in 1806 in the so-called 'Ministry of All the Talents'.

Romilly's first success came about in 1808 when he persuaded Parliament to repeal an Elizabethan statute which prescribed the death penalty for any offenders convicted of picking pockets, and to substitute the punishment of transportation for life. In 1810 he introduced three more Bills aimed at mitigating the severity of the Bloody Code by abolishing the death penalty for the theft from a shop of goods worth five shillings or more, the theft of property valued at over two pounds from a private house, and theft of a similar value from a ship afloat on any navigable river. The House of Commons accepted the first of these measures, but not the latter two; however, the House of Lords was in no mood to make even this modest concession, and encouraged by the bitter opposition of the Lord Chancellor, the Lord Chief Justice, the Archbishop of Canterbury and six other bishops they firmly rejected the Bill. Also in 1810 Romilly urged Parliament to review the whole system of penal administration; he denounced the prisons in Britain as a disgrace to the country. 'Imprisonment on board the hulks,' he said, 'is still more pernicious and productive of still greater evils even than imprisonment in our common gaols.' As a result of his efforts a House of Commons Committee was set up to investigate the laws relating to Penitentiary Houses. They reported in 1811 expressing their opinion, 'that many offenders may be reclaimed by a system of Penitentiary imprisonment by which [the Committee] mean a system of imprisonment not confined to the safe custody of the person, but extending to the reformation and improvement of the mind and operating by seclusion, employment and religious instruction'.

Outside Parliament, too, the cause of penal reform was being actively promoted by a small band of faithful adherents, foremost amongst whom were the members of several well-known Quaker families. In 1811 James Nield set out on a tour of the prisons very similar to the one John Howard had undertaken forty years before. Nield found, in his own words, that:

the great reformation produced by Howard was in several places merely temporary: some prisons that had been ameliorated under the persuasive influence of his kind advice were relapsing into their former state of privation, filthiness, severity or neglect.

Many new dungeons had aggravated the evils against which his sagacity could but remonstrate.

The conditions at Newgate early in the nineteenth century have been amply described in various authentic accounts. Nield reported on the gaol in 1811; A House of Commons Committee carried out an inspection in 1814; the Hon. H. G. Bennett, M.P., went there in 1817, and Sir Thomas Buxton in 1818. It is apparent that there had been little general improvement since Howard had made his recommendations. The wards were perpetually overcrowded; Nield found that there was a total of twelve hundred prisoners in the gaol at the time of his visit in 1811, comprising nine hundred felons and three hundred debtors. The keeper of Newgate, when he gave evidence before the House of Commons Committee in 1814, attributed the habitual congestion as being partly due to the slowness of the authorities in removing prisoners who had been sentenced to transportation; many of these people, he said, were kept waiting in the gaol for periods of between six and twelve months, or even longer. Indiscriminate mixing of different types of criminal and different age-groups still persisted.

H. G. Bennett said:

The City of London should be called upon to cease confining the wretched prisoners in a manner against which common sense and the most ordinary humanity revolt. Boys of thirteen and fourteen, and even infants of nine are confined in the same yard as hardened offenders. The shameless victims of lust and profligacy are placed in the same chamber with others who, however they may have offended the laws in particular points, still preserve their respect for decency and decorum.

Although men and women prisoners were now kept apart, the immorality in the men's wards continued. Bennett suggested:

The principal evil, perhaps, is the introduction into the prisons of the most profligate and abandoned females who are to be found in the Metropolis. A woman has only to state herself to be the wife of a prisoner, and although she may be well-known as a street walker by every turnkey she must pass, she is admitted without further enquiry. It is certain that females are not excluded at the time of locking up the prison; but every woman who chooses to remain through the night may do so upon the small fee of one shilling being paid for this permission. The perquisite of the turnkeys is technically called 'the bad money' and is divided between them.

Nield considered Newgate to be well supplied with water, dust-bins and sewers, but thought that the prisoners had few comforts beyond the occasional chance of a bath, which was regarded as a very special favour. Although mops and brooms were supplied out of garnish money and charitable funds, 'dirt prevailed everywhere'. The tap-rooms in the gaol had been closed, but prisoners were allowed to have beer and wine sent in from a public house in the vicinity; no attempt was made to curtail these supplies and drunkenness was still very prevalent especially in the Press Yard, which was now used for the confinement of men under sentence of death. 'Capital prisoners', said Bennett, 'lessened the ennui and despair of their situation by unbecoming merriment, or sought relief in the constant application of intoxicating stimulants.' He had observed some malefactors a few hours before their executions, 'smoking and drinking with the utmost unconcern and indifference'. The capital prisoners could use the Press Yard and a large association room during the day, but were locked in the fifteen condemned cells, two, three or more together, at night. They were watched continuously for fear that they would attempt to commit suicide and were constantly searched for weapons and for poison. However, their right to receive visits from relatives or friends was almost unrestricted. The most comfortable part of the gaol was known as the State Ward. It was 'large and fairly commodious' and, naturally, accommodation there was very expensive. On the Common Side the food, as in the past, was mostly provided out of charitable sources, and in place of bedding two rugs were issued to each prisoner by the City authorities when these were available. According to Bennett, every prisoner committed to Newgate for felony, whether tried or untried, was ironed, but it seems that a felon could still purchase his easement. Heavier irons were applied to the unruly, and those who attempted to escape were usually chained to the floors of their wards.

Perhaps the greatest cruelties suffered by the inmates at
Newgate during this period were perpetrated by their fellow-
prisoners. Those who could not afford to pay garnish were
forced to scrub out the wards, and were prevented from
coming near to the fireplaces or forbidden the use of the
communal cooking facilities. Thomas Buxton has recounted
the appalling experiences of a young lawyer who declined to
participate in the general drinking which was taking place
in his ward when he was committed to the gaol. As a result
he was brought repeatedly before a prisoners' court on a
series of turned-up 'charges', such as 'touching objects
which should not be touched', 'coughing maliciously to the
disturbance of his companions', or 'leaving a door open'. A
selected prisoner would preside over the court with an
imitation judge's wig on his head, made of a towel tied into
knots, and a jury of prisoners would be sworn in to try each
case. The only chance of an acquittal was for an accused to
offer a sufficiently large bribe to the judge and jury; if he
failed to do so he would be sentenced to 'the pillory', which
consisted of having his head forced through the legs of a chair
and his arms being tied to it on either side. Eventually the
lawyer's powers of resistance to his new associates were overcome. 'By sensible degrees', Buxton wrote, 'he began to lose
his repugnance to their society, caught their flash terms and
sang their songs, was admitted to their revels and acquired,
in place of habits of perfect sobriety, a taste for spirits.' Even
then the amicability of his new companions was only ephe-
meral, for his wife had visited him in the ward some time
later and had found him 'pale as death, very ill and in a
dreadfully dirty state, the wretches making game of him and
enjoying my distress'.

The debasing effects of Newgate were corroborated by
another House of Commons committee which conducted an
enquiry soon after Buxton's visit to the gaol. 'The promiscuous assemblage of persons of all descriptions, ages, and
characters of crime', they reported, 'have deeply impressed
[them] with the opinion that no-one can enter the walls of
Newgate without going out from thence more depraved and
corrupted than when first committed thereto.' On the other
hand, they found that boys below the age of sixteen were now

kept apart from the other male prisoners and a school had been opened for them in which they were taught by a convict. The Committee also commented favourably upon the fact that outside visitors had recently been excluded from the interior of the gaol, and in consideration of this change the untried prisoners were no longer put in irons. The Committee also found that the familiar overcrowding at Newgate had been eased considerably by the opening of Whitecross Street debtor's prison in 1815; since then no prisoners for debt had been sent either to Newgate or to the City compters.

In 1813 the Government had decided to erect a large new-style penitentiary at Millbank in Westminster on the site which had previously been acquired by Jeremy Bentham. This massive building, which was to accommodate a thousand prisoners, would be shaped like a six-jointed star, with a chapel at the centre and each of its six separate radiating wings being three stories high. The whole block was to occupy a space of about seven acres and was to cost over half-a-million pounds. Even this development did not wholly appease some of those who were avid for speedier penal reform and in 1814, in the House of Commons, George Holford, M.P., introduced a motion drawing attention to the terrible conditions existing in the London gaols; during the ensuing debate one member declared that he had never in his life seen a worse-managed prison than Newgate. In that same year the grand jury at Middlesex presented Newgate Gaol as a public nuisance. The first part of Millbank Penitentiary was opened in 1816. The design of the prison accorded partly with the principles of Howard and partly with those of Bentham. The prisoners occupied separate cells, with stone walls and small barred windows; each cell contained a toilet, a hand basin, a hammock and a loom. On arrival at the prison men and women were shut up alone for five days 'to awaken them to reflection and a due sense of their situation'; thereafter, none of the inmates were kept in a state of absolute solitary confinement except as a punishment for disciplinary offences, although for the first half of their sentences they worked alone in their cells, before graduating to the privilege of labour in association. The staff at Millbank included a medical officer, a chaplain, a master-manufacturer and a matron in charge of the women. The first intake of prisoners, which arrived soon after the official opening, included a contingent transferred from Newgate. The remaining sections of the prison were built by stages, the final wing being completed in 1821.

In 1816 Samuel Romilly again attempted to procure the repeal of the ancient statute which prescribed the death peanalty for the offence of stealing articles worth five shillings or more from a shop: as before, his measure passed through the Commons and was defeated in the Lords. Romilly was now approaching the end of his brilliant career, but there were others with an equal dedication and a similar fervour for humanitarian reform who were waiting to step into his place, notably Sir Thomas Fowell Buxton and Sir James Mackintosh. About this time Buxton had been walking past Newgate Gaol with his brother-in-law Samuel Hoare when they had started to discuss the activities of Elizabeth Fry. During the conversation they had decided to form an organization which would have for its object the bringing about of a complete overhaul of the prison system. The Society for the Reformation of Prison Discipline, which came into being as a result, and was mostly composed of Quakers, played a prominent part in publicizing the abuses and oppressions of the British gaols. Like Howard and Mrs Fry, Buxton was impelled and inspired by his Christian beliefs; after visiting some condemned prisoners at Newgate in 1817 he wrote to his wife, 'It has made me long much that my life may not pass quite uselessly; but that, in some shape or other, I may assist in checking and diminishing crime and its consequent misery. Surely it is in the power of all to do something in the service of their Master?'

In the course of his work for the new society Thomas Buxton visited many prisons throughout the country and reported on their condition. For the most part he was horrified by what he saw. In the Borough Compter, he said, the overcrowding was so desperate that the inmates only had sufficient room to sleep on their sides; a prisoner there had told him, 'In the morning the heat was so oppressive that he and everyone else on waking rushed unclothed into the yard.' At Guildford Gaol in 1818 Buxton found that there was no infirmary, no chapel and no classification; and the prisoners were so heavily ironed that they could not undress at night. At Bristol Gaol one hundred and fifty prisoners of all ages were confined in a prison which had been built to accommodate fifty-two; the floors were damp; there were sick lying in every ward; and the stench was 'something more than can be expressed by the word "disgusting" '. None of these faults were occasioned by the gaolers, said Buxton; 'without exception I have had reason to approve, and sometimes to applaud their conduct'.

Samuel Romilly died in 1818 after his Bill to abolish capital punishment for shoplifters had been frustrated for the third time by the House of Lords, but during March 1819 the peers, in a less obdurate mood, accepted a proposal by Lord Castlereagh that they should appoint a select committee to enquire generally into the state of prison discipline in Britain. A short while later the House of Commons agreed to a motion, proposed by Sir James Mackintosh and seconded by Sir Thomas Buxton, that their own select committee should be set up 'to consider so much of the criminal law as relates to capital punishments or felonies'. During the following year the Society for the Reformation of Prison Discipline issued a statement in which it was disclosed that 'of the 519 Gaols and Houses of Correction in the United Kingdom, and to which in 1818, upwards of 107,000 persons were committed, twenty-three only of these prisons are divided for the classification of offenders; fifty-nine have no division whatever to separate male from female prisoners: one hundred and thirty-six have merely one division; and in seventy-three only has employment been introduced.'

In the course of their report the House of Commons Committee on capital punishment recommended the repeal or amendment of a number of obsolete statutes prescribing the death sentence for various less grave offences. The members of the committee had been divided in their opinions, with Buxton favouring the abolition of hanging for every crime except murder and the others merely seeking to reduce the incidence of capital punishment. The Lords Committee on prison discipline achieved a more immediate result, for in 1821 a Bill was introduced in Parliament 'for the better regulation of prisons'. Unfortunately, as so frequently in the past, this measure was mostly confined to declarations of general principle rather than to devising a means to ensure their implementation. However, despite its imperfections the Prison Act, 1821, clearly demonstrated that the cause of penal reform was gathering momentum.

CHAPTER SIXTEEN

NEW CONCEPTIONS

ALTHOUGH there was a general consensus of opinion in Britain that prisoners should no longer be left to spend their days in dissipation and idleness there were two contradictory schools of thought as to the manner in which they should be employed. There were those who acceded to Jeremy Bentham's view that prison-labour should be productive and commercial: others considered that it should be pointless and wearisome so as to enhance its value as a deterrent. Whilst the argument was still at its height Mr Cubitt designed the first prison tread-wheel. William (later Sir William) Cubitt was a Lowestoft engineer. In 1818 he had had occasion to visit the Suffolk County Gaol in Bury St Edmunds and he had noticed a crowd of prisoners lounging about just inside the entrance gates in what he later described as 'repulsive groups'. Presently he had been joined by a local magistrate who said to him, 'I wish to God, Mr Cubitt, you could suggest to us some mode of employing these fellows. Could nothing like a wheel become available?' Cubitt had promised that he would try to devise a simple means to keep the prisoners occupied, and a short while later he had developed his human tread-wheel, which was to form one of the central features of the British prison system for the remainder of the century. The tread-wheel fulfilled a dual function; it could be used for a practical purpose such as operating a mill, grinding corn or raising water: on the other hand, it was a tiring, monotonous and degrading form of labour. The Reverend Sydney Smith had welcomed enthusiastically this new addition to the regimen of the gaols; it was, he said, 'economical, certain, well-administered, little liable to abuse, capable of infinite division, a perpetual example before the eyes of those who want it, affecting the imagination only with horror and disgust, and affording great ease to the Government'. The less draconian penologist C. C. Western wrote in 1825, 'The superiority of the tread-wheel over every other means of applying hard labour is obvious to those who have seen it: so exactly suited is it to the purpose, that I have little doubt of its universal adoption, and that ere long imprisonment to hard labour will be considered as a sentence to labour on the tread-wheel.'

With the advent of the tread-wheels the lives of prisoners in the gaols appeared suddenly to have become better regulated and more meaningful. The county magistrates in particular had placed an infinite reliance on the disciplinary and remedial effects of this novel innovation, and men and women of all ages, quite irrespective of their physical limitations, were ranged side-by-side in rows of a dozen or more to rotate their individual wheels until they had reached the point of exhaustion. Later on it became the established practice for prisoners to toil for shifts of fifteen minutes; then to be relieved by others for a fifteen minute rest before returning once more to the endless ascent; this process was continued for hours on end and sometimes for a whole day. Strangely enough Elizabeth Fry was not opposed to women being put on the tread-wheel, but she suggested that their stints there might be of comparatively short duration. One of the first criticisms of this new device came from J. I. Briscoe in 1824 when he wrote, 'My firm and deliberate opinion is that the labour is of a nature tending in all cases to injure the prisoner in a greater or less degree; according to the duration of his sentence and the constitutional strength he may possess to enable him to resist the effects of the wheel.' The governor of Coldbath Fields prison voiced a similar misgiving in 1837 when he said that men in general were 'greatly distressed' when they went on the tread-wheel and this applied particularly to heavy men and hard drinkers. He added, however, 'With regard to women I believe tread-wheel labour, if judiciously used, is highly beneficial to health, particularly in cases of disorderly women, prostitutes etc.'

Naturally there were many to whom the tread-wheel seemed to provide a wholly unsatisfactory solution to the perplexing problem of prison labour; for the basic question which still remained unanswered was whether the future purpose of imprisonment was to be retributory, reformatory or deterrent. James Mill, who was a disciple of Jeremy Bentham, in a thoughtful analysis of the subject in the *Encyclopaedia Britannica* of 1823 concluded that the object of a prison sentence should be 'reform by industry'. Such a process had been attempted in the new penitentiary at Millbank where at the start about twenty different trades had been introduced, including tailoring and shoe-making for men, and weaving and needlework for women. But one by one of these were gradually abandoned, some because they necessitated the prisoners being provided with sharp and dangerous implements, and others because of a lack of skilled supervisors, until weaving was the only truly commercial trade which remained. Quite apart from this involuntary restriction in the scope of its prison-labour the officials at Millbank, during its initial years, had encountered a spate of far more serious troubles. In 1818 the inmates rioted for two days in protest against the standard of the prison bread, which formed a substantial part of their diet: in 1823 there were epidemics of scurvy, dysentery and cholera amongst the prisoners which assumed such alarming proportions that the Government decided temporarily to close the penitentiary, and to transfer the women to an empty hospital in London and the men to the hulks at Woolwich. Millbank had remained unoccupied for several months whilst it was thoroughly cleaned and fumigated before being reopened with a new intake of prisoners. A parliamentary commission which investigated the causes of the epidemics decided that none of the staff had been to blame, but recommended that an improved system of ventilation should be installed in the building, that the prisoners should be allowed more facilities for games and recreation, and that all the cells should be lit with candles during winter evenings.

At the time of its reopening in 1823 both the structure and the system at Millbank were still regarded as an interesting and imaginative penal experiment. The prisoners of both sexes were carefully selected, only those considered as potentially responsive being sent to the penitentiary; these consisted solely of young persons, first offenders, and others whose 'early habits and good character [afforded] reasonable hope of their being restored to society, corrected and reclaimed by the punishment they had undergone'. Apart from Mill-bank, conditions in the majority of the British gaols remained almost completely unchanged, for despite the interest which had been stimulated by the evangelical zeal of the Quakers and the emotional fervour of a small group of reformers, no administrator had ever officially formulated a comprehensive scheme for improved prison management. It was left to Robert Peel, who on becoming Home Secretary in 1822 immediately embarked upon a number of far-sighted and radical domestic policies, to introduce what the Webbs have referred to as 'the first measure of general prison reform to be framed and enacted on the responsibility of the national executive'. The Prison Act, 1823, sought to eradicate some of the principal abuses which had corrupted the British gaols for centuries past. The payment of fees by prisoners was finally abolished and gaolers became the salaried servants of the local authorities. Men and women were to be confined in separate parts of prisons, and the women were to be super-vised entirely by female wardresses. The general use of irons was prohibited, and whenever a prisoner was ironed or sub-jected to a 'tyrannical punishment' the matter was to be re-ported to the visiting justices of the peace. Prisoners were to be classified in five groups: debtors, unconvicted felons, un-convicted misdemeanants, convicted felons, and convicted misdemeanants. Rules were prescribed with regard to the health, clothing and education of prisoners in addition to the regulation of their labour, and the justices of the peace were required to organize the gaols according to a prescribed pattern and to furnish the Home Secretary with quarterly reports concerning 'every department' of their administration. Peel's measure rejected the concept of solitary confinement and directed that a 'reformatory régime' should be applied to every prisoner.

The 1823 Act suffered from two substantial defects. First, it had failed to authorize the creation of an inspectorate to ensure the implementation of the new provisions; and secondly, it only applied to the one hundred and thirty county gaols, to the prisons in the Cities of London and Westminster, and to those in seventeen designated provincial towns. At any rate Britain had belatedly achieved a national prison policy, even though its fulfilment was to be dependant on the whims of the local magistracy. Another important innovation which occurred in 1823 was the introduction by the Surrey justices of covered vans for the conveyance of prisoners through the streets; the idea was soon adopted by other authorities and by 1830 it was used fairly universally throughout the country. The standard type of prison van was just over eight feet long, four and a half feet wide, and had an internal height of five and a half feet. To save additional journeys, between twenty and thirty prisoners were often carried in a single load. Some years later an official report stated, 'No officer, either male or female, is inside the van. It can excite no surprise that under such circumstances scenes of gross indecency constantly occur.' When the destination had been reached, it was said, profligate characters of both sexes descended from the van, 'with clothing not sufficient to cover their nakedness'. Some prisoners were drunk, some were verminous, and some diseased. 'The desperate burglar, the notorious pickpocket, the abandoned prostitute, and even the unnatural offender, are here crowded together in the smallest possible space.'

Although the House of Lords had persisted in blocking any attempts to seriously reduce the number of capital offences the proportion of prisoners who were sentenced to death and were later reprieved was showing a steady and appreciable increase. In the year 1785 there had been ninety-six hangings in London alone: in 1825 there were fifty executions in the whole of England, of which only seventeen took place in the capital. James Mackintosh and Thomas Buxton were perpetually agitating in the Commons for a drastic review of the criminal law and for a greater humanity in the scale of punishments. During Robert Peel's period of office as Home Secretary between 1823 and 1830, he managed to pass five statutes which exempted no less than a hundred offences from the capital penalty; in 1832 the process of amelioration was continued when housebreaking, horse and sheep stealing, and coining ceased to be hanging offences; in 1837 forgery was also exempted and, in fact, from that year until the close of the nineteenth century no executions took place in Britain for any crimes other than murder or attempted murder. If the public outlook was becoming more compassionate at the time when Peel had assumed office, a similar forebearance had not permeated to the interior of Newgate where the ritual of hanging was still conducted with the same degrading formalities as had been enacted in the past. The burial service was described by a prisoner who was at the gaol about the year 1820:

Three unfortunate men were ordered for execution. On the Sunday morning they were placed in the condemned pew, which is an oval-shaped, sable-coloured box, with a coffin on the table in the middle. The pew is large enough to contain thirty individuals. It is in the centre of the chapel. Here the condemned are the gazing blocks of the other prisoners and of those who paid a shilling for admission to the gallery.

The Ordinary began by telling the three men this was the last sermon they would ever hear, 'and then proceeded at great length to scold the wretches already worn to the bone with misery' for having committed their crimes. The account continued:

Next morning at half-past seven the clergyman's voice was heard in the vaulting passages, 'I am the resurrection and the life . . .' Christianity appears more hateful to me every time I reflect on this circumstance.

From 1824 visitors from outside were not allowed to attend the condemned service at Newgate, and another salutary change occurred in 1832 with the discontinuation of the practice of sending corpses of executed murderers to the Surgeons' Hall for dissection; instead, after a brief inquest, the bodies were buried in quicklime in the Newgate cemetery – which was, in fact, the narrow passage connecting the gaol with the Old Bailey, along which the condemned prisoners had passed going to and coming from their trials.

The vast majority of reprieved felons underwent transportation to Australia. In 1823 two convict ships set sail for Botany Bay; in 1826 and 1827 there was a total of five ships each year; from then on an average of five or six fully laden convict ships left English ports annually. However, there was a growing disenchantment with the scheme both at home and in New South Wales. Many people in Britain thought

that transportation was a wastage of man-power and that
plenty of useful work in their own country could be found
for this conscripted labour force; on the other hand, the free
Australian settlers bitterly resented the continual inflow of
murderers, robbers, pickpockets, housebreakers and prostitutes. In addition to all else, it was becoming increasingly
doubtful whether or not, from the long-term view, transportation was proving an effective deterrent. As the Reverend
Sydney Smith declared, a criminal might well be told by the
judge:

Because you have committed this offence, the sentence of the
court is that you shall no longer be burdened with the support
of your wife and family. You shall be immediately removed from
a bad climate and a country overburdened with people to one of
the finest regions on earth where the demand for human labour
is every hour increasing and where it is probable you may ultimately regain your character and improve your future.

Eight years after the passing of the Prison Act of 1823 it
was becoming increasingly apparent that it would be necessary to define in much clearer detail the 'reformatory régime'
it had sought to introduce. In 1831 a select committee was
set up by the House of Commons for this purpose. They reported that:

It is almost impossible for any but the most degraded criminal
to be confined even for a short period within the walls of any
prison, as at present regulated, without injury to his morals.
They, therefore, recommend that prisoners, when committed
for trial, should be placed in light, solitary sleeping cells, provided with employment where practicable, and furnished with
moral and religious books; that although they should be strictly
confined to their cells at night, and while at their meals, they
should be allowed to receive visits from their friends, under proper superintendence, and also to walk in the airing yards of the
prison, in company with the other untried prisoners.

After conviction, said the committee, prisoners should sleep
and eat in the solitude of their own cells, but should be
allowed to work together in silence. These proposals were
largely academic as most of the local authorities were avoiding
the expense of constructing new prison buildings, and at that

time very few of the existing gaols in the country had separate
cellular accommodation. Millbank had continued to practise
partial isolation for the first part of a prisoner's sentence, and
labour in association for the second part. During 1832 this
second phase was abolished and there was a general tightening
up of regulations to make the complete separation of all the
inmates more effectual. At the same time a greater emphasis
was placed on religious instruction, more services were held
in the prison chapel, and more Bibles and tracts were distributed among the cells.

During the early 1830s the number of prisoners in the gaols
was rapidly increasing and there was a general recognition in
Britain that the ancient system of imprisonment with its corruption, idleness, indiscriminate association, and its complete
absence of any reformatory influence would have to be
entirely replaced. There were three distinct, but partially
overlapping theories on the way in which prison discipline
should be shaped for the future. Some had followed Jeremy
Bentham in the belief that the reformation of prisoners could
be best achieved by industrial employment; others adhered
to Mrs Fry's opinion that they might be reclaimed by religious
and moral instruction; and others, like the Reverend Sydney
Smith, held that the conditions in the gaols should reflect
the basic fact that the sole purpose of punishment was to
deter. The first supervisors at Millbank were still working
on the simple principle that their function was merely to
eradicate the bad habits of the prisoners and to replace these
with a more assiduous mode of life. The distinguished French
writer Alexis De Tocqueville shared in this uncomplicated
view of the basic objective of imprisonment. 'Its essential
value,' he wrote, 'is in the habit of order, work, separation,
education and obedience to inflexible rule.' De Tocqueville
considered that the moral reform of an individual was a matter for the clergy rather than the prison keepers. In a model
prison system, he said, 'if a man is not made honest, he con-
tracts honest habits.' The more idealistically inclined peno-
logists were still seeking after a form of confinement that
would both expiate and purify, and many had pinned their
faith to the remedial impulsion of solitude, holding that isolation combined with a régime of hard, compulsory labour

and moral and religious teaching would be capable of reclaiming all but the most hardened criminals. This theory had originated amongst the evangelists and Quakers in the state of Pennsylvania in America and had become formulated into what was known as the 'separate system'. It was the method which had been operated at the Walnut Street Gaol in Philadelphia since its opening in 1792, and had also been adopted by the Western Penitentiary at Pittsburg, completed in 1818, and by the Eastern Penitentiary at Cherry Hill which was opened ten years later. In these prisons the inmates might remain in solitary confinement for their entire sentences, reading their Bibles in their barren cells and even taking their exercise alone in small, individual compounds. Another type of imprisonment which was being tried out in America was called the 'silent system'; in this the prisoners worked in association and slept either in wards or in cells; the rule of silence was at all times strictly enforced, and at Auburn prison in New York, where labour was performed in a central hall, both men and women were flogged if they so much as lifted their eyes from their work.

The American prison methods were attracting a great deal of attention from European observers and in 1832 the British Government sent out a special representative, Mr William Crawford, to carry out his own investigations. Crawford returned to England as a convinced supporter of the separate system and he recommended the establishment of a new national penitentiary closely modelled on the Eastern Penitentiary at Cherry Hill. In his report to the Home Secretary he said:

So greatly does increasing experience prove the importance of solitude in the management of prisoners that I could not, if circumstances admitted, too strongly advocate its application in Britain for every class of offender, as well as for persons before trial, under modifications which would divest seclusion of its harshest character.

Although he had such faith in the reformative influence of the separate system Crawford was by no means oblivious of its punitive effects, as he commented, 'The whip inflicts immediate pain, but solitude inspires permanent terror.' In

1835 a House of Lords Committee was appointed to carry out a complete survey of the prisons in Britain; later that year an Act of Parliament was passed for the purpose of 'effecting greater uniformity of practice in the government of the several prisons in England and Wales'. Perhaps the most important provision in the Prison Act, 1835 was that which empowered the Home Secretary to appoint up to five Prison Inspectors whose duty would be to visit 'every Gaol, Bridewell, House of Correction, Penitentiary or other Prison or Place kept and used for the confinement of Prisoners, in any part of the Kingdom of Great Britain'. The Home Secretary was also enabled to make his own prison rules whenever he wished to do so. As a result of this statute a partial governmental control was substituted for the former autonomy of the local authorities in the field of prison management, and it was not without significance with regard to future penal policy that William Crawford was one of the first Prison Inspectors to be appointed.

During 1835 William Crawford and another of the newly-created Inspectors carried out a thorough survey of the conditions in Newgate. In the autumn of that year the twenty-three-year-old Charles Dickens had also visited the gaol, 'this gloomy depository of the guilt and misery of London', as he called it, with the intention of describing its interior in his first book *Sketches By Boz,* which he was just completing. The Inspectors' factual report and Dickens's impressionistic commentary together provide a full, complementary and authentic portrayal of the lives of the prisoners at this period. It was not surprising, in view of the penal philosophy recently adopted by the central authorities, that the Inspectors should have been highly critical of the state of Newgate. 'The association of prisoners of all ages, and every shade of guilt, in one indiscriminate mass', they said, 'is a frightful feature of the system which prevails here; the first in magnitude, and the most pernicious in effect.' They were also appalled at 'the utter absence of employment for the prisoners'. Dickens carried out his inspection during the daytime and first of all entered one of the women's wards. He wrote:

It was a spacious, bare, whitewashed apartment, lighted, of course, by windows looking into the interior of the prison, but

far more light and airy than one could reasonably expect to find
in such a situation. There was a large fire with a deal table before it, round which ten or a dozen women were seated on forms
at dinner. Along both sides of the room ran a shelf; below it, at
regular intervals, a row of large hooks were fixed in the wall, on
each of which was hung the sleeping mat of a prisoner: her rug
and blanket being folded up, and placed on the shelf above. At
night, these mats are placed on the floor, each beneath the hook
on which it hangs during the day; and the ward is thus made to
answer the purposes both of day-room and sleeping apartment.

The arrangements in the men's wards were the same, he
said, the main apparent difference being the complete idleness
of the male inmates. The Inspectors entered the men's wards
by night and saw the prisoners lying 'two, three and even four,
under the same covering, and much crowded together on the
floor'. The blankets were insufficient in number and were
usually ragged and dirty. As a general rule the prisoners were
not allowed to take water into the wards for personal washing but were obliged to perform their ablutions at pumps in
the yards. 'The women sometimes while washing themselves
expose their necks', said the Inspectors; 'this is not decent, as
the female yards are overlooked by the principal male turnkeys apartments.' There was a limited issue of free clothing,
which was wholly inadequate and was only made to prisoners
who were unable to clothe themselves. The free issues of
food were also meagre and the size of a person's ration, 'depended on the good-will of the wardsman who doled it out'.
Prisoners with money could obtain unlimited quantities of
provisions from outside the gaol and visitors were allowed
to bring in gifts of food.

'In every ward on the female side, a wardswoman is
appointed to preserve order,' said Dickens, 'and a similar
regulation is adopted among the males. The wardsmen and
wardswomen are all prisoners selected for good conduct. They
alone are allowed the privilege of sleeping on bedsteads; a
small stump bedstead being placed in every ward for that
purpose.' The wardsmen, according to the inspectors' report,
enjoyed other favours as well, including the receipt of double
rations of food. The Inspectors considered that they had far
too much power; they could accuse prisoners of disciplinary

offences and have them punished whenever they chose; they sold small luxuries like tea, coffee, sugar and tobacco at their own prices; they charged 'ward dues' for the use of knives, forks and plates; and generally they exercised a despotic authority over their charges. The keeper had admitted that quite recently a prisoner of weak intellect had been savagely assaulted by a wardsman and had not dared to complain because he had 'more fear of the power of the wardsman to injure him, than confidence in the [keeper's] power to protect him'. Mr Cope, the keeper of Newgate in 1835 was censured by the Inspectors for his laxity in carrying out his responsibilities. He very rarely went round his gaol, they said; in fact he only entered the wards about once a fortnight, and a condemned man had told them that he had not seen the keeper more than four times during the previous two months. Inevitably, perhaps, most of the turnkeys took their cue from their master and left the prisoners in charge of the wardsmen all day, merely unlocking the wards in the morning and locking them up again at night. The Ordinary was no more diligent than any of the other Newgate officials; he had complained to the Inspectors that, 'For years he gave his whole time to his duties, from an early hour in the morning until late in the afternoon. He left off because he was so much interfered with and laughed at, and seeing that no success attended his efforts owing to the evils arising from association.'

The Inspectors declared from their observations that the average prisoner at Newgate was spending his days 'in riot, debauchery and gaming, vaunting his own adventures or listening to those of others; communicating his own skill and aptitude in crime, or acquiring lessons from greater adepts'. Discipline was negligible, according to the Inspectors; 'Rioting, uproar and fighting are frequently going on, the serious nature of which may be best understood from the severe accidents which have occurred.' Drunkenness was rife amongst both the men and the women prisoners; the potman from a local public house was allowed into the gaol every day from twelve noon until one o'clock and each inmate was officially permitted to buy one pint of beer, but no one restricted the amounts which were actually sold. In the evening, after the wards were locked up, obscene conversation, swearing, singing, gaming, revelry and violence continued far into the night. Classification in the gaol was only of the most cursory nature; the Inspectors mentioned a small ward which had contained a middle-aged man, charged with attempting to commit an indecent assault on a boy, and two youths of seventeen and eighteen, one of whom was still untried. They also found that the separation of the sexes was not being strictly enforced: neither was the regulation that women prisoners should always be placed in the charge of female officers.

The untried prisoners at Newgate were allowed to receive visitors on three days a week, and the convicted, on one day. No check was made as to the identity or the characters of the people entering the gaol on visiting days and strangers were not searched at the gates, but they could only speak to the prisoners through a double iron railing. Charles Dickens described how part of one side of the women's yard was railed off 'and formed into a kind of iron cage, about five feet ten inches in height, roofed at the top, and defended in front by iron bars, from which the friends of the female prisoners communicate with them'. While he had been passing through the yard, a 'yellow, haggard, decepit old woman' was visiting her daughter, 'a good-looking robust female, with a profusion of hair streaming about in the wind'; and a little farther off a prostitute had come to see her mother, 'a squalid-looking woman in a thick-bordered cap'. Dickens also went round the section of Newgate, consisting of a yard and two wards, which had just been set apart for boys under fourteen years of age:

In a tolerable-sized room, in which were some writing materials and some copy-books, was the schoolmaster, with a couple of his pupils; the remainder having been fetched from an adjoining apartment, the whole were drawn up in line for our inspection. There were fourteen of them in all, some with shoes, some without; some in pinafores without jackets, others in jackets without pinafores, and one in scarce anything at all. The whole number, without exception we believe, had been committed for trial on charges of pocket-picking; and fourteen such terrible little faces were never beheld. There was not one redeeming feature among them — not a glance of honesty — not a wink expressive of anything but the gallows and the hulks, in the whole collection. As to anything like shame or contrition, that was entirely out of the question.

The Press Yard at Newgate was still reserved for the condemned male prisoners, who often numbered between fifty and sixty persons of widely-differing ages; when the Prison Inspectors first entered this part of the gaol they found that five of the inmates were under sixteen; 'one of them was no more than thirteen years old,' they reported, 'and in appearance as well as in years, quite a child.' Dickens described the Press Yard as:

A long narrow court, of which a portion of the wall in Newgate Street forms one end and [the entrance gate] the other. At the upper end, on the left hand – that is, adjoining the wall in Newgate Street – is a cistern of water, and at the bottom a double grating (of which the gate itself forms a part). Through these grates the prisoners are allowed to see their friends; a turnkey always remaining in the vacant space between during the whole interview.

Prisoners with the hope of a reprieve had the use of a separate day-room. At the time of Dickens's visit he found twenty-five or thirty people there, who were, he said:

All under sentence of death, awaiting the result of the recorder's report – men of all ages and appearances, from a hardened old offender with swarthy face and grizzly beard of three days growth to a handsome boy, not fourteen years old, and of singularly youthful appearance even for that age, who had been condemned for burglary. There was nothing remarkable in the appearance of these prisoners. One or two decently dressed men were brooding with a dejected air over the fire; several little groups of two or three had been engaged in conversation at the upper end of the room, or in the windows; and the remainder were crowded round a young man seated at a table, who appeared to be engaged in teaching the younger ones to write.

Before the recorder's report on a condemned prisoner was received he was locked up in a cell from five o'clock in the afternoon until seven the following morning, and he was allowed to have a lighted candle up to ten o'clock at night. Dickens continued:

When the warrant for a prisoner's execution arrives, he is removed to the cells and confined in one of them until he leaves it for the scaffold. He is at liberty to walk in the yard; but, both in his walks and in his cell, he is constantly attended by a turnkey who never leaves him on any pretence. We entered the first cell. It was a stone dungeon, eight feet long by six wide, with a bench at the upper end, under which were a common rug, a Bible, and prayer-book. An iron candlestick was fixed to the wall at the side; and a small high window in the back admitted as much air and light as could struggle in between a double row of heavy, crossed iron bars. It contained no other furniture of any description.

The number of prisoners awaiting trial who required to be accommodated at Newgate increased in 1834 when the Sessions House in the Old Bailey was converted into the Central Criminal Court, with a jurisdiction for the trial of any treasons, murders and other felonies committed within the City of London, the County of Middlesex, and in certain parts of the counties of Essex, Kent and Surrey. Originally the Sessions House only had one court but by the middle of the nineteenth century it possessed three, and sometimes a fourth court sat in the Grand Jury Room. In the old courtroom the judges continued to sit on crimson cushions and the panelling behind them was covered with crimson cloth. Over the centre of the bench there was a wooden canopy surmounted by a carving of the Royal coat-of-arms. When the court was in session a sword of justice with a gold handle and an ornamented scabbard was usually supended under the canopy. The sessions at the Central Criminal Court took place twelve times a year, and the intimate connection between the court and Newgate was preserved by the tradition that the keeper of the gaol should always sit at the corner of the dock when a trial was taking place.

CHAPTER SEVENTEEN

THE SILENT AND SEPARATE SYSTEMS

It had become apparent by the year 1830 that the much-vaunted scheme of developing New South Wales by a combination of voluntary settlement and convict labour had proved an utter failure – and an expensive failure at that, because quite apart from the ineffectual nature of transportation as a punishment the project was costing about £300,000 annually for the shipment of prisoners, in addition to an outlay of at least £100,000 a year on the upkeep of military garrisons in the colony. In 1836 a select committee which had been appointed by the House of Commons to examine the New South Wales scheme, strongly recommended that the whole system of transportation should be abolished as quickly as possible and that for the future convicts should serve terms of between two and fifteen years imprisonment with hard labour in gaols either at home or overseas. This proposal accentuated the need for a complete overhaul of the British prisons and the introduction of some uniform penal policy for the whole country.

Separate confinement was being used at a few local gaols, but there were, as yet, hardly any prison buildings constructed on a cellular design. As has been noted the Millbank Penitentiary, still regarded as a prototype, had introduced a more rigorous regime of isolation since 1832. The Middlesex House of Correction at Coldbath Fields and the Westminster Bridewell at Tothill Fields had both branched out on their own and adopted the silent system. Captain George Chesterton, a retired army officer, had become Governor of Coldbath Fields in 1829. At the time he took over the prison, he said later, he had found it to be a sink of abomination. The entire administration, in his own words, had 'betokened the most appalling abuse' and he had found everything around him 'stamped with iniquity and corruption.' Nearly all the members of the staff had been making a second income out of bribes, perquisites, and the sale of liquor, tobacco and food to the inmates; every afternoon one of the attics in the prison was set aside for male and female prisoners to meet together for erotic enjoyment; and the infirmary was filled at night with perfectly healthy prisoners who were paying a set fee of two-and-sixpence for the privilege of sleeping in a bed. After five years of reorganization Chesterton suddenly announced in 1834 the immediate imposition of the silent system. From then on, he told the prisoners, any form of communication between them, whether by word, sign, or gesture, would be regarded as a serious offence. Although the prison had very few separate cells the rule of absolute silence was strictly applied both by night and by day and the smallest infringements of it were severely punished. Chesterton was a great believer in the use of the whip to enforce discipline; he once described flogging in prisons as being 'beneficial – nay indispensable'. He kept his prisoners locked up in their wards and cells for twelve hours out of the twenty-four at all times of the year without any form of heating or lighting. There had been no instruction and no productive employment at Coldbath Fields for the period from 1834 until 1854 while the silent system was in force; the male prisoners spent the whole day at the tread-wheel, the crank, oakum picking or shot-drill: the females were mostly engaged at the tread-wheel. Caroline Fox, who visited the prison in 1842, commented, 'It was sad to see the poor exhausted women ever toiling upward without a chance of progress.' Tothill Fields Bridewell, the governor of which was a retired naval officer, was conducted on much the same lines.

The Prison Inspectors in their reports published in 1837 and 1838 continued to advocate the separate, and to condemn the silent, system of imprisonment. They doubted whether the prevention of communication between the prisoners could ever be properly enforced. 'The truth of this is demonstrated by the following among other remarkable facts,' they said, 'that in the prison of Coldbath Fields, in which the Silent System is believed to be brought to the greatest degree of perfection, there were in the year 1836 no less than 5,138 punishments for "talking and swearing".' They went on to provide an example of the way in which these 'conversations' took place:

Although there is a turnkey stationed in each tread-wheel and two monitors, or wardsmen, selected from the prisoners, stand constantly by, the men on the wheel can, and do, speak to each other. They ask one another how long they are sentenced for and when they are going out; and the answers are given by laying two or three fingers on the wheel to signify so many months, or by pointing to some inscriptions carved on the tread-wheel as to the terms of imprisonment suffered by former prisoners, or else they turn their hands to express unlockings or days.

Another feature of the silent system to be severely criticized by the Inspectors was 'the employment of prisoners as wardsmen and monitors' to aid in the enforcement of discipline. 'This practice,' they declared, 'is directly opposed to every principle of justice.' Having thus disposed of the silent system the Inspectors repeated William Crawford's suggestion that the Government should now erect a new, model penitentiary in which the separate system could be demonstrated 'as a pattern for county and borough gaols' all over Britain.

The silent system found no favour with the Reverend Joseph Kingsmill, an experienced prison chaplain at the time. Whilst admitting that it put a stop to 'open blasphemy, profaneness, riot and obscenity', he was certain that it failed 'in some essential particulars, if reformation of morals, as well as correction of the offender, be desired'. This system, he said, presented so many temptations to prisoners to communicate with each other that they had to be subjected to constant surveillance and had to undergo perpetual punishments. When they were together, 'the winking of an eye, the movement of the finger, a sneeze or a cough is enough to indicate what is desired.' During the daytime there were many opportunities of holding quite lengthy conversations without much chance of being discovered. 'At meals, in spite of the strictness with which they are watched, the order is constantly infringed; but the time of exercise affords an almost unlimited power of communicating with each other. The closeness of their position and the noise of their feet render communication an easy matter.' At daily Chapel, according to Kingsmill, the prisoners held their books close to their faces and pretended to read with the chaplain, whilst in reality they were chatting with their neighbours.

The Government were so impressed with the arguments in support of the separate system that Lord John Russell, the Home Secretary, sent a circular letter to all the local magistrates in 1837 drawing their attention to the Inspectors' condemnation of silent association and urging them to construct their future prisons for the application of the separate system and, indeed, to adapt their existing gaols for its immediate introduction as far as was practicable. Two years later Parliament gave its approval to a measure which officially recognized the separate system as forming the basis of official British prison policy. The Prison Act, 1839 laid down that, 'in order to prevent contamination arising from association of prisoners in any prison in which rules for the individual separation of prisoners shall be in force, any prisoner may be separately confined during the whole or part of the period of his or her imprisonment.' At the same time the Home Secretary was granted increased powers over the design of prison buildings and the local authorities were provided with specific details as to the manner in which the separate system was to be implemented. The statute also prescribed a standard code of prison regulations which was intended to eradicate many of the principal, long-standing abuses which were still debasing the British gaols. No officer was to gain any illicit profit from his position; no prisoner was to be employed in a custodial or supervisory capacity; liquor and tobacco were only to be allowed into a prison on the recommendation of a doctor; keepers were to inspect the whole of their prisons every day; no prisoner was to be kept in irons for more than twenty-four hours at a time; and chaplains were to be appointed to every gaol. During 1839 the Inspectors achieved another of their aims when Parliament empowered the Government to build and administer a new model penitentiary, which would afford a national example of the benefits of the separate system. A few months after this decision the construction of Pentonville prison was commenced. In the spring of 1840 Lord John Russell announced to the House of

Commons that transportation to New South Wales was to be indefinitely suspended; in its place a far more limited scheme was started by which a certain number of convicts were transported annually to Van Diemen's Land and Norfolk Island.

Those who shared the illogical faith in the universal regenerative effects of prolonged solitude seemed to overlook the fact that the criminal, unlike the mystic, was neither trained nor disciplined for introspection. In the United States of America the separate system of imprisonment had resulted in deaths, insanity and suicides on a considerable scale. At Walnut Street Gaol in Philadelphia the prisoners spent most of their sentences alone in a cell which, according to a contemporary description, contained 'one small window, placed high up and out of reach; the window well secured by a double iron grating, so that, provided an effort to get to it was successful, the person could perceive neither heaven nor earth, on account of the thickness of the wall. The criminal, while confined here, is permitted no convenience of bench, table, or even bed, or anything else but what is barely necessary to support life.'

In 1842 Charles Dickens inspected the Eastern Penitentiary at Cherry Hill. Five days after his visit he wrote in a letter:

I went last Tuesday to the Eastern Penitentiary near Philadelphia, which is the only prison in the States, or I believe, in the world, on the principle of hopeless, strict, and unrelaxed solitary confinement, during the whole term of the sentence. It is wonderfully kept, but a most dreadful, fearful place . . . I shall never be able to dismiss from my mind the impressions of that day. Making notes of them, as I have done, is an absurdity, for they are written, beyond all power of erasure, in my brain. I saw men who had been there, five years, six years, eleven years, two years, two months, two days; some whose term was nearly over, and some whose term had only just begun. Women too, under the same variety of circumstances. Every prisoner who comes into the gaol, comes at night; is put into a bath, and dressed in the prison garb; and then a black hood is drawn over his face and head, and he is led to the cell from which he never stirs again until his whole period of confinement has expired. I looked at some of them with the same awe as I should have looked at men who had been buried alive, and dug up again.

Later on, in his book *American Notes,* Dickens was to comment, 'Very few men were capable of estimating the immense amount of torture and agony which this dreadful punishment, prolonged for years, inflicts upon the prisoner.'

After making his own study of prison conditions in the United States of America, De Tocqueville concluded that whereas the separate system was more likely to reform prisoners, the silent system was better calculated to deter them in the future: the former would produce more honest men and the latter more obedient citizens. On a visit to one of the separate penitentiaries in Philadelphia, De Tocqueville had asked a prisoner, 'Do you find it difficult to endure solitude?', to which the man had replied, 'Ah sir, it is the most horrid punishment that can be imagined.' De Tocqueville had then enquired, 'Does your health suffer from it?' and had received the answer, 'No, but my soul is very sick.' However, the Reverend John Field, an English prison chaplain who had witnessed the separate system in operation, could still bestow upon it the fulsome and incredibly smug commendation, 'seclusion, under such circumstances, renders society more inviting, whilst its corrective tendency prepares the subject of it for the increased pleasure which more virtuous companionship shall afford.' After the prisoner is released, said Field, 'the advantages of his seclusion will be thankfully borne in mind, and occasional secrecy therefore chosen; but converse will have increased charms; the deprivation will have made it a privilege; company therefore, but of a better character than before, will be sought, and will prove a source of more profitable enjoyment.' Elizabeth Fry, from her intimate acquaintanceship with the mentality of prisoners, deprecated both these new penal methods; her dislike of the separate system, said her daughters, 'was only augmented by further knowledge of its consequences. As a permanent punishment, she considered it was too cruel to contemplate even for the most heinous crimes.' With regard to the silent system, 'she considered it little likely to benefit the criminal, and particularly adapted to harden the heart.'

Pentonville prison, with just over five hundred separate

cells, was completed in 1842. It possessed, said Joseph Kingsmill, 'every advantage which a philanthropy enlightened by long experience of the evils of the other systems could suggest, or a wise and powerful Government could bestow'. Certainly Pentonville had far more amenities than the older gaols. Each cell was thirteen feet long, seven feet wide and nine feet high, with a small, barred window in its outer wall, and on the inner side a door leading to a central gallery; they were furnished to a uniform pattern with a table, a stool, and a hammock, and contained a shaded gas-burner, a water closet and a copper wash-basin supplied with running water. The whole prison was heated in cold weather by the circulation of warm air. Yet owing to the regime which was imposed on the prisoners, during the initial eight years of its existence the rate of insanity at Pentonville was ten times as great as the normal rate for gaols in the rest of the country. The upholders of the separate system in British prisons, or the Pentonville system as it was sometimes called, were always eager to distinguish this method of captivity from solitary confinement. Joseph Adshead wrote in 1856:

It differs from it in the following particulars: in providing the prisoners with a large, well-lighted, well-ventilated apartment, instead of immuring him in a confined, ill-ventilated and dark cell; in providing the prisoner with everything that is necessary for his cleanliness, health and comfort during the day, and for his repose at night, instead of denying him these advantages: in supplying him with sufficient food of wholesome quality, instead of confining him to bread and water; in alleviating his mental discomfort by giving him employment and regular visits by officers in the prison.

The prisoner, Adshead continued, maintained contact with the prison chaplain and was allowed to attend Divine Service and to take exercise in the open air. The object of Separate Confinement was:

the permanent moral benefit of the prisoner – an object which he can plainly see the system has in view. Under the Separate System, an appeal is made to the moral sense and understanding of the prisoner: he is treated as a man with the respect and benevolence due to humanity even in its lowest debasement.

Originally Pentonville was intended to be a 'convict academy' where specially-selected prisoners would undergo a course of moral training before fulfilling their sentences of transportation; they would also be taught a trade which would enable them to earn their own living when they eventually graduated to 'ticket-of-leave' status in the land of their exile. Every inmate of the prison was supposed to be veiled with an absolute anonymity; he was known and addressed by the number of his cell which was inscribed on a brass badge he wore permanently pinned to his chest. Whenever he left his cell he was obliged to wear a peculiar brown cloth cap to which was attached a mask, completely covering his face. A visitor to Pentonville remarked that the prisoners had a half-spectral appearance:

For the eyes glistening through the apertures in the mask give the notion of a spirit peeping out from behind it, so that there is something positively terrible in the idea that these are men whose crimes have caused their features to be hidden from the world.

The period of time spent at Pentonville was initially between fifteen and twenty-two months, but some men stayed there for a full two years. The routine was always the same except on Sundays. At 6 a.m. the cells were unlocked and the whole prison was scrubbed out. Labour commenced at 6.30 a.m., the principal trades being weaving, mat-making, tailoring, and shoe-making; the majority of the prisoners worked in their own cells with the doors wide open, under the constant surveillance of the warders and instructors. There were short breaks for meals and for letter-writing, all outgoing mail being censored by the governor or the chaplain. Half-an-hour in the morning was spent at exercise, tramping in silence round a quadrangle; and a further half-an-hour at prayers in the chapel, where the prisoners sat in individual stalls, completely hidden from their neighbours, whilst warders on elevated stands kept watch to see that they did not communicate with one another. Work finished at 7 p.m. and the prisoners were then allowed to read library books until 9 p.m. when the lights were extinguished and the cell doors locked. Those who attended classes in the school-room had to sit in compartments similar to those in the chapel, and a small number were allowed to spend part of the time in the communal workshop. There was no labour on a Sunday, but the monotony and the solitude were broken by prolonged church services in the morning and afternoon. Every prisoner was permitted to see his relations or friends in the visiting room for fifteen minutes every three months; later this was varied to twenty minutes every six months.

Most of the disciplinary offences under the separate system consisted of various methods of inter-communication between the prisoners. A certain amount of conversation always occurred in the chapel and on the exercise ground. Sometimes a convict would fling a note into the cell of another as he was passing the door, and elaborate forms of sign-language were devised with the use of the fingers, scraping dinner-cans, or tapping on the dividing walls between the cells; one obvious code which was constantly used was that one scrape or tap represented the letter A, two represented B, three represented C, and so on; it was thus possible for the prisoners to spell out complete words to each other. Some men, it was said, 'accustom themselves to talk without moving their lips, so that they can look a warder full in the face while conversing with their neighbour'. The usual punishment inflicted for communication was a spell in the refractory ward where the prisoner remained in a dark cell on a diet of bread and water. The prison governor was permitted to impose a sentence of three days in the refractory ward and the Governing Board had a jurisdiction extending up to twenty-eight days. Kingsmill, who had himself been a chaplain at Pentonville, wrote, 'I have tried the experiment of a dark cell for a little while during the day, and, allowing for the voluntariness of the confinement, better mental resources, etc., I came out with an increased sense of the terrible nature of the punishment, when at all prolonged.' After visiting Pentonville in 1841 Elizabeth Fry declared that penal dark cells 'should never exist in a Christian and civilized country'. Another form of punishment used in the prison, which was also much-dreaded by the inmates, was depriving a man of his work and keeping him in his cell in a state of complete idleness for the whole day.

Joseph Kingsmill, while eulogizing the separate system,

admitted that almost all the prisoners, while experiencing it, complained of 'great loss of strength'. And another prison chaplain, John Clay, remarked that, 'It took all the starch out of the prisoners' characters and rendered both their wits and their wills limp and flabby.' In spite of this, between 1842 and 1848 no less than fifty-four new prisons on the Pentonville model were completed in Britain, altogether accommodating over 11,000 inmates. With the expansion of the separate system came the introduction of a new form of prison-labour, the crank, which must rank as one of the most useless and soul-destroying methods of employing a prisoner's time that has ever been invented. The crank was described in 1862 as being:

A narrow drum, placed on legs, with a long handle on one side, which on being turned, causes a series of cups or scoops in the interior to revolve. At the lower part of the interior of the machine is a thick layer of sand, which the cups, as they come round, scoop up, and carry to the top of the wheel, where they throw it out and empty themselves, after the principle of a dredging machine. A dial-plate, fixed in front of the iron drum, shows how many revolutions the machine has made.

A crank was usually fixed in a prisoner's cell, so that he might labour on it in silence and in solitude. Every prison settled its own figure for the number of revolutions demanded as a day's work, and failure to fulfil the necessary stint would probably result in disciplinary punishment such as the dark cells or a flogging. Another form of tedious drudgery which was started in the prisons about this time was oakum-picking. A prisoner was presented with a quantity of old rope cut up into lengths, each of which he had to unravel down to its thinnest strands. At the end of the day his pile of threads was collected by a warder and placed on the scales; if it did not attain the minimum weight prescribed by the governor the prisoner was disciplined for his indolence. A third 'reformatory occupation' which became very familiar under the separate system was shot-drill; this was compulsory at many prisons for all men who were not excused on medical grounds. After watching one of these sessions in progress Henry Mayhew declared that it was 'impossible to imagine anything more ingeniously useless than this form of hard labour'. Shot-drill took place in the open, the prisoners being arranged three-deep on three sides of a square with the supervising warder standing at the centre. At one end of the files of prisoners a number of cannon balls were piled in a pyramid; on a word of command from the warder the three men closest to the pyramid took up a cannon ball each and placed these on the ground at their feet. On another word of command they lifted the balls and passed them to the men alongside who in their turn placed them at their own feet. The process was repeated with the balls passing down the ranks in continuous succession, and eventually being built up into another pyramid by the men in the last three files. When all the cannon balls were stacked in their new position the operation was reversed and they were passed back again. The sessions usually lasted, with the pyramids being formed at alternating ends of the lines of prisoners, for over an hour at a time.

There was another system of imprisonment during this period which was tried out in Ireland, and at Birmingham Prison between 1849 and 1851 when Captain Alexander Maconochie was governor there, but which was never adopted elsewhere in Britain. Maconochie, a humane and thoughtful penal reformer, has originally served as Superintendent of Norfolk Island where he had developed the Marks System. The basis of his scheme was a departure from the orthodox form of prison discipline which, he said, attached too much importance to submission and obedience. He wrote later:

I sought generally by every means to recover the man's self-respect, to gain his own goodwill towards his reform, to visit moral offences severely, but to reduce the number that were purely contraventional, to mitigate the penalties attached to these, and then gradually to awaken better and more enlightened feelings among both officers and men.

Under the Mark System the prisoners' disciplinary offences, for the most part, were punished with fines, and instead of obtaining his automatic release after serving a sentence defined in terms of months or years, he was obliged to attain a prescribed number of marks for his good conduct and his dili-gence. A similar theory had been formulated at an earlier date by Archdeacon William Paley, a man whose draconian penal views were otherwise completely alien to those of Captain Maconochie; in 1785 the archdeacon had written, 'I would measure the confinement [of prisoners], not by the duration of time, but by quantity of work, in order both to excite indus-try, and to render it more voluntary.'

The Government were endeavouring, as far as a partially-centralized system of administration would permit, to bring about a greater uniformity in every aspect of prison conditions than had ever existed before. In 1843 the Home Secretary, Sir James Graham, requested the Prison Inspectors to enquire into the standards of feeding in the gaols. In their report they stated their opinion that 'a quantity of food should be given in all cases, which is sufficient, and not more than sufficient, to maintain health and strength, at the least possible cost.' Since there was no consistency in the amount, the type or the quality of the rations supplied in the prisons throughout the country, the Home Office drew up and circulated a diet-sheet meticu-lously setting out the quantities of solid and liquid food which should be allotted to each prisoner every week. The Prison Inspectors, also in 1843, expressed their view that tread-wheel labour could be injurious to health if it was used too indiscriminately; they affirmed that the tread-wheel should never be operated by women, boys under fourteen years of age, the medically unfit, or by prisoners who were not serving specific sentences of hard labour. In 1845 the Govern-ment created the new office of Surveyor-General of Prisons; Colonel (afterwards Sir Joshua) Jebb, who received the first appointment, was to play an important part in the co-ordination of the layout of British prison design.

The project, commenced in 1840, of transporting convicts to Van Diemen's Land soon ran into difficulties. During the first four years over sixteen thousand prisoners were sent out from Britain, about half of whom were later released on ticket-of-leave; unfortunately there was little employment to be obtained on the island and this swarm of idle and penniless exiles were obliged to batten on an economy which was already on the verge of bankruptcy. In 1846 the British Government decided to reconsider the position, and all transportation to Van Diemen's Land was suspended for a period of two years. Once again there seemed to be no alternative to keeping all the convicts, whilst serving their sentences and thereafter, in their own country. The Home Secretary, Sir George Grey, quickly prepared a penal scheme consisting of three stages. In the first stage the convicts would undergo a period of separate confinement in a cellular prison, during which they would receive industrial employment and moral training. The second stage would consist of a spell of hard labour on public works, either at home or overseas; and the third stage was designed, rather optimistically as it turned out, to be an indefinite exile to some British colony on ticket-of-leave. Sir George Grey's scheme was put into effect immediately. There were few suitable prisons for phase one except Pentonville and Millbank, but accommodation was also hired at several provincial gaols including those at Wakefield and Leicester. For phase two, work was commenced without delay on the construction of a harbour of refuge at Portland in Dorset; 1,500 convicts who had been selected for this task were drafted to a specially built prison in the vicinity. During the next few years new prisons were also erected at Portsmouth and Chatham so that convicts could be detailed to work at the busy dockyards in these two towns. In 1850 the disused prison at Dartmoor, originally built in 1806 to accommodate French and German prisoners-of-war, was reconstructed as a modern gaol, and thereafter it formed the base for convicts employed on the waste lands nearby. The conception of phase three completely miscarried owing to the natural reluctance shown by the colonies at the prospect of becoming permanent dumping-grounds for the mother-country's partially reformed criminals; in the event, in reply to a circular letter from the British Government inviting their co-operation in the scheme, only the colony of Western Australia replied in the affirmative. It was as a direct result of this predicament that a form of imprisonment known as 'penal servitude' came into being.

A new statutory body, the Directors of Convict Prisons, was

created in 1850 with Sir Joshua Jebb as its first chairman. This was a move to bring under direct Government control all those establishments which were dealing with prisoners sentenced to terms of transportation. The Directors were to be responsible, firstly for the prisons of separate confinement, which meant at that time Millbank, Pentonville and special sections at eight local prisons; secondly, for prisons accommodating convicts employed on public works, such as Portland and Dartmoor; thirdly, for the hulks; and fourthly, for the juvenile convict prison at Parkhurst in the Isle of Wight. For a few years Sir George Grey's scheme was operated in its original conception with an initial phase of eighteen months' separate confinement – later, for health reasons, this was reduced to twelve months. However, the third, or ticket-of-leave phase, was drastically amended by the Penal Servitude Act, 1853 which stipulated that in the future no convict was to be transported for a term less than fourteen years and, indeed, that even sentences of over fourteen years transportation or transportation for life might be commuted into periods of penal servitude to be served entirely in Britain. A set scale was prescribed for converting transportation sentences into sentences of penal servitude; for instance, between ten and fifteen years transportation would be equivalent to eight years penal servitude; between seven and ten years transportation would become four to six years penal servitude, and so on. The period of penal servitude was always considerably shorter than the term of transportation to allow for the fact that a transported prisoner could have expected to spend the last portion of his sentence on ticket-of-leave in the place of his exile. A term of penal servitude would be divided between the first two stages of the Grey scheme, a period of separate confinement followed by one of labouring in silent association on public works. Having served his term in full, the prisoner would then be released on licence until his original sentence of transportation was finished. The Penal Servitude Act, 1857 eliminated the clumsy procedure for converting transportation into penal servitude, and enabled courts to pass sentences of penal servitude in the first place. A prisoner could be granted a remission for good behaviour of up to one sixth of his full term in the case of any sentence of between three and fifteen years penal servitude, and up to one third of the term for a sentence of fifteen years or more. Prisoners were to be released on licence for unexpired portions of the remitted sentences.

CHAPTER EIGHTEEN

LONDON PRISONS IN THE MID-NINETEENTH CENTURY

'Few prisons in this country are in a satisfactory moral state,' wrote Hepworth Dixon in 1850, 'for the very nature of the institution, so liable to abuses and neglects – to faults of over-severity on one side, and injudicious indulgence on the other – makes it difficult to preserve even the appearance of moral order in them; but such grossness of abuse, such wanton neglect of every chance of doing good, such wicked connivance at corruption, as may be found in some of the London prisons, will probably shock every manly and generous sentiment.' Hepworth Dixon also complained of the paucity of information concerning conditions of the gaols of London which had permeated through to the outside world, and he attributed this to the difficulty of obtaining access to any of them; for no one was allowed to carry out an inspection without a permit signed by a magistrate who happened to be at the time one of the visiting justices to the prison in question. 'Practically,' he said, 'these prohibitions prevent the general public from gaining admission to these gaols, and learning what is going on in them'.

In spite of the difficulty Hepworth Dixon managed to enter several London prisons himself. He found that the Giltspur Street Compter was so overcrowded that the prisoners in some wards barely had room to lie down:

I have seen five persons locked up at four o'clock in the day, to be there confined, in darkness, in idleness, to pass all those hours, to do the offices of nature, not merely in each other's presence, but crushed by the narrowness of their den into a state of filthy contact which brute beasts would have resisted in the last gasp of life.

In the course of his enquiries he visited Newgate which he described as being 'surrounded by high walls, between which a scanty supply of air and light find their way downwards as into a well'. And yet, he was impressed by the grandeur of the building. 'Inside and outside it is equally striking,' he said. 'Massive, dark, and solemn, it arrests the eye and holds it. Of all the London prisons, except the Tower, it alone has an imposing aspect.' Hepworth Dixon was extremely critical of the conditions at Newgate, particularly of the absence of classification among the untried prisoners. He quoted the example of a servant-girl, about sixteen years old, and only recently up from the country, who had been charged by her mistress with the theft of a brooch:

She was in the same room – lived all day and slept all night – with the most abandoned of her sex. They were left alone; they had no work to do; no books – except a few tracts for which they had no taste – to read. The whole day was spent as is usual in such prisons, in telling stories – the gross and guilty stories of their own lives. There is no form of wickedness, no aspect of vice, with which the poor creature's mind would not be compelled to grow familiar in the few weeks she spent in Newgate awaiting trial.

When the girl eventually appeared at the Central Criminal Court the evidence against her was found to be so flimsy that she was acquitted. Hepworth Dixon commented feelingly:

Society can never make reparation to its innocent member for his or her immurement in Newgate. In such a place the heart becomes tainted in spite of itself. Vices undreamt of become familiar to it. The mind must be more than human that can come out of the companionship of Newgate as pure as it entered in.

He was almost as condemnatory about the other City prisons because:

The chief negative features to be seen there – no work, no instruction, no superintendence; the chief positive features – idleness, illicit gaming, filthiness, moral and material disorder, unnatural crowding together, unlimited licence – broken at time by severities at which the sense of justice revolts – and universal corruption of each other.

Hepworth Dickson's impressions of the state of the London prisons under the associated system, formed as an outside

observer, were corroborated by the experiences of one seemingly intelligent prisoner, as recounted to the Reverend
Joseph Kingsmill. This man had been committed in company
with ten others to an unspecified gaol, all charged with different offences – mostly concerned with dishonesty. The party
consisted of both men and women and on their way to prison
they amused themselves by singing obscene songs. 'The persons who drove the van,' he told Kingsmill, 'indulged us by
stopping at every public house on the road.' When the prisoners arrived at the gaol their fetters were removed and they
were all placed in a pen, a kind of dungeon, from which they
were taken out one at a time to be searched and documented.
Kingsmill's informant was then taken to the felon's yard, an
enclosure about twenty yards square and crowded with
people, where a fire was burning. Here he was issued with a
quart wooden pail and a wooden spoon. Presently a bell rang
for prayers, followed by another for supper, which consisted
of a pint of gruel and a half-pound of bread, after which the
prisoners queued up at the pump in the yard to wash their
spoons and pails. The bell rang again, signifying 'prepare for
bed', and the men formed a single line for the evening roll
call; they were then taken inside by the warders, divided up
into groups of eight and locked into cells. 'The bedsteads were
of iron,' said the prisoner, 'each one fastened to the wall with
a long chain. I threw myself on the one I chanced to select
without undressing.' Once the warders had departed the men
began a sing-song which continued until about eleven o'clock,
when one-by-one they dropped off to sleep. Next morning they
were turned out of their cells and taken down into the yard
where the warders supervised their washing – there was, in
fact, a total of only four towels to go round. Breakfast consisted once again of gruel and bread. The day was passed
idling in the association hall. 'I observed a few Bibles and
books on the shelves with some slates,' the prisoner said; 'but
on a closer inspection I found, from the dust that was accumu-
lated on them, that they had not been removed for some
time.' The prisoners spent most of the time crowded around
the fire telling stories in turn. 'Each as he finished would call
upon another prisoner who, if he refused, must forfeit two

potatoes out of his daily allowance.' The monotony of this was only broken by one hour's compulsory walking in the yard. A turnkey, true to the tradition of his trade, approached the prisoner and told him that if there were any little things which he wanted the turnkey would be his 'humble servant'. The prisoner says he replied that 'whether I wanted his assistance or not, I would recompense him. This is what he was waiting to hear.'

After the opening of Holloway Prison in 1852, Newgate Gaol became principally a place of confinement for male and female prisoners awaiting trial at the Central Criminal Court and for those who had been sentenced to death. Ten years previously the City authorities had decided to replace Giltspur Street Compter with a new House of Correction. In 1843 a committee had considered ten possible schemes for the proposed building, one of which was for the enlargement of Newgate. The committee had reported in favour of a prison outside the walls of the City, on a site in Holloway originally purchased by the City Corporation in 1832 for use as a cemetery during a serious epidemic of cholera. It was intended at one stage to close down Newgate completely as soon as Holloway was ready for use, but this proposal was abandoned and the new House of Correction, designed on the Pentonville pattern with 438 separate cells, became a prison solely for men and women serving short sentences.

In the spring of 1857 the Court of Aldermen decided to rebuild Newgate Gaol on the cellular system. In accordance with this plan the whole of the north side of the prison, the part closest to Newgate Street, was demolished; this comprised the oldest surviving section of the gaol, including the condemned cells, the press room, and the dungeon in which Jack Sheppard was said to have been confined. The redesigned block, which was completed in 1859, consisted of 130 cells for male prisoners built in galleries round a central corridor; there were also eleven reception, six punishment, and two condemned cells. In 1861 the women's wing of Newgate was also demolished, the prisoners being temporarily accommodated in Holloway while the work was in progress. A year later the reconstruction was complete, the new

women's section consisting of forty-seven separate cells and a
prison laundry.

After the introduction of Sir George Grey's scheme and the
penal servitude system, convicts from the London area were
sent to Pentonville, Millbank, the Hulks at Woolwich, and
the women's prison in Brixton. These were all under the
control of the Government. The so-called 'Correctional Prisons', to which prisoners were sent if they were serving sentences of two years or less, were the City House of Correction
at Holloway, the Middlesex Houses of Correction at Coldbath
Fields and Tothill Fields, and the Surrey House of Correction at Wandsworth. Men and women in custody awaiting
trial were committed to Newgate, Horsemonger Lane, or the
Middlesex House of Detention at Clerkenwell.

In 1862 Henry Mayhew and John Binny published their
massive volume describing a series of visits they had paid
during the previous few years to all of the prisons in London.
At that time prisoners who had just been sentenced to terms
of transportation or of penal servitude were returned first of
all to the prisons at which they had been held in custody
whilst awaiting trial. As soon as possible after their convictions they were transferred to Millbank to undergo a probationary period of separate confinement. Every inmate of
Millbank, other than those who were excused on medical
grounds, had to spend six months in fairly strict solitude,
during which time they worked twelve hours a day for six
days a week in the privacy of their cells, Sundays being devoted to worship and meditation. During this stage the prisoners were given a certain amount of moral and religious
instruction, and were allowed an hour's exercise daily, which
consisted of walking silently in single file around a gravelled
courtyard. The treadmill had been abandoned at this particular prison and labour comprised oakum-picking, tailoring,
shoemaking and weaving. After six months the prisoners graduated from solitude to silent association, and although the
hours and the type of work remained the same they were
allowed to sleep, to take their meals, and to perform their
labour in one of the large association wards. The principal
form of punishment for disciplinary offences was confinement
for a few hours or a few days in one of the refractory cells, of

which a warder remarked, 'It's impossible to describe the darkness – it's pitch black; no dungeon was ever so dark.' From Millbank the male convicts went on to Pentonville, except for a few who were sent straight to Portsmouth, Portland or to the hulks; women convicts were transferred to Brixton, juvenile males to Parkhurst, and very young girls to the Manor Hall Institution.

Mayhew and Binny watched a party of prisoners arriving at Pentonville from Millbank. They wrote:

> The miserable wretches were chained together by the wrists in lines. Some were habited in the ordinary light, snuff-brown convict suits, and others wore grey jackets, all having Scotch caps and small bundles of Bibles and hymn-books tied in handkerchiefs under their arms. Jackets, trousers, caps and grey stockings were all marked with red stripes.

The object of Pentonville was to form an intermediary stage between Millbank and transportation or hard labour public works; Mayhew and Binny described it as 'a kind of penal purgatory where men are submitted to the chastisement of separate confinement so as to fit them for the afterstate'. Solitude was enforced more strictly at Pentonville than at Millbank and discipline was harsher. The period of rigorous separate confinement generally lasted for nine months from the date of admission.

The female convict prison at Brixton had been enlarged gradually until it was capable of holding between 700 and 800 prisoners. On arrival the women underwent a four-month probationary period of separate confinement; they then advanced into silent associaton when they were allowed to work together without talking. Eventually they reached the stage of association with intercommunication, in which they were permitted to speak to each other at certain times of the day, but they still slept in their individual cells at night. They could gradually gain various privileges with regard to visits, letters, and payment for labour, and might ultimately qualify to be released on ticket-of-leave for the unexpired portion of their sentences. Employment at this prison consisted of shirt-making, hemming, stitching and laundry. The airing yards at Brixton, Mayhew and Binny said, 'have little of the bare gravel playground character, so common with other gaols, for here there are grass-plots and flower-beds, so that, were it not for the series of madhouse-like windows piercing the prison wall, a walk in the exercising grounds of Brixton would be pleasant and unprison-like enough.' After watching some prisoners out walking, they commented:

> It is a somewhat curious and interesting sight to see near upon two hundred female convicts pacing in couples round and round the Brixton exercising yards, and chattering as they go like a large school, so that the yard positively rings, as though it were a market-place, with the gabbling of many tongues.

They found the prisoners' uniform 'simple and picturesque' and remarked that the women 'had none of the repulsive and spectral appearance of the brown masked men at Pentonville, nor had they even the unpleasant grey, pauper look of the male prisoners at Millbank'. Their dress consisted of a loose, dark, claret-brown robe with a blue apron and neckerchief and a white muslin cap.

A Prison Matron, who had been on the staff both at Millbank and Brixton, published an anonymous book of recollections in 1862. Speaking of women prisoners in general she said:

> As a class they are desperately wicked – deceitful, crafty, malicious, lewd, and void of common feeling. In the penal classes of the male prisons there is not one man to match the worst inmates of the female prisons . . . some women are less easy to tame than creatures of the jungle.

Mayhew and Binny, surveying the prisons during a similar period, commented with chivalrous compassion on the ability of these women, no matter how degraded, to perform the highest sacrifices of their lovers:

> The majority of the habitual female criminals are connected with some low brute of a man who is either a prize-fighter, or cab-driver, or private soldier, or pickpocket, or coiner, or costermonger, or indeed, some such character. And for this lazy and ruffian fellow, there is no indignity nor cruelty they will not suffer, no atrocity that they are not ready to commit, and no

infamy that they will hesitate to perform, in order that he may continue to live half-luxuriously with them in their shame.

The Prison Matron described the arrival of a new party of women prisoners at Millbank. When the outer bell was rung, the gate-keeper unlocked and swung open the massive gates and the second gate-keeper unfastened the inner entrance. The prison-van passed through and deposited the prisoners at the reception room where a female officer took the particulars of each woman in turn. Next their hair was cut. 'They weep, beg, pray, occasionally assume a defiant attitude, resist to the last,' the Matron continued, 'and are finally overcome by force.' Sometimes it was even necessary to summon the assistance of male warders to handcuff the struggling prisoners.

The maintenance of discipline in the female wings and the women's prisons was always a major problem. Since the abolition of flogging as a penalty for women in 1820, dark cells, dietary restrictions, and loss of privileges had been the only sanctions which the authorities could impose. 'The dark cells,' said the Prison Matron, 'have been long secretly acknowledged as failures. Confinement in these cells is an objectionable punishment; it affects the prisoner's health; it has never worked any good, and it has done much moral, physical, and even mental injury. It has always appeared, in my eyes, a relic of the old barbarous times.' Prisoners often became violent and hysterical when sentenced to a spell in the dark cells and had to be forcibly removed by male warders. 'The strength of some of these women during their fits of frenzy,' according to the Prison Matron, 'is greatly in excess of the men's. It always required two, very often three, of the guards to force one fighting, plunging woman from her cell into the "dark".' A lot of female prisoners, especially the Irish girls who formed a considerable proportion of the total, were by no means inexperienced in a brawl. Monsieur Simmond, who visited London in 1810–11, has told how the Irish colony there used to indulge in pitched battles every Saturday night, when 'heroes and heroines' showed their prowess at fisticuffs and wrestling. The Prison Matron recounted how one girl, of no great muscular power in appearance, to the delight of her fellows used to rush up to a six-foot warder, 'fling her arms round his capacious waist, lift him bodily from the ground, and run with him a distance of thirty or forty yards'. In addition to their physical aptitude the women prisoners could be ruthless and cunning. She wrote:

The schemes to obtain a place in the infirmary are unceasing. Among them are many instances of self-mutilation, personal damage, and wanton destruction of health, which appear to be regarded as nothing in the balance with a few privileges and a higher scale of diet. A woman will coolly pound a piece of glass to powder, and bring on an internal haemorrhage, nay often bring herself to the dark threshold of death's door, for the mere sake of the change. Bad hands, and arms, and feet will be studiously contrived by means of scissors, a thimble, or a half-penny fastened to the wound; madness will be feigned, stay-laces will be twisted round the neck till respiration almost ceases; women, more desperate still, will run the risk of hanging themselves, in the hope of being cut down in time and taken to the infirmary.

Women who were pregnant were always transferred from Millbank to Brixton when the time for their confinement was approaching, as the latter prison had a special ward accommodating up to twenty mothers with their babies. Formerly the child had remained with its mother until it reached the age of two, when it had been sent out to her relatives or friends, but by 1860 a prisoner was allowed to keep her child with her until she had completed her sentence.

During the year 1841 there had been three 'convicts' serving on the hulks who were less than ten years of age, as well as 213 aged between ten and fifteen, and 958 between fifteen and twenty. In those days there were frequent outbreaks of cholera on board and it was said that the shirts of the prisoners, hung out on the rigging, were 'so black with vermin that the linen positively appeared to have been sprinkled over with pepper'. In 1850 Hepworth Dixon, in a forthright condemnation of the hulks, said, 'the system was continued notwithstanding its disastrous consequences, soon become patent to all the world; and it still flourishes – if that which only stagnates, debases, and corrupts, can be said to flourish.' A considerable reduction in the hulk establishments took place in 1852 after the opening of the Portsmouth Convict Prison. At the time when

Mayhew and Binny carried out their survey there were, in fact, four hulks, a hospital ship, and an invalid depot ship moored at Woolwich, and only one hulk remaining at Portsmouth. Mayhew and Binny commented that the men were herded together on board these ships and they were free to plot and plan as they pleased. They wrote:

Convicts who have undergone the reformatory discipline of Millbank and Pentonville are on the hulks suddenly brought into contact with offenders who have undergone no reformatory discipline whatever. All the care which has been taken at Pentonville and at Millbank to prevent the men talking together, and associating with one another, is thrown away.

Apart from this, they added, if a prisoner had been taught a trade during his period of separate confinement, on his transfer to the hulks 'he has to lay aside the craft that he has only just learnt, and is set to scrape the rust from shells, or else stack timber.'

A correctional prison, or a House of Correction, according to Mayhew and Binny, was a place for 'safe custody, punishment and reformation, to which criminals are committed when sentenced to terms of imprisonment varying from seven days up to two years'. The régime at most of these short-term prisons followed a familiar pattern. The City House of Correction at Holloway operated the separate confinement system for all its prisoners – males, females and juveniles. Seven hours of hard labour was performed each day, and these were interspersed with meals, school, exercise, and services in the chapel. The work consisted of oakum-picking, tread-wheel, tailoring and shoe-making for the men; and oakum-picking, needlework and laundry for the women. Children under fifteen years of age were exempted from every form of hard labour. By a general prison rule extending to this and all similar prisons, two relations or 'respectable friends' were allowed to visit a prisoner, in the presence of a warder, at the end of every three months. The Surrey House of Correction at Wandsworth, opened in 1851, was also a prison for men, women and juveniles; the inmates there passed their time in much the same manner as the inmates of Holloway, except that there was no tread-wheel and extensive use was made of the crank. When Mayhew and Binny visited the dark cells at Wandsworth they saw in one of them a twelve-year-old girl who had been locked up there for forty hours on a diet of bread and water for tearing her clothing. In the course of their inspection they noticed a whipping post in a basement cell at which juveniles could be flogged with a birchen rod on the authority of a visiting magistrate.

In 1850 the justices at the Middlesex quarter sessions had decided to introduce the novel idea of segregating the short-term prisoners in their county between their two existing Houses of Correction. From then on the adult males were sent to Coldbath Fields, while the females and the boys below the age of seventeen went to Tothill Fields. At the time of May-hew and Binny's visit Coldbath Fields was still operating the silent system and they were told that prison-labour was treated as a punishment rather than as a means of industrial training or self-support; in consequence, apart from a very limited amount of tailoring and shoe and mat-making, the prisoners spent their working hours on oakum-picking and shot-drill or at the tread-wheel and the crank. The routine in this prison was extremely arduous and severe; so much so, according to the Deputy-Governor, that at the conclusion of their sentences the prisoners were beyond exhibiting any form of joy or excitement at their impending liberation, but merely 'stood staring stupidly about them, and answered calmly, pre-cisely in the same manner as a day or two since, they had replied to any question put to them by the warders'. Tothill Fields, which was run on the silent system as well, had been rebuilt in 1836 after the style of Jeremy Bentham's panopti-con. The women, most of whom had committed offences concerned with prostitution, slept in cells and dormitories which were very cold and dark during the winter months, and in which they were shut up for twelve hours out of twenty-four. This prison always contained a large number of boys and girls below the age of fourteen. Mayhew and Binny saw a crowd of them picking oakum in an association ward:

It was indeed a melancholy sight to look on children in prison clothes. Some were so young they seemed to need a nurse, rather than a jailer to watch over them; others, again, had such frank and innocent-looking faces, that we could not help fancying they had no business there; whilst others had such shamelessness and cunning painted in their features, that the mind was led insensibly towards fatalism.

They spoke to a girl of eight who was serving a three months sentence for stealing a pair of boots; when they asked her why she had taken them, they received the reply, ' 'cause I hadn't got none of my own'.

In addition to the introduction of segregation amongst their short-term prisoners the Middlesex magistrates had also originated Houses of Detention for those who were still awaiting trial. The foundation-stone of the Clerkenwell House of Detention was laid in 1849 and the prison, containing three hundred separate cells, was opened the following year. Most of the prisoners there were charged with petty offences, as those alleged to have committed more serious crimes were sent to Newgate because of its greater security. The Surrey magistrates followed this lead by converting the immense Horsemonger Lane gaol, on the southern side of Newington Causeway, into a House of Detention for their county; Horsemonger Lane could hold close on 1,500 inmates, a thousand of whom could be accommodated in separate cells.

Mayhew and Binny described their visit to Newgate in great detail. They entered the gaol through a door in the Old Bailey, 'flanked by dark huge masses of stone, forming part of the wall, which is about four feet thick', Inside was another massive oaken door, faced with iron of enormous strength, which was only closed at night. They were shown around by the Deputy-Governor who led them through gloomy passages and ponderous iron-bolted doors to the Bread-Room, where in a cupboard were preserved a collection of ancient fetters, including the leg-irons worn by Jack Sheppard, and 'also a leathern belt about two and a half inches wide for pinioning persons about to be executed'. The bread was kept in another cupboard with a weighing machine, and as the alarm bell was operated from this room a warder slept there every night. They were then taken to the Governor's Office, where there was an arsenal of pistols, muskets, bayonets and cutlasses for use by the officers in the event of a riot. Along

two shelves above the door – another relic of the Newgate of
the past – were three rows of the busts of murderers who had
been executed at the gaol. The Deputy-Governor explained
that they had probably been moulded after death. 'You will
remark,' he said, 'the upper lip of the group is thick, which
might be caused by the process of hanging.'

The male section of Newgate, with its four galleries of cells
surmounted by a glass roof, struck Mayhew and Binny as
presenting 'a very cheerful appearance, very unlike the remaining portion of the old prison'. They inspected one of the
cells, which measured thirteen feet by seven feet and was just
over eight feet high. It contained a small table, folding against
the wall, a shelf for cleaning materials, a three-legged stool,
and 'a copper basin well supplied with water from a water-
tap; on turning the handle of the tap in one direction the
water is discharged into a water-closet, and on turning it the
reverse way it is turned into the copper basin for washing'.
Daylight seeped into the cell through a heavily-barred window, and there was a gas lamp covered with a bright tin
shade, which was lit at a specified time in the evening. Bedding was stacked on three triangular shelves in a corner
every morning and was laid out by the prisoner on the asphalt
floor every night. The cells in the female wing of Newgate
were very similar to those in the male section; however, they
faced to the south and east and Mayhew and Binny declared
that they were 'more gloomy and lonely in appearance than
[those] in any other prison we have visited – partly caused by
the overhanging clouds of smoke which loom over the City,
and partly by the sombre lofty surrounding walls of the prison'. The refractory cells for both men and women were in
the basement. They were about the same size as the ordinary
cells but had stone floors and were sparsely furnished with a
wooden bench, which also served as a bed, and a chamber-pot.
'When shut,' said Mayhew and Binny, 'they not only exclude
a single beam of light, but they do not admit the slightest
sound.'

There were six association rooms in Newgate, four for
males and two for females, in which some of the prisoners
still slept. The chapel had been retained from the past, and
so had the exercise yards, four of which were allocated to men

and one to women. The laundry in the new female wing contained two large coppers and six washing-boxes; four women prisoners were constantly employed there to do the washing and ironing for the whole gaol. Mayhew and Binny were also shown round the infirmaries and the solicitors room, in which those awaiting trial might confer with their legal representatives. There were still no facilities for private visiting by relatives and friends; in the male section, the prisoners had to stand in a long, narrow cage running across an exercise yard, flanked on either side by two iron-grated railings about four feet apart, whilst their visitors were allowed to speak to them from either side of the outer rail. In the female wing the position was reversed, the visitors standing inside, and the prisoners outside the cage, with prison officers patrolling the space between the two gratings.

During the year 1860 a total of 1,059 males and 277 females had passed through Newgate, out of which nine boys and six girls were less than twelve years old, and forty-three boys and five girls were aged between twelve and sixteen. Prison uniform was issued to those of all ages when it was available; this comprised for males, a dark grey jacket, vest and trousers and a Scotch cap, and for women, a blue gown, blue check apron and neckerchief, and a white cap. Mayhew and Binny saw a party of felons marching round an exercise yard in their own 'miserable, poverty-stricken attire'. In the boys' yard, a narrow court adjoining the condemned cells, there were also a number of prisoners dressed in their own clothing. They were told that one youth, wearing 'a shabby black dress', was charged with attempted suicide, and another, 'a pale-faced, knock-kneed lad of about fourteen years of age, with a very sinister look', who was dressed in dark clothes, was to be tried for a forgery offence. The regulation costume was worn by almost every inmate of the female wing, where, said Mayhew and Binny, 'most of the prisoners were ordinary-looking people, charged with common offences.'

CHAPTER NINETEEN

A POLICY OF DETERRENCE

When Captain Alexander Maconochie became Governor of Birmingham Prison in 1849 he obtained permission from the local justices to introduce the Marks System which he had operated so successfully during his term as Superintendent of Norfolk Island. Later, however, the justices had complained that the discipline in the prison was becoming unduly lax and had transferred a large part of the control to the Deputy-Governor, Lieutenant Austin, a man who believed that prisoners should be treated with the utmost severity. It must have been obvious that two persons with such widely differing views would find it impossible to co-operate in this sort of joint-administration and in 1851 Maconochie was dismissed, Austin receiving the appointment of Governor in his place. During the following year there were a succession of disquieting rumours about the oppression and brutality to which Austin was subjecting his prisoners and eventually, after a fifteen-year-old youth had committed suicide by hanging himself in his cell, a Royal Commission was set up to investigate the conditions in the prison. The Commission published its report in 1854. They found that Austin had practised deliberate cruelties upon the prisoners. Whippings had been savage and prolonged, two boys in particular being sentenced to receive a beating every day; an especially arduous type of crank, invented in Leicester Prison, had been used habitually at Birmingham and any prisoner who had failed to complete his stint upon it had been left in the crank cell all night without any food; and a form of strait-jacket had been employed on violent or hysterical prisoners which the Commission described as 'an engine of positive torture'. They concluded by finding that Austin had shewn 'a lamentable indifference to human suffering, until the penal system of the gaol became almost a uniform system of the application of pain and terror'. The relevations aroused an outburst of general indignation in consequence of which Austin was prosecuted and sentenced to three months imprisonment. A further report, dealing with the conditions at Leicester Prison, was published by the Commission a short while later. They stated that discipline in this gaol was also too severe and they condemned a custom there by which the prisoners had to qualify for their eligibility to receive every meal by performing a set, and usually excessive, number of revolutions on the crank.

The reports on conditions at the Birmingham and Leicester prisons strengthened the growing belief that all the gaols in Britain should be brought under centralized Governmental control, but no immediate steps were taken to bring about this much-needed reform. During the early 1860's there was an appreciable hardening of public opinion towards the criminal, brought about by a wave of crime which swept the whole country; London was affected particularly by an outbreak of robberies with violence in which gangs of professional garotters half-strangled their victims to render them incapable of resistance. Not only was there a sudden demand for the sterner punishment of offenders, but there were many who began to question the advisability of returning to freedom so many ticket-of-leave convicts who, they alleged, were neither adequately reformed nor properly purged of their crimes. In 1863 the House of Lords appointed a Select Committee on prison discipline under the chairmanship of Lord Carnarvon, whose recommendations marked the eve of an era in which prisoners were to suffer conditions even more rigorous than before, and in which separate confinement was acknowledged to be, not a curative and cleansing process, but a grim and sustained punishment.

The Carnarvon Committee declared unequivocally:

The system generally known as the separate system must now be accepted as the foundation of prison discipline, and that its rigid maintenance is a vital principle to the efficiency of county and borough gaols. The Committee are of the opinion that the principle of separation should be made to pervade the entire system of the prison, and no adequate reason has been assigned for the relaxation of the rule in school, in chapel and at exercise.

The underlying theme of the report was the need for deterrence. 'Penal servitude,' said the Committee, 'appears not to be sufficiently dreaded either by those who have undergone it, or by the criminal class in general.' They did not accept that the moral reformation of the offender should hold a primary place in the concept of imprisonment:

The Committee fully admits that it forms part of a sound penal system, but they are satisfied that, in the interests of society and the criminal himself, it is essential that the other means employed for the reformation of offenders should always be accompanied by due and effective punishment.

According to their formula, a prison régime should be based on the components of solitude and toil, and they urged that there should be a statutory definition of the term 'hard labour'. Of the various types of labour then applied in British gaols they considered that the tread-wheel, the crank and shot-drill were the most appropriate. 'Of these,' they said, 'the tread-wheel and the crank form the principal elements of penal discipline;' industrial work, though it might vary in amount and character, was 'so much less penal, irksome and fatiguing, that it can only be classed under the head of light labour'. On the other hand they thought it important that prisoners should graduate by stages from 'the penal and disciplinary labour of the tread-wheel, crank, or shot-drill, into the higher and less irksome forms of employment'. For offences committed in prison the Committee considered that the best penalty would be 'degradation from a higher to a lower and more penal class, combined with harder labour and a more sparing diet'. They also recommended solitary confinement in a dark cell, 'but where the offender is hardened, and the offence deliberately repeated, corporal punishment is the most effective, and sometimes the only remedy.'

Both the spirit and the substance of the Carnarvon Committee proposals were embodied in the Prison Act of 1865. In the first place, this statute enforced the separate system throughout Britain by providing that in any prison where criminal prisoners where confined, 'such prisoners shall be

H

prevented from holding any communication with each other, either by every prisoner being kept in a separate cell by day and by night except when he is at chapel or taking exercise, or by every prisoner being confined by night in his cell and being subjected to such superintendence during the day as will prevent his communicating with any other prisoner.' Hard Labour, which was officially defined for the first time, was divided into two classes. The first class was deliberately devised to be tiring, monotonous and distasteful, and consisted of the tread-wheel, the crank, shot-drill, the capstan, stone-breaking 'or such other like description of hard bodily labour', with the proviso that no prisoner should be placed upon the tread-wheel without the prior consent of a Medical Officer. The second class, although termed rather vaguely as 'such other description of bodily labour as may be appointed', was intended to be less onerous and less punitive than the first class; it was laid down that every prisoner aged sixteen or over should serve the first three months of his sentence doing first class hard labour before becoming eligible for graduation to the second class.

The 1865 Act was designed to make imprisonment more uncomfortable, and to place greater emphasis upon deterrence than on education or moral reform. For example, hammocks were immediately removed from prison cells to be replaced by bare wooden beds; the use of chains, irons, and other methods of restraint was officially approved for troublesome prisoners; and prison governors were empowered to punish disciplinary offences with up to three days and three nights solitary confinement in a dark cell on a diet of bread and water, whereas visiting justices could impose a similar penalty for a duration of one month, or could order a flogging if they thought it necessary. However, as well as its more draconian clauses, the statute did introduce a number of beneficial measures. It was provided that every prison should henceforth employ a Medical Officer and an Anglican Chaplain on its regular staff. Arrangements were to be made for payments to prisoners out of public funds when they were discharged at the end of their sentences. The old, anomalous distinction between ordinary gaols and Houses of Correction was abolished, and a universal code of regulations was authorized for every prison in the country. Above all, a major step was taken towards the centralization of control by granting the Home Secretary the right of withholding grants-in-aid to any prisons which did not comply with the mandatory provisions of the Act. As a result, a number of smaller gaols closed down because they were unable to meet the cost of the new statutory requirements.

Meanwhile the transportation system was coming to an end. Although no woman had been transported since 1852, men and boys were still being shipped to Western Australia during the early 1860s, amidst the mounting resentment of the local population. In 1861 out of 2,678 prisoners sentenced to penal servitude by courts in Britain, 306 suffered transportation: in 1862 a total of 3,369 prisoners received sentences of penal servitude and 782 of these were transported. But the stream of protests, petitions and memorials could not be indefinitely ignored by the Government; in 1867 the last convict ship set sail for the shores of Western Australia and thereafter the whole ill-fated system of transportation disappeared irrevocably from the British penal code.

A public hanging outside the walls of Newgate Gaol still featured as one of the most popular spectacles in London. Executions generally took place at eight o'clock on a Monday morning, the workmen having erected the portable scaffold during the previous night. On the Sunday evening, said Hepworth Dixon:

> The low taverns and beer-houses about Newgate Street, Smithfield, and the Fleet district are gorged with company, who sally out at intervals to see how the workmen get on with the preparations for the morrow, and to have a brush with the police who are on duty in great force. Knots of queer-looking fellows form here and there, and in their own slang phrases discuss their plans; for an execution is as good as a Lord Mayor's Show for the race of pickpockets. And in this way the time wears on till morning.

Mayhew and Binny wrote, 'The crowd generally musters on the Sabbath evening at eight o'clock, and increases during the night, consisting, to a certain extent, of boys and girls. The greater portion of the spectators assemble between six and seven o'clock.' Just before the execution was to take place, and while the condemned prisoner was still in his cell, the bell of St Sepulchre's Church began to toll the service of the dead, and then on the first stroke of the prison bell he was led from the gaol to mount the scaffold. The Deputy-Governor of Newgate, who had witnessed twenty-nine hangings, commented in 1861:

I find the murderers to be of different characters. Some are callous and ruffian-like in demeanour, but others are of more gentle and peaceable disposition, whom you heartily pity, as you are convinced from all you see about them, that they had been incited to the commission of their crime through intemperance or other incidental causes, foreign to their general character.

The corpse of an executed criminal was left to hang for an hour before being cut down and placed in a coffin which was then carried into the gaol. A formal examination was made by the Medical Officer, in the presence of the sheriffs, to ensure that life was extinct. Prior to the burial, which took place later in the day in the Newgate cemetery, a cast was usually taken of the dead prisoner's head and face.

In July 1840 two celebrated novelists, Dickens and Thackeray, had stood outside Newgate and watched the hanging of the Swiss valet François Courvoisier who had been sentenced to death for the murder of his elderly employer Lord William Russell. Courvoisier's trial had aroused a great deal of interest as his victim was the uncle of a Cabinet Minister, and it has been estimated that as many as 40,000 people turned out to witness his execution. During the following month Thackeray described the scene in an article in *Fraser's Magazine*:

I feel myself ashamed and degraded at the brutal curiosity which took me to that brutal sight. It seems to me that I have been abetting an act of frightful wickedness and violence, performed by a set of men against one of their fellows.

It was not until 1846 that Charles Dickens, in the course of his campaign against capital punishment, set out his own impressions of Courvoisier's execution in a letter published in the *Daily News*. He said:

I was, purposely, on the spot, from midnight of the night before;
and was a near witness of the whole process of the building of the
scaffold, the gathering of the crowd, the gradual swelling of the
concourse with the coming-on of day, the hanging of the man, the
cutting of the body down, and the removal of it into the prison.
From the moment of my arrival, when there were but a few score
boys in the street, and those all young thieves, and all clustered
together behind the barrier nearest to the drop – down to the time
when I saw the body with its dangling head, being carried on a
wooden bier into the gaol – I did not see one token in all the
immense crowd; at the windows, in the streets, on the house-tops,
anywhere; of any one emotion suitable to the occasion. No sorrow,
no salutary terror, no abhorrence, no seriousness; nothing but
ribaldry, debauchery, levity, drunkenness, and flaunting vice in
fifty other shapes. I should have deemed it impossible that I could
have ever felt any large assemblage of my fellow-creatures to be
so odious. I hoped, for an instant, that there was some sense of
Death and Eternity in the cry of 'Hats off!' when the miserable
wretch appeared; but I found, next moment, that they only raised
it as they would at a Play – to see the stage the better, in the final
scene.

Of the effect upon a perfectly different class, I can speak with no
less confidence. There were, with me, some gentlemen of education and distinction in imaginative pursuits, who had, as I had,
a particular detestation of that murderer; not only for the cruel
deed he had done, but for his slow and subtle treachery, and for
his wicked defence. And yet, if any one among us could have saved
the man (we said so, afterwards, with one accord), he would have
done it. It was so loathsome, pitiful, and vile a sight, that the law
appeared to be as bad as he, or worse; being very much the
stronger, and shedding around it a far more dismal contagion.

When a murderer whose crime had been committed out-
side London or Middlesex was sentenced to death at the Old
Bailey he was transferred from Newgate to the appropriate
county gaol for his execution. If the murder had been in
Kent, the hanging took place at Maidstone, if it had been
committed in Essex it was at Chelmsford, and if in Surrey, at
Horsemonger Lane prison. In November 1849 Dickens wit-
nessed the execution at Horsemonger Lane of Mr and Mrs
Manning, who had been condemned to death at the Old
Bailey for the murder of their lodger Patrick O'Connor.
Again the repulsive spectacle was witnessed by a huge, unruly

mob, and Dickens had long been haunted, as he later confessed, by the memory of 'those two forms dangling at the top of the entrance gateway – the man's limp, loose suit of clothes as if the man had gone out of them; the woman's fine shape, so elaborately corseted and artfully dressed, that it was unchanged in its trim appearance as it slowly swung from side to side.'

During the week following the double hanging Dickens published two letters in the *Times*; this time he was advocating, not the total abolition of capital punishment, but the cessation of public executions. The *Times* replied to his arguments in a leading article, stating their opinion that the mystery of private executions would be intolerable as the populace must be able to see that the rich as well as the poor murderers were really hanged. To meet this criticism Dickens suggested that a special 'witness jury', comprising twenty-four persons drawn from all classes of society, should be summoned to attend at every private execution.

William Ewart, a radical Member of Parliament, had attempted unsuccessfully in the House of Commons in 1840 to secure the total abolition of the death penalty. However, in the ensuing years the campaign against public hangings had slowly gathered momentum, with the support of a group of well-known authors and the consistent backing, rather incongruously, of the pages of *Punch* – mainly through the influence of the writer Douglas Jerrold. In 1856 the Commons accepted the findings of a Select Committee which had declared in favour of private execution, but this proposal was rejected by the House of Lords. The matter was referred to a Royal Commission in 1864, a year in which the *Times* altered its policy and began to support the views which Dickens had expressed in its columns fifteen years before. The Royal Commission on Capital Punishment, after hearing witnesses of widely-differing opinions, eventually recommended that all future executions should be carried out inside a prison, 'under such regulations as might be considered necessary to prevent abuses, and to satisfy the public that the law had been complied with'. A Bill to abolish public executions received its first reading in March, 1866 and passed into law in the summer in 1868. The Home Office immediately circulated all prison governors with a list of rules for the procedure at private hangings. It was suggested they should be timed for eight o'clock in the morning, 'on the first day after the intervention of three Sundays from the day on which sentence is passed'. The prison bell, or the bell of a neighbouring church, was to toll for fifteen minutes before and fifteen minutes after the execution, and a black flag was to be flown conspicuously over the prison for a period of one hour following the death of the condemned prisoner. Apart from these requirements, 'the mode of execution, and the ceremonies attending it [were] to be the same as heretofore in use. The last public hanging in front of Newgate took place on 26 May, 1868 when Michael Barrett, a Fenian, was executed for causing a bomb explosion at Clerkenwell prison. A gallows shed was then built inside the walls of the gaol, adjacent to the chapel and at the end of a passage leading from the condemned cells. It was first used on 8 September 1868, the victim being a man called Alexander Mackay, who had been sentenced to death for the murder of his mistress.

The Prison Act of 1865 had directed that prisoners for debt should be separated from prisoners for crime; but as long as these two different categories of inmate were housed together in the same gaols there could be no absolute uniformity of treatment, as the debtors were allowed to have food, tobacco and other articles sent in to them from outside and were, of course, exempted from compulsory labour. Not that prisoners for debt were in a particularly favourable position as they continued to be treated with excessive neglect. In 1869 an Act of Parliament abolished imprisonment for debt, thus erasing from the British judicial process one of its harshest and most illogical features. After 1869 debtors could only be committed to prison for contempt of court, or for wilfully refusing to comply with an order for payment made by the justices.

During the next fifteen years after the 1865 statute it became apparent that its provisions were not bringing about the uniformity in prison conditions which had been desired. It was not sufficient that the Inspectors were carrying out routine checks and that government grants were conditional on the receipt of their satisfactory reports; certain extensive varieties in practice were still permissable under the regulations. Each gaol was entitled to set its own limits for the number of feet a prisoner must climb to constitute his stint on the tread-wheel; there were appreciable differences between the amounts and the standards of food; and every local authority could use its own discretion with regard to extent and severity in its application of hard labour. An equally cogent reason for absolute national control of prisons was that whilst they were under the semi-autonomous administration of the local justices there was no co-ordinated distribution of gaol accommodation throughout the country; as a consequence, some prisons were hopelessly overcrowded and others were almost empty. In 1874 a Government came into power which was pledged to reduce the county rates. At this time there were more than a hundred local gaols, many of which fell considerably below the standards prescribed by Parliament, and it was estimated that by closing down some of the older ones and reallocating the prison population on a centrally-organized basis about £500,000 a year could be saved in administrative expenses. Accordingly, a Bill was introduced in the House of Commons for the purpose of bringing the entire prison system under the direct control of the Home Office. The measure was bitterly criticized in some sections of the press as being 'a gigantic and almost unparalleled centralization' and a 'distinct slur upon local government'; it also encountered a certain amount of parliamentary opposition, but it finally passed into law in 1877.

The Prison Act of 1877 was a milestone in British penal history, as it vested the control of all the gaols in the country in a body of five Prison Commissioners, who were to be appointed by, and responsible to the Home Secretary. These officials were given authority to close down all the gaols which they considered to be superfluous, and they decided immediately to discontinue the use of no less than thirty-eight out of the existing 113 local prisons; within five years the total number of prisons remaining open had been further reduced to sixty-seven. The Commissioners were also empowered to establish a single, universally-applicable code of prison discipline, and to bring about a uniform standard of conditions in every gaol. The first Chairman of the Prison Commissioners,

Colonel (later Sir Edmund) Du Cane, Royal Engineers, was a man of set and rigid beliefs who succeeded, during his eighteen years of office, in moulding the British system of imprisonment to his own inflexible concepts. Du Cane may have been an austere and insensitive autocrat, but he was, at the same time, a most efficient administrator. He compelled prison governors to keep proper accounts; he standardized the hours of work and the rates of payment for all members of prison staffs; he introduced a uniform scale of diet and labour for prisoners; he improved sanitary and hygienic arrangements, reformed hospital and nursing facilities, rationalized spending, and he obliged every prison to operate, so far as possible, as a self-contained, economic unit.

In spite of the benefits which it produced the Du Cane régime is principally remembered for its severity, its nihilism, and its implacable emphasis on a policy of deterrence. There were two types of penal detention at that time – an ordinary prison sentence which could last up to two years, and a sentence of penal servitude which could be for any period from five years to life. The scheme of imprisonment for both sorts of sentence was the same and was planned almost entirely in accordance with the recommendations of the Carnarvon Committee. Every prisoner was confined in a solitary cell and the rule against communication was strictly enforced. On the reformatory aspect of isolation Du Cane wrote:

The mind is thrown in upon itself. During this time [the prisoner] becomes open to lessons of admonition and warning; religious influences have full opportunity of obtaining access to him; he is put in that condition when he is likely to feel sorrow for the past and to welcome the words of those who show him how to avoid evil for the future.

Prison food during this era was intentionally meagre and plain. Prison labour, which consisted mainly of oakum-picking, the crank and the tread-wheel, was designed to be tedious, useless and exhausting. 'I believe that the penal element is so necessary,' Du Cane explained, 'that the feeling of degradation I must place altogether on one side of my mind.' Nevertheless, he acknowledged that this type of drudgery was apt to be 'decidedly brutalizing' in its consequences. 'To men of intelligence it is irritating, depressing and debasing to the mental faculties; to those already of a low type, it is too comfortable to the state of mind out of which it is desirable they should be raised.' Some effort was made to counteract these tendencies by the adoption of a marks system based on the scheme which had been put forward by Captain Maconochie. The prisoner's sentence was divided into four stages. During the first stage, which lasted for at least a month, he slept on a plank bed without a mattress and worked for ten hours a day. In the second stage he was allowed a mattress on five nights each week; he was employed at slightly less onerous labour; he was entitled to take exercise every Sunday, to receive a limited amount of school instruction, and to study educational books in his cell. When the prisoner had earned sufficient marks in the second stage he qualified for the third, during which he was issued with a mattress on six nights of the week, he did easier and more interesting work such as tailoring, shoe and basket-making, book-binding or printing, and he was permitted to read books from the prison library. In the fourth and final stage he became eligible for employment in an office of trust in the service of the prison, he could sleep on a mattress every night, and he was entitled to write and receive a letter and to see a visitor every three months. During the second, third and fourth stages the prisoner could earn small cash gratuities. These stages were the same whatever the age or the sex of the prisoner, except that females, youths under sixteen, and men of over sixty had mattresses every night throughout their sentences. The basic purpose of his system, said Sir Edmund Du Cane, 'was that of setting before the prisoners the advantages of good conduct and industry by enabling them to gain certain privileges and modifications of the penal character of the sentence by the exertion of these qualities. Commencing with severe penal labour – hard fare and a hard bed – he can gradually advance to more interesting employment, somewhat more material comfort, full use of library books, the privilege of communicating by letter and word with friends, finally the advantage of a moderate sum of money to start again on discharge.'

Like all the other prisons in Britain Newgate passed into

the control of the Government in 1877, but it was hardly affected by the changes brought about under the Du Cane régime. Despite its continued operational role the ancient gaol had come to be regarded by the public as a sort of penal museum and it was visited every week by crowds of fascinated sightseers. In 1873 the *Illustrated London News* had published a series of articles entitled *Sketches in Newgate,* and had stated by way of introduction, 'The prison is a stern and necessary reality in our civilization. It is one which we cannot refuse to contemplate, though it is unpleasing as a spectacle and in the feelings associated with it.' In subsequent issues the journal proceeded to conduct its readers on a descriptive tour of the gaol, pausing in the entrance hall to inspect the collection of plaster-casts of executed criminals – an exhibition which, they thought, should now be discontinued. They inspected the exercise yards, the soup kitchen, the workshop and the attorney's consulting room; and they explained the structure of the Newgate flogging-box which seemed to be 'a combination of the principle of the pillory with that of the stocks, as the hands are held fast in an erect frame before the patient's face, while his legs are secured in two holes in the lid of a wooden box, where he stands during the process of manual expostulation, applied by means of a nine-lashed scourge, or a birchen rod for boys'. These articles revealed very little about the daily lives of the prisoners at this period, except that 'they rise at six o'clock in the morning, and go to rest at eight in the evening; and most of them being untried, have no labour imposed on them while in this prison. They are not permitted to converse with each other when they meet in the exercise-yards.' After a prisoner had been convicted during the few days before he was transferred to another prison, he was 'required to pick a certain daily quantity of oakum – that is old ships' rope and cordage – three pounds of which must be reduced to fine soft tow by the bare fingers of each man before he lays down to rest; while the women are commonly employed in laundry work'.

During the winter of 1881 it was decided, in the interests of economy, that for the future Newgate would only be used when there was a session in progress at the Old Bailey. This gave rise to a widespread report that the gaol was about to close down completely. On 3 January 1881 the Under-Secretary of State at the Home Office sent a letter to the Common Serjeant, partly to refute the rumour and partly to outline the new arrangements. 'There appears to be a great deal of misapprehension abroad,' he said, 'with regard to the real intentions of the Government as to the future of Newgate prison.' From then on prisoners for trial at the Central Criminal Court would be committed to Clerkenwell, and Newgate would be temporarily unoccupied. At the commencement of the sessions the prisoners would be transferred to Newgate and kept there until after their trials. 'I am to add,' he concluded, 'that there is no intention of pulling down, or of altering the present buildings.'

CHAPTER TWENTY

THE DEMOLITION OF NEWGATE

The final closure of Newgate Gaol and the termination of the Du Cane régime coincided within a matter of a few years. In 1894 the Government set up a Departmental Committee under the chairmanship of Mr Herbert (later Lord) Gladstone to conduct a thorough enquiry into the state of the prison system. The Committee examined many witnesses, out of whom two men in particular made a deep impression on its members because of their especial experience. The first of these was a Colonel Baker of the Salvation Army, who had assisted many ex-convicts immediately after their discharge from prison. 'I should like to say,' he stated, 'that we find a greater number of them incapable of pursuing any ordinary occupation. They are mentally weak and wasted, requiring careful treatment for months.' The second was Sir Godfrey Lushington, Permanent Under-Secretary at the Home Office, who in one dialectical passage of his evidence not only criticized the Du Cane system but threw considerable doubt upon the entire concept of remedial imprisonment. He said:

I regard as unfavourable to reformation the status of a prisoner throughout his whole career; the crushing of self-respect, the starving of all moral instinct he may possess; the absence of all opportunity to do or receive a kindness; the continual association with none but criminals; the forced labour and the denial of liberty. I believe the true mode of reforming a man, or restoring him to society, is exactly in the opposite direction to all these. But, of course, this is a mere idea. It is quite impracticable in prison. In fact, the unfavourable features I have mentioned are quite inseparable from prison life.

The Gladstone Committee's report was published in 1895; whilst it praised Du Cane's administrative achievements in the prisons, it totally condemned the basic features of his scheme. They said:

The great, and as we consider, the proved danger of this highly centralized system has been and is that while much attention has been given to the organisation, finance, order, health of the prisoners, and prison statistics, the prisoners have been treated too much as a hopeless and worthless element in the community, and the moral as well as the legal responsibilities of the Prison Authorities have been held to cease when they pass out of the prison gates.

The Committee disagreed with Sir Godfrey Lushington's view that reformatory influences were incompatible with imprisonment. They stated:

We think that the system should be made more elastic, more capable of being adapted to special cases of individual prisoners; that prison discipline and treatment should be more effectually designed to maintain, stimulate or awaken the higher susceptibilities of prisoners, to develop their moral instincts, to train them in orderly and industrial habits, and wherever possible to turn them out of prison better men and women physically and mentally than when they came in.

Apart from their more visionary notions the Gladstone Committee made a series of specific proposals aimed at mitigating the excessive severity of prison conditions and fostering a climate in which, they believed, the incidence of moral reformation would be increased. They doubted the wisdom of separate confinement and the 'terrible ordeal' of enforced silence. They recommended that useless penal drudgery, such as the tread-wheel and the crank, should be abolished and that productive labour and technical instruction should gradually be extended; that habitual criminals should be separated from other offenders; that prisoners should be allowed more books and longer periods for reading in their cells; and that there should be increased educational facilities, more prison visits from friends or relations, and a more varied prison diet.

Sir Edmund Du Cane retired immediately after the publication of the Gladstone Committee's report and Herbert Asquith, the Home Secretary, appointed Sir Evelyn Ruggles-Brise as his successor, with instructions to implement the Committee's proposals in every way possible. By dint of the

Prison Act of 1898 and a new set of prison regulations introduced the year after Sir Evelyn set about this assignment. He
retained the period of solitude at the commencement of every
prison sentence, but purely as a form of punishment. He
wrote later:

The public enquiry of 1894 into prison administration was a
practical condemnation of the separate or cellular system, except
for short periods. It swept aside the old-fashioned idea that
separate confinement was desirable on the ground that it enables
the prisoner to meditate on his misdeeds.

Instead, a prisoner was to serve the first six months in
isolation if sentenced to penal servitude, and the first month
if he had received an ordinary sentence of imprisonment,
followed by graduation to labour in association. The tread-
wheel and the crank were to be phased out and replaced by
productive and industrial employment. Every prisoner was to
have the opportunity of earning remission of his sentence by
good conduct. Classification of prisoners was to be made more
effective; first offenders were to be separated from habitual
criminals, and young prisoners from adults. And corporal
punishment for prison offences was only to be awarded in
cases of mutiny, incitement to mutiny or gross violence to a
prison officer.

However, Newgate was not destined to partake in this
ameliorated penal era. By the turn of the century a final,
irrevocable decision had been taken to pull down the
medieval gaol and to utilize the site for the erection of a
larger and more impressive Central Criminal Court. Newgate
continued to fascinate the public to the end. In July 1900 the
Sphere published an illustrated article describing the origins
of the gaol and saying that it was soon to be demolished. 'This
is not to be regretted,' the journal commented, 'for its history
is of the most unsavoury order.' Prisoners were, in fact,
accommodated at Newgate until the early months of 1902,
and the execution shed was last used on 2 May of that year
when a man named George Woolfe was hanged for murder.
The work of demolition commenced on the afternoon of 15
August 1902. The following day the *Daily Mail* gave a short

and whimsical account of what had taken place. Their reporter wrote:

Just below the statue of liberty at a quarter past three o'clock, a piece of stone about the size of a foot fell on the pavement, and a hand with a chisel in it was seen working away in the breach. A little crowd soon gathered to watch the operations. The old pigeons, rough and grimy as the prison itself compared with the other flocks in London, fluttered about the statue, evidently talking over the event with much excitement. The doom of the gaol was being carried out at last.

On 7 February 1903 the City Press described a sale of the relics of Newgate Gaol which had taken place a few days earlier, 'within the gloomy precincts of crime-stricken Newgate', and attended by crowds 'of the curious and the speculative who were naturally attracted to the fortress prison site'. The toll bell was sold for one hundred pounds and the flagstaff, on which a black flag used to be flown after an execution, fetched eleven and a half guineas. 'The appointments of the condemned cells, both male and female, realised fairly good prices,' said the report, 'the former in particular;' the equipment of the execution shed sold for five pounds fifteen shillings, and the plaster casts of hanged criminals for five pounds each. Other items disposed of included the chapel pulpit, 'the famous oak and iron-cased, half-latticed door, associated with Mrs. Fry', 'the old massive oak and iron-bound main entrance door', and a large number of copper washing-bowls. Most of the buyers were probably attracted by the morbid association of the various objects, but one Scottish gentleman had a more practical purpose and purchased the staunch iron gates of the gaol to have them re-erected at the entrance of his estate in Bishopton, Renfrewshire. 'Altogether,' concluded the City Press, 'it was a sale in which monotony and curiosity singularly intermingled and, withal, one to be remembered by those who happened to be present.'

The disappearance of Newgate Gaol at such a time might have seemed to symbolize an absolute abandonment of all the prison policies of the past. But in reality time was to prove that the Gladstone Committee had failed to solve a number of fundamental problems. If a prison sentence was to be partially-punitive and partially-reclamatory how could these two components be co-ordinated, or even reconciled with one another? To what extent might the conditions of confinement be improved without neutralizing the deterrent effect of imprisonment? And finally, what practical methods were possible to bring about the moral reformation of the average criminal? These are questions to which we have still discovered no satisfactory answers.

ACKNOWLEDGEMENTS

I would like to express my deepest gratitude to Mr Philip E. Jones, lately Deputy Keeper of the Records at the Corporation of London Records Office, and also to his successor, Miss Betty R. Masters. No trouble has been too much for either in advising me where to find material about Newgate Gaol and the other City of London prisons, and I am indebted to them for their great assistance and encouragement when I was writing this book.

I would like to thank as well Mr Leslie Boyd, Clerk of the Court at the Central Criminal Court, Mr Philip Bean, Cropwood Fellow of the Institute of Criminology, University of Cambridge, and Mr Ronald Ryall, all of whom have given me valuable advice. The task of carrying out the necessary research has been considerably simplified by the kindness and help I have received from the staffs at the London Library and the Reading Room of the British Museum.

BIBLIOGRAPHY

Bibliographical sources include:

ANGELO, Henry, *Reminiscences of Henry Angelo*, London, Kegan Paul & Co., 1904

ANTAL, Frederick, *Hogarth and his Place in European Art*, London, Routledge & Kegan Paul, 1962

BENTHAM, Jeremy, *The Works of Jeremy Bentham* (edited by John Bowring), Edinburgh, William Tait, 1843

BLACKSTONE, Sir William, *Commentaries on the Laws of England*, London, John Murray, 1876

BOSWELL, James, *The Life of Samuel Johnson* (edited by George Birbeck Hill), Oxford, The Clarendon Press, 1887
    Boswell's London Journal 1762-73, London, William Heinemann, 1950

BUXTON, Thomas Fowell, *An Enquiry whether Crime and Misery are Produced or Prevented by our Present System of Prison Discipline*, London, 1818
    The Substance of the Speech of Thos. Fowell Buxton Esq. M.P. in the House of Commons, March 2nd, 1819, London, 1819
    Memoirs of Sir Thomas Fowell Buxton (edited by Charles Buxton), London, John Murray, 1848

DE CASTRO, J. Paul, *The Gordon Riots*, London, Oxford University Press, 1926

CLAY, Walter Lowe, *The Prison Chaplain, A Memoir of the Reverend John Clay*, London, Macmillan, 1861

COLLINS, Phillip, *Dickens and Crime*, London, Macmillan & Co., 1965

COLQUHOUN, Patrick, *A Treatise on the Police of the Metropolis*, London, 1797

COLSON, Percy, *The Strange History of Lord George Gordon*, London, Robert Hale & Co., 1937

CRABBE, *The Life of George Crabbe by his Son*, London, the Cresset Press, 1947

DEFOE, Daniel, *Moll Flanders*, London, the Folio Society, 1965

DICKENS, Charles, *Sketches by Boz*, London, Richard Edward King, 1850

DICTIONARY OF NATIONAL BIOGRAPHY, London, Smith, Elder & Co., 1896

DIXON, Hepworth, *John Howard and the Prison-World of Europe*, London, Jackson & Walford, 1849
 The London Prisons, London, Jackson & Walford, 1850
DOTTIN, Paul, *The Life and Strange and Surprising Adventures of Daniel Defoe* (Translated from the French by Louise Ragan), London, Stanley Paul & Co., 1930
DU CANE, Edmund F., *The Punishment and Prevention of Crime*, London, 1885
EVELYN, John, *John Evelyn's Diaries* (edited by Philip Francis), London, the Folio Society, 1963
FIELDING, Henry, *An Enquiry into the Causes of the Late Increase of Robbers etc.*, London, 1751
FOX, Lionel W., *The English Prison and Borstal Systems*, London, Routledge & Kegan Paul, 1952
FOXE, John, *The Acts and Monuments*, London, the Religious Tract Society, 1877
FRY, Elizabeth, *Memoir of the Life of Elizabeth Fry with Extracts from her Journal and Letters* (edited by Two of her Daughters), London, 1847
GEORGE, M. Dorothy, *London Life in the Eighteenth Century*, Harmondsworth, Peregrine Books, 1966
GORDON, Charles, *The Old Bailey and Newgate*, London, T. Fisher Unwin, 1902
GRIFFITHS, Arthur, *The Chronicles of Newgate*, London, Chapman & Hall, 1884
HEALEY, George Harris, *The Letters of Daniel Defoe*, Oxford, The Clarendon Press, 1955
HIBBERT, Christopher, *The Roots of Evil, A Social History of Crime and Punishment*, London, Wiedenfeld & Nicolson, 1963
HINDE, R. S. E., *The British Penal System 1773–1950*, London, Gerald Duckworth & Co., 1951
HOLCROFT, Thomas, *Memoirs of the Late Thomas Holcroft, written by himself and continued at the time of his death from his Diary, Notes, and other Papers*, London, 1816
HOWARD, John, *The State of the Prisons*, London, J. M. Dent & Son, 1929
HOWELL, T. B., *A complete Collection of State Trials*, London, 1813
JOHNSON, Samuel, *The Lives of the English Poets*, London, the Folio Society, 1965
KINGSMILL, John, *Chapters on Prisons and Prisoners*, London, Longman, Green, Brown & Longmans, 1852

KNAPP, Andrew and BALDWIN, William, *The New Newgate Calendar*, London, circa 1813

LANE, Jane, *Titus Oates*, London, Andrew Dakers, 1949

LECKEY, W. E. H., *A History of England in the Eighteenth Century*, London, Longmans, Green & Co., 1887

MACAULAY, Thomas Babington, *The History of England from the Accession of James the Second*, London, Longman, Brown, Green & Longmans, 1849

MAYHEW, Henry and BINNY, John, *The Criminal Prisons of London and Scenes of Prison Life*, London, Griffin, Bohn & Co., 1862

MOBERLY, Sir Walter, *The Ethics of Punishment*, London, Faber, 1968

MONTAGUE, Basil, *Hanging Not Punishment Enough*, London, 1812 (first published 1701)

MOORE, T. Inglis (editor), *A Book of Australia*, London and Glasgow, Collins, 1961

NIELD, James, *The State of the Prisons in England, Scotland and Wales*, London, 1813

THE PARLIAMENTARY HISTORY OF ENGLAND (London, 1811)

PEARE, Catherine Owens, *William Penn*, Philadelphia and New York, J. B. Lippincott Company, 1957

A PRISON MATRON, *Female Life in Prison*, London, Hurst & Blackett, 1862

PUGH, Ralph B., *Imprisonment in Medieval England*, Cambridge, Cambridge University Press, 1968

QUENNELL, Peter, *Hogarth's Progress*, London, Collins, 1955

RUGGLES-BRISE, Sir E., *The English Prison System*, London, Macmillan, 1921

SIMOND, L., *Journal of a Tour and Residence in Great Britain, 1810 and 1811*, London, 1815

SMITH, Captain Alexander, *A Complete History of the Lives and Robberies of the Most Notorious Highwaymen, Footpads, Shoplifts and Cheats of Both Sexes*, London, George Routledge & Sons, 1926 (first published 1719)

SMITH, Ann D., *Women in Prison*, London, Stevens & Sons, 1962

SMITH, John Thomas, *A Book for a Rainy Day*, (edited by Wilfred Whitten), London, Methuen, 1905

STEPHEN, Sir James Fitzjames, *A History of the Criminal Law of England*, London, Macmillan & Co., 1883

STOUGHTON, John, *William Penn, The Founder of Pennsylvania*, London, Hodder & Stoughton, 1882

STOW, *Survey of London*, London, J. M. Dent & Sons, 1960

SUTHERLAND, James, *Defoe*, London, Methuen & Co., 1937

TREVELYAN, G. M., *English Social History*, Longmans, Green & Co., 1944

THORNBURY, Walter, *Old and New London*, London, Cassel, Petter & Galpin, undated

WALPOLE, Horace, *The Letters of Horace Walpole, Fourth Earl of Oxford* (edited by Mrs Paget Toynbee), Oxford, The Clarendon Press, 1903–5

WATSON, J. Steven, *The Reign of George III, 1760–1815*, Oxford, the Clarendon Press, 1960

WEBB, Sidney & Beatrice, *English Prisons Under Local Government*, London, Longmans, Green & Co., 1922

WHITNEY, Janet, *Elizabeth Fry, Quaker Heroine*, London, George Harrap & Co., 1938

WILKINSON, George Theodore, *The Newgate Calendar*, London. 1816

WILLIAMS, Basil, *The Whig Supremacy, 1714–1760*, Oxford, the Clarendon Press, 1939

WOODWARD, Sir Llewellyn, *The Age of Reform, 1815–1870*, Oxford, the Clarendon Press, 1962

WRIGHT, Robert, *A Memoir of James Oglethorpe*, London, Chapman & Hall, 1867

Articles

'Henry Goodcole, Visitor of Newgate', by C. Dobb in the *Guildhall Miscellany*, February 1955

'Newgate in the Middle Ages', by Margery Bassett in *Speculum* Vol XVIII (1943)

'Prison Discipline', by Major Arthur Griffiths in the Ninth Edition (1875) and the Tenth Edition (1902) of the *Encyclopaedia Britannica*

Pamphlets, Tracts and Letters

England's Calamities Discovered (1696)

The London Spy, by Edward Ward (1696)

A New View of London (1708)

Memoirs of the Right Villainous Jack Hall (1717)

The History of the Press Yard (1717)

An Accurate Description of Conditions in Newgate etc., by B.L. Twickenham (1724)

*A letter to the Common Council and Livery of the City of London
on the Abuses existing in Newgate,* by the Hon. H. G. Bennett,
M.P., published in the *Pamphleteer* (1818)
Note on Newgate Prison, by Nellie J. M. Kerling, Wardens of
Cornwall Ltd., Penzance, undated

Documents in the Corporation of London Records Office

The Repertories of the Court of Aldermen
*Proclamation for the Reformation of Abuses in the Gaol of New-
gate* (September 1617)
Estimated Expenses for the Repair of Newgate Gaol (February
1628)
*Orders Devised and Agreed by the Lord Mayor and Court of
Aldermen for the Good Government of Newgate Gaol* (March
1632)
Bills for Rebuilding the Gaol and the Press Yard (1660–1672)
*Report of the Justices on the Abuses to Poor Debtors in Newgate
Gaol* (September 1702)
*Letter to the Lord Mayor and the Court of Aldermen relating to
escapes from Newgate Gaol* (May 1716)
*Answer of the Keeper of Newgate Gaol to Articles Exhibited
against him re Debtor Prisoners* (November 1730)
*An Account of Several Persons seized with the Gaol Distemper,
working in Newgate etc.,* by John Pringle, M.D., F.R.S. (January
1753)
*Minutes and Reports of a Committee appointed to enquire into
the Gaol of Newgate and to consider how the same may be
Enlarged and rendered more Healthy and Commodious* (1755–
1765)
Printed Broadsheets of the Returns of Prisoners in Newgate Gaol
(1785 and 1786)

Newspapers and Periodicals

The *City Press*
The *Daily Mail*
The *Daily News*
Fraser's Magazine
The *Gentleman's Magazine*
The *Illustrated London News*
The *Sphere*
The *Times*

INDEX

Accurate Description of Newgate Gaol . . ., 70
Acton, William, 87–9
Adshead, Joseph, 196
after-care, 144–5
Akerman, Richard, 135, 137
  approves improvements to Newgate, 101; condemns Newgate, 99; his house burned, 120–21; tributes to, 119–20
Alexander, Andrew, 42–3
American prison methods, 183–4, 194–5
Andrews, Mary, 30
Angelo, Henry, 33, 122
Annual Register, 163
Armstrong, Sergeant, 164
Asquith, Herbert, 234
assize circuits, 10–11
Assizes of Clarendon, 3, 4, 8
Auburn, New York, 183
Austin, Lieutenant, 219

Baker, Colonel, 233
Bambridge, Thomas, 84–7, 89
Barnaby Rudge, 121
Barrett, Michael, 227
Baston, T., 81–2
Beccaria, Cesare, 112, 132
  postulates 'the social contract', 125
  views on penal reform, 126–30
Beggar's Opera, The, 117–18
begging, 7, 22, 44, 65
beheading, 34
Benefit of Clergy, 27–9
Bennett, H. G., 168–9
Bentham, Jeremy, 112, 125, 171, 175, 177, 182, 215
  his panopticon, 132–5
  views on penal reform, 130–31
  wishes to build penitentiary, 144
Bentham, Sir Samuel, 132
Birmingham prison, 200, 219–20
Bishops' prisons, 4
Black Assizes, the, 8, 97
Blackstone, Sir William, 4, 11, 37, 141
'Bloody Code', the, 94, 163, 167
Bonner, Edmund, 41, 42
Borough compter, 172

Boswell, James, 90, 119, 120–1
Botany Bay, 142–3, 180
Bowen, Thomas, 161
de Bracton, Henry, 8
branding, 8, 11
Bray, Thomas, 67
Briscoe, J. I., 176
Bridewell, Palace of, 20, 47
Bridewells – *see* Houses of Correction and individual prisons
Bristol gaol, 173
Brixton prison, 209, 210–11, 213
Bromley, Sir Thomas, 44
Burke, Edmund, 90, 94
burning at the stake, 37–8, 146
Bushell, Edmund, 60
Buxton, Anna, 153
Buxton, Sir Thomas Fowell, 153, 179
  on prison usage, 161–2, 170
  reports on prison conditions, 172–3

Cambridge assizes, 7
Cambridge gaol, 6
Du Cane, Sir Edmund, 229–32, 233–4
capital punishment, 27, 93–4, 173–4, 179–80; *see also* executions
Carlyle, Thomas, 102
Carnarvon, Lord, 220–1
Castell, Robert, 84
Castlereagh, Viscount, 173
Cato Street conspirators, 163
Central Criminal Court, 189, 206, 208, 232, 235; *see also* Old Bailey
Charles II, 62
Chatham prison, 202
Chesterton, George, 190–91
Chomley, 42
Christ Church, 45
Christian Knowledge, Society for Promoting, 67
City Press, 236
Clarence, Duke of, 139
Clark, William, 41
Clay, John, 199
Clerkenwell bridewell, 96, 227, 232
'Clinke', the, 20
Coldbath Fields prison (Middlesex House of Correction), 176, 190–91, 209, 215
Coleman, Edward, 62

245

Colquhoun, Patrick, 94, 144, 162–3
Common Pleas and Exchequer, court of, 14
compters, 22, 41
  Broad Street, 19
  Poultry, 19, 40, 63
  Wood Street, 19, 63
'county allowance', 51
convict-ships, 177, 203, 209, 210
  condemned by Romilly, 167
  conditions on, 213–14
  first employed, 141
Cope, Mr, 186
Court of Aldermen (City of London), 23, 24, 97
  assigns minor felons to Ludgate, 16
  attempts to improve gaols, 6, 17–18
  rebuilds Newgate, 208
  records of administration of gaols, 39, 41, 43–4, 45, 46
  regulates prisoners' begging, 22
Court of Chancery, 14
Courts of Conscience, 90–91
Courvoisier, François, 224–5
Cowdery, Walter, 54–5
Crabbe, George, 121–3
crank, the, 191, 215, 219, 221, 222, 229, 235
  defined, 199
Crawford, William, 183–4, 192
Cressey, Mr, 65
Cromwell, Oliver, 56
Crowder, William, 43–4
Cubitt, Sir William, 175
Cuthbert, Mr, 85

Daily Mail, 235
Daily News, 224
Dance, Sir George, 58, 100, 136
Dartmoor prison, 202, 203
death penalty, abolition of, 226
debtor prisoners, 6–7, 51, 70–71, 81–91, 106, 117
  conditions criticized by Howard, 109
  duty of creditor to support, 9
Defoe, Daniel, 68–9
Dickens, Charles, 121
  on executions, 224–5, 226
  on Newgate, 184–5, 187–8
  on solitary confinement in American prisons, 194–5
Dixon, Hepworth, 136, 205–6, 213, 223
Dow, Robert, 34

Eastern Penitentiary, Cherry Hill, 183, 194
Eden, William, 141

Edgworth Bess – see Lion, Elizabeth
Edward III, 16, 25
Edward V, 13
Edward VI, 20
Elizabeth I, 11
Encyclopedia Britannica (1823), 177
England's Calamities Discovered, 66–7
escapes, 50, 65, 85, 115–16
  capital offence, 122
  gaolers punished for, 6, 22
  Jack Sheppard's, 113–15
  methods of, 23, 56
Essay on Crimes and Punishment, 125
Evelyn, John, 57, 62, 63
Ewart, William, 226
executions, 8, 26, 30–38, 119, 131, 145–7, 163–4, 180, 225–7
  outside Newgate, 146, 223–5
  procession to Tyburn, 32–3
Execution Dock, 34, 36

fees, 5, 41, 47, 48, 63, 178
  admission fees, 5, 9, 71–3, 86, 87
  release fees, 5, 9, 41, 103
  garnish, 10, 73–5, 83, 88, 95–6, 108–9, 170
Fell, James, 65
Field, John, 195
Fielding, Henry, 36–7, 93
Flanders, Moll, 68–9
Fleet prison, 3, 22, 23, 84–7, 89
  first London prison, 14
flogging, 26–7, 130, 191, 219
Flower, Mr, 65
Forde, Doctor, 164–5
Forster, William, 151
Fox, Caroline, 191
Foxe, John, 41, 42, 43
Franklin, James, 53
Fraser's Magazine, 224
Fry, Elizabeth, 162, 166, 172, 176, 182, 195, 198, 236
  life and work, 148–60
Fry, Joseph, 150

'gaol delivery', 10–11, 25, 40
gaol fever, 63–4, 97–9, 100, 105, 135, 139
  form of typhus, 7–8
gaols, county, 3–4, 11–12, 107
gaolers, 4–6, 40–44, 103; see also Newgate, keepers
garnish – see fees
garrotting, 220
Gay, John, 117–18
Gentleman's Magazine, 96, 123, 140
George III, 30, 144
Georgia, 83, 90
Giltspur Street compter, 205, 208
Gladstone, Viscount, 233–4, 236

Goodcole, Henry, 46
Gordon, Lord George, 137–9
Gordon Riots, 14, 120–2, 136, 148
Goree, West Africa, 164
Graham, James, 201
Great Fire (1666), 14, 57, 59, 63
Grellet, Stephen, 151, 152
Grey, Sir George, 202–3, 209
Grotius, Hugo, 126–7
Guildford gaol, 172

habeas corpus, 61
Haggerty, Owen, 163
de Hakford, John, 27
Hales, Doctor, 97–8
Half-way House, Holborn, 35
Hall, John, 70
  memoirs quoted, 73–4, 75, 76, 77,
    79, 80
Hand, Clayton, 98
hanging, drawing and quartering,
    37
Hanging Not Punishment Enough, 92
Hanway, Jonas, 131
Harcourt, Lady, 159
hard labour, 141–2, 222
Harris, Phoebe, 146
Haughton, Simon, 47
Hawes, Nathaniel, 32
Hay, William, 94
Hayes, Catherine, 37–8
Henry II, 10, 14
Henry III, 15, 17, 22
Henry IV, 15
Henry VI, 13
Henry VIII, 11, 41
History of the Press Yard, 70, 71–3,
    74, 78
Hoare, Samuel, 172
Hodges, Doctor, 63–4
Hogarth, William, 118
Holcroft, Thomas, 121–2
Holford, George, 171
Holinshed, Raphael, 24
Holloway, John, 163
Holloway prison, 208, 209, 214
Houses of Correction, 11–12, 20, 107,
    140; see also individual prisons
Howard, John, 131, 132, 136, 137,
    140, 141, 142, 158, 167, 168, 171
  commends Akerman, 120
  his first journey, 143–4
  life and work, 102–12
Huggins, John, 85, 89
'hulks, the' – see convict ships
Hunter, John, 8
Husband, Richard, 19–20

Illustrated London News, 231

Imprisonment
  conditions of, 39–46, 105–11, 140–
    41, 175–6, 178, 201, 205–8, 209–
    18, 222–3, 227–31; see also
    Newgate, conditions
  purpose of, 3, 8–9, 125–35, 161,
    177, 182
Insolvent Debtors Relief Act, 89
irons, 5–6, 17, 41, 96, 101, 107–8,
    161–2, 173, 222
  injuries caused by, 23, 42, 87
  used at will of keeper, 70–71

Jamaica, 49
James I and VI, 50
Jebb, Sir Joshua, 201, 203
Jerrold, Douglas, 226
Johnson, Richard, 53–4
Johnson, Samuel, 90, 123
  commends Akerman, 119
  on The Beggar's Opera, 117
  on the condemned procession, 147
  opposes imprisonment for debt, 9

Kidd, 'Captain', 36
King's Bench prison, 20, 55, 89, 95
Kingsmill, John, 32, 35
Kingsmill, Joseph, 196, 198, 199, 207
  opposes silent system, 192–3
Knolles, Thomas, 24

Lancaster Castle, 162
Laurence, John, 33
Leckey, W. E. H., 93, 94, 102
Leicester prison, 202, 219, 220
Levi, Polly, 139
Lion, Elizabeth (Edgworth Bess),
    113–15, 143
Locke, John, 125
Logate, Bartholomew, 47
le Lorimer, Edmund, 23
Ludgate gaol, 19, 22, 39, 43, 44, 45,
    65
  opened for minor felons, 16–17
  receives extra water supply, 24
Lushington, Sir Godfrey, 234
Lutterell, 82

Macaulay, Thomas Babington, 65
Mackay, Alexander, 227
Mackintosh, Sir James, 172, 173, 179
Mackpheadris, John, 87
Maclane, James, 117
Maconochie, Alexander, 200, 219,
    230
Malcolm, Sarah, 33, 118
Malden, Daniel, 116
Manning, Frederick George, 225–6
  Maria, 225–6
Manor Hall Institution, 210

marks system, 200–1, 219, 230
Marsden, Samuel, 166
Marshal, James, 83
Marshalsea prison, 6, 20, 22, 39, 81,
    87–9
    first opened, 20
    Oglethorpe Committee report on,
        87–9
Mary, Queen, 42
Maryland, colony of, 49
Mayhew, Henry, 199
Mayhew and Binny (*The Criminal
    Prisons of London and Scenes of
    Prison Life*), 32, 209–11, 214–18,
    223
Mead, William, 59–61
*Memoirs of the Right Villainous
    John Hall*, 70, 73–4, 75
Mill, James, 177
Millbank penitentiary, 182, 190, 202,
    203, 209, 210, 211, 212, 213, 214
    design of, 171
    opening of, 171–2
    type of prisoners in, 177–8
Montagu, Basil, 92
Moral and Political Philosophy, 141
mutilation, 26

Newgate Calendar, 31, 37, 46, 113,
    114, 115
Newgate gaol, 6, 14–16, 17, 18, 19,
    24–5, 27, 30, 31, 32, 34, 35, 38,
    40–46, 47–8, 52, 56–7, 59, 60, 62,
    65, 67–8, 72–3, 79, 87, 94, 111,
    135, 137, 140, 145, 151–8, 171, 172,
    208, 209, 231–2, 233, 235–6
    condemned procession from, 33–5,
        62, 63
    conditions in, 20–24, 43–4, 47–8,
        50–51, 55–7, 61, 63, 66–9, 70–79,
        83–4, 84–7, 97–9, 116–117, 151–
        8, 168–71, 184–9, 205–6, 216–18
    first built, 14–15
    executions at, 146–7, 163–5, 180,
        223–7
    gaol delivery at, 40
    keepers of, 18–19, 42–3, 47, 53–5,
        83, 99, 116–17, 119–20
    mystique of, 113–24
    rebuilding, 24, 49–50, 52, 57–8,
        99–100, 136–7, 208
    women in, 151–3, 157
Newman, Mr, 151
New South Wales, 163, 181, 190
    conditions in penal colony, 165–6,
    growth of, 165
    prisoner convoys to, 142–3, 180
    transportation suspended, 194
Nield, James, 167–8, 169

Nollekens, Joseph, 164
Norfolk Island, 194, 200, 219
Norton, Sir George, 66

oakum-picking, 191, 209, 214, 215,
    229, 231
    defined, 199
Oates, Titus, 61–3
O'Connor, Patrick, 225
Oglethorpe, James, 83, 84, 87, 89
    forms colony of Georgia, 90
    Oglethorpe Committee reports,
        84–9, 95
Old Bailey, 8, 24, 25, 41, 59, 62, 79,
    89, 97, 114, 162, 189, 216, 225,
    231; *see also* Central Criminal Court
    erection of, 40
    plundered in Gordon riots, 123
Oneby, 'Major', 35
Oxford assizes, 7

Paley, William, 141, 201
panopticon, 132–5, 215
Panopticon or Inspection House, 132,
    144
Parkhurst prison, 203
Peel, Robert, 178–9
peine forte et dure, 29–30, 79
penal reform, 94–5, 166–8, 172–4,
    179–80
    Howard's attempts at, 109–11
    Romilly's attempts at, 166–7, 172,
        173
penal servitude, 203–4, 209, 221, 223,
    229, 235
Penitentiary House, 142
Penn, William, 59–61
Pentonvile prison, 195–8, 202, 203,
    208, 209, 210, 211, 214
    building commenced, 193
Philpot, John, 43
pillory, 8, 27
Pitt, William, 116–17, 142, 144
Player, Sir Thomas, 58
Pocklington, Mr, 83
poor law, 11
Pope, Alexander, 90, 117
Popham, Alexander, 104
Porter, John, 41–2
Portland prison, 202, 210
Portsmouth prison, 202, 210, 213
Poulteney, Sir John, 22
Poyntz, Sir Nicholas, 55
Prance, Miles, 62
'press, the'—*see* peine forte et dure
Pringle, John, 98–9
Prison Acts, 174, 178, 181, 184, 193,
    221-2, 227, 228, 235

prisoners, spiritual welfare of, 45–6,
52–3, 64
Privy Council, 14, 19, 55
Pryor, Mrs, 162
Public Advertiser, 138
public executioner, 36, 94
Pugh, Ralph B, 8
Punch, 226
punishment, 26–7, 92–3, 125–35; *see
also* individual headings

Quennell, Peter, 118

Rann, Jack (Sixteen String Jack), 32,
35
*Report of the Justices on the Abuses
to Poor Debtors in Newgate Gaol*,
83
Reynolds, Frederick, 122–3
Richard II, 13
Robinson, Mr, 83
Rogers, John, 43
Romilly, Sir Samuel, 166–7, 172, 173
Ruggles-Brise, Sir Evelyn, 234–5
Russell, Lord John, 193
Russell, Lord William, 224

St Alban's gaol, 140
St Bartholomew, Hospital and Priory
of, 24, 45
St Giles's Roundhouse, 113
St Sepulchre's Church, 32, 42
associated with Newgate, 34–5
bell as funeral knell, 34, 69, 224
Scot, Dr, 123
Scott, Alexander, 115
separate system, 190, 191–2, 193–8,
199, 209, 210, 214, 220–21, 222,
229, 235
defined, 182–3
in America, 194–5
Sheppard, Jack, 34, 118, 208, 216
escapes of, 113–15
shot-drill, 191, 215, 221, 222
defined, 199–200
Shrewsbury, Duke of, 65
silent system, 181, 183, 190, 191,
192–3, 195, 215
in America, 183, 195
Simmond, Monsieur, 212
Sinclair, Captain, 87
Sketches by Boz, 184
Smith, John (Half-hanged Smith),
31
Smith, John Thomas, 164–5
Smith, Sidney, 161, 175, 181, 182
Smith, William, 101, 119
Society for the Reformation of Prison
Discipline, 172, 173

Society for the Relief of Persons
Imprisoned for Small Sums, 90
Solas, Jacob, 86–7
solitary confinement, 101, 141, 158,
161, 171, 181, 183, 221, 222
early supporters of, 131–2
Somerset assizes, 7
Southwark, 20
Sphere, the, 235
Stafford, Earl of, 84
Star Chamber, 14, 47
starvation, 6, 7
*State of the Prisons in England and
Wales*, 104
Statute of Escapes, 23
Stephen, Sir James, 27
stocks, 11
Story, Mr, 42
Stow, 7, 15, 19–20, 24
Strype, John, 40
Suffolk County Gaol, 175
Sussex, Duke of, 139
Swift, Jonathan, 117

Thackeray, William, 224
Thornhill, Sir James, 118
*Thoughts on Trade and a Publick
Spirit*, 81
Thrale, Hester, 123
tickets-of-leave, 203, 210, 220
Times, The, 226
Tocqueville, Alexis de, 182, 195
torture, 6, 88
Tothill Fields prison (Westminster
Bridewell), 190–91, 209, 215
Tower Hill, 34
Tower of London, 13–14, 137
Townshend, Lord, 84
transportation, 138, 140, 159, 162,
163, 167, 209
first mentioned, 49
to America, 49, 141
to Australia, 142–3, 163, 165–6,
180–81, 190, 223
to Van Diemen's Land and Norfolk
Island, 194, 201–2
tread-wheel, 142, 191, 201, 209, 214,
215, 221, 222, 229, 235
defined, 175–6
tuns, 4, 20
Turner, John, 56
Turpin, Dick, 32
Tyburn, 1, 59, 70, 77, 78, 113, 116,
118, 119, 145–7
procession to, 32–5
scene at, 35–8

Underhill, Edward, 43

vagrancy, 11
Van Diemen's Land, 194, 201–2
Virginia, colony of, 49

Wakefield prison, 202
Wall, Joseph, 164
Walnut Street gaol, Philadelphia, 183, 194
Walpole, Horace, 117, 139
Walpole, Sir Robert, 90
Wandsworth prison (Surrey House of Correction), 209, 214–15
Watson, Doctor, 139
Webb, Sidney and Beatrice, 49, 102
Wesley, John, 138
Western, C.C., 176
Western Penitentiary, Pittsburg, 183
whipping, 6, 8, 11

White, Charles, 163
Whitechapel gaol, 81–2
Whittington, Richard, 24
Wilberforce, William, 142
William the Conqueror, 13, 26
Williams, Renwick, 139–40
Wilmot, Thomas, 98–9
Woodhouse, Henry, 52
Woolaston, Henry, 53–4
    John, 53
Woolfe, George, 235
work, for prisoners, 53, 65, 182, 191, 196, 199–200, 203, 209, 214, 215, 221, 230, 235
    for women, 156–7
    in Bentham's panopticon, 134

Yong, Thomas, 41
York, Duke of, 139